In the Opinion of the Court

IN THE

O·P·I·N·I·O·N

OF THE COURT

William Domnarski

◆

UNIVERSITY OF ILLINOIS PRESS

URBANA AND CHICAGO

© 1996 by the Board of Trustees of the University of Illinois
Manufactured in the United States of America
1 2 3 4 5 C P 5 4 3 2 1

This book is printed on acid-free paper.

Library of Congress Cataloging-in-Publication Data
Domnarski, William, 1953–
In the opinion of the court / William Domnarski.
p.   cm.
Includes bibliographical references and index.
ISBN 0-252-02257-2 (acid-free paper)
ISBN 0-252-06556-5 (pbk. : acid-free paper)
1. Law reporting—United States. 2. Judicial opinions—
United States. 3. Legal composition. I. Title.
KF255.G66   1996
347.73'12—dc20   96-4493
[347.30712]   CIP

To Kathleen, Colleen, and Erin—
Suddenly, bloom in the desert

Contents

Preface

Issuing forth in a steady stream from courts around the country, judicial opinions make decisions for the litigants in individual cases and provide answers for the populace at large on the full range of societal questions, both by speaking to the litigants and by offering interpretations to third parties. Yet underlying this straightforward definition of judicial opinions we find complexity and tension, in part because opinions are speaking both for the courts and for the individual judges authoring them. As a result they function on two levels, the one institutional and public, the other individual and personal. Moreover, in deciding cases and writing opinions judges are engaged in two separate exercises. In deciding cases and setting into motion the consequences of decisions—which can range from ordering school desegregation to obligating one party to pay damages to another—judges are exercising power. But they are also writing legal literature. Here their obligations and interests go beyond the litigants and conclusory statements explaining why one party won and the other lost. Their audience is all those interested in law, and their obligations are to the law that has gone before them. "To whom am I responsible?" the great Learned Hand once asked a law clerk. "No one can fire me. No one can dock my pay. Even those nine bozos in Washington, who sometimes reverse me, can't make me decide as they want. Everyone should be responsible to someone. To whom am I responsible?" Pointing to the shelves of his law library, he then answered, "To those books about us! That's to whom I'm responsible!"[1]

Contradictions and ironies surround judicial opinions and their place in society and in legal literature. Even definitions and descriptions of them from respected sources are vague and at odds with each other. Fred Rodell, for example, thought opinions were "fancy rationalizations of legal action,"[2] while Benjamin Cardozo likened opinions to a desert wasteland, referring to the "Sahara of judicial opinions."[3] In a different vein, William Gaddis, one of America's best writers, parodies judicial opinions in his 1994 novel *A Frolic of His Own*. The novel's characters include a federal judge who tries to untangle problems such as the case of an artist seeking an injunction against the destruction of his civic sculpture to rescue a dog trapped within. Gaddis's point seems to be that just as judicial opinions are inadequate responses to hyperbole and lunacy, judges are also unable to handle quotidian experience and the cases it produces. Surprisingly, however, reviewers seemed to miss the parodic element of the opinions and considered them examples of the most sensible writing in the novel.[4]

On the other hand, Charles Wyzanski, a former federal judge and distinguished essayist, articulated the answer to Rodell, Cardozo, and Gaddis when he identified the importance of judicial opinions in America, writing that "from the time of Chief Justice Marshall, the opinions of the Supreme Court have been a text unto the people. Read in the daily press, studied in the common school, knotted into the rope of enduring history, they may well be the largest single contribution to the philosophy of the American way of life."[5] Seen in this light, as the essence of American life, it is not surprising that the U.S. State Department thought the opinions of the High Court so reflective of America that in 1938 it presented the government of Burma with the three hundred volumes of the *U.S. Reports* that had thus far been written.

Some have argued that in their public, institutional role, judicial opinions are the life blood of our democracy and a testament to its operation merely because they are followed. As former Supreme Court Justice Tom Clark noted, "we don't have money at the Court for an army and we can't take out ads in the newspaper, and we don't want to go out on a picket line in our robes. We have to convince the nation by the force of our opinions."[6] But at the same time, while a decision such as *Brown v. Board of Education* does represent the best of American values, President Eisenhower had to order troops into the deep south to fulfill its integration promise. In addition, significant numbers of Americans called for Chief Justice Earl Warren's impeachment rather than follow the Court's lead.

Another contradiction, which goes to the heart of the opinion-writing process, embodies the essence of the problem that courts face today. Commentators such as Karl Llewellyn have argued that the genius of judicial opinions is that the judges who write them are "a body of specialists only in being unspecialized." "It still seems to me," Llewellyn reflected, "that increasingly as technological complexity piles high, our ancient institution of ultimate review by those complete nonspecialists, the general Supreme Court, stands out as one of the wisest institutions man has thus far managed to develop."[7] But at the same time we permit this very institution to be undermined by allowing fledgling law clerks rather than their nonspecialist bosses to do the court's work. Wisdom, for Llewellyn, was a function of the reasoning process in opinion writing. We lose the judge's processed involvement in the reasoning of an opinion when technically proficient law clerks write the opinions and the judge understands his role more as a decision maker and editor, if that, than as a writer. That law clerks should write so many opinions is especially ironic because no judicial system in the common law world has featured the judicial opinion to the extent that the American system has. In England, for example, only the highest courts regularly issue written decisions. Appellate judges give opinions from the bench and then later polish their remarks for publication. Only in Australia, which has always been more eager than England to import American customs, has there been an increasing tendency for judges to use their law clerks to help them write their opinions.

It is against this backdrop that my study is set. The controlling thought throughout is that judicial opinions are too important, both to the law and to the country, not to be better understood. Bits of the story of judicial opinions as I have sketched it can be found in the vast primary and secondary literature relating to the Supreme Court, the lower federal courts, and federal judges. My goal has been to describe and examine judicial opinions from the perspective of a general essay, with the hope that if the story is told we will better appreciate the judges who have contributed to the literature of the law with their judicial opinions.

◆   ◆

Portions of this book appeared originally in *Style and Justice Holmes*, 60 CONN. B.J. 251–65 (1986) and *Shakespeare and the Law*, 67 CONN. B.J. 317–51 (1993) and are used here with the permission of the editors.

In the Opinion of the Court

Introduction

We have, surprisingly, no comprehensive study of the opinions that judges such as Learned Hand, answering to his law books, have labored at in interpreting our statutes and our Constitution. Though critical theorists from the schools of feminism, deconstruction, reader response, and critical legal studies have taken on and taken apart judicial opinions,[1] much of the work to date has looked at them from two points of view. The first sees courts as institutions and studies their role in society. These commentators have examined courts for the decisions they make and the legitimacy of the language they use in fashioning legal principles. They have, for example, scrutinized the function of tropes in articulating legal doctrines, such as the metaphors of standing, mootness, ripeness, the marketplace of ideas, the wall of separation between church and state, and the captive audience.[2] Commentators examining such language take their cue first from Cardozo, who warned that "metaphors in law are to be narrowly watched, for starting as devices to liberate thought, they often end by enslaving it,"[3] and then from Justice Stanley Reed, who, in a dissenting opinion in a case involving the metaphoric wall of separation between church and state, noted that "a rule of law should not be drawn from a figure of speech."[4] They stress the indeterminacy of figurative language — the subjectivity of its meaning — in arguing that its use creates mischief.

The second point of view looks to style in judicial opinions and argues that it matters. Style here goes beyond individual rhetorical devices to the total effect. Griffin Bell summarized the significance of style, writing that "in judicial writing [style] is an important factor in the growth of the law. The style of an opinion may affect the manner in which it's interpreted by the reader. It may also govern the frequency with which the opinion will be cited in other cases and thus determine the influence the opinion will ultimately have."[5] Judge Richard Posner, our preeminent explicator of style, has shown its importance, with specific reference to Holmes and Cardozo.[6] The reputations of both are due in part, he argues, to their rhetorical strategies and felicitous language, which, at times, deflect attention from the major changes in the law that the opinions are producing.

Little, however, has been written about judicial opinions as a form of legal literature specifically or as a form of literature generally. Putting the studies of rhetorical strategies to one side, opinions have not been analyzed as a literary form, as communications between the court and society. Nor have they been studied for what they are at their best, a place where life and law meet in a language available to the general, educated reader. Lastly, opinions have not been examined as illustrations of the care judges sometimes take in writing for an audience. I hope to change that with this book.

I, too, have an interest in examining the style of judicial opinions. But here my attention goes beyond the rhetorical strategies of individual opinions and is but one aspect of an interest in the broader subject of the judicial opinion. To understand judicial opinions we need to know who writes them, how they are written, and how they are reported and published. We need to canvass and examine the opinions that are being written around the country by scores of judges, and we need as well to know the traditions within which they are working. For this, we need to know the evolution of judicial opinions, both in the Supreme Court and the lower federal courts.

This book examines judicial opinions from the U.S. Supreme Court, the U.S. Court of Appeals, and the U.S. district courts in the manner of a general, comprehensive essay that describes their history, function, and place in legal literature. It is organized by three overarching themes. The first is the connection between judges and their audiences on the one hand and judicial opinions and their functions on the other. The second is the path of the judicial opinion process, from writing to dissemination. And the third is the evolution in judicial opinion style and substance as a function of court business, dominant personalities, and the influence of law clerks. In addition I examine the relationship between style and substance in important Supreme Court cases; the key roles played by the reporting and publication of judicial opinions in establishing and advancing distinctly American jurisprudential values; the dominance exercised by competent and talented opinion writers; the rise of the law clerk; the current widespread interest of lower federal court judges, as opposed to Supreme Court Justices, in distinguishing their opinions stylistically and rhetorically; and the work of one federal judge, Richard Posner, in writing judicial opinions that transcend the genre and make important jurisprudential and legal literature contributions.

Chapter 1 examines the reporting and publication of judicial opinions and describes the current state of activities in the Supreme Court and lower federal courts. It sketches the evolution of judicial opinion reporting and publication, including the effect of money and markets. It briefly contrasts the American experience with the English and concludes by looking at the communications revolution and its effect on the dissemination of judicial opinions in the federal system. Chapter 2 investigates the question of who writes judicial opinions, first by describing the current state of affairs and then by selectively charting the opinion-writing process. It concentrates on the great opinion writers such as Holmes and a quartet of Justices in the forties and fifties—Douglas, Black, Frankfurter, and Jackson—and then examines the rise of the law clerk as a writer of judicial opinions in the twentieth century. Chapter 3 examines the evolution of style and substance in Supreme Court opinions and discusses the forces that have shaped the changes. These include dominant Justices, increasing work-load pressures, and the stylistic and substantive values that law clerks have brought to the writing process. Chapter 4 continues the study of the Supreme Court and constructs a canon of its greatest judicial opinions. It discusses the rhetorical and substantive approaches taken by the Justices as a way of highlighting both the prevailing legal and literary values of the opinions and their status as communications between the Supreme Court and the public. Chapter 5 examines the evolution of lower court opinion in the same way that chapter 3 examines Supreme Court opinions. Chapter 6 then extends the look at lower court opinions and examines the career of Richard Posner of the U.S. Court of Appeals. It explores Posner's insight that the judicial opinion writer can shape the genre and that the genre of the opinion can, in turn, shape the opinion writer. It provides as well a portrait and extended analysis of Posner as the successor to Hand and Holmes and as the great expositor of modern common law, with its legal doctrines and animating principles of law and economics.

My examination of judicial opinions extends only to those coming from the federal courts. To include state courts would be too large a project for the general interest book I have tried to write. More important, federal statutes increasingly affect our lives as a result of an explosion in the last few decades in federal statutory law. Congress has created an expansive array of rights and remedies in the workplace and elsewhere. Legislation in the areas of education, employment, and housing, more than any force coming from state or local governments, affects the way we live today. The federal judicial system has not been able to keep pace with the legislative explosion, which by itself has caused some of the developments in the opinion-writing process described here. Not only are the federal courts covering this vast array of federal law—to say nothing of diversity jurisdiction—they have the final say in all but those few cases that are appealed from the circuit courts and reviewed by the Supreme Court. This perforce makes their work important. Ours, as some commentators have pointed out, is a legislative rather than a judicial age.[7] This is not to say that the Supreme Court no longer issues rulings that affect the way we live. But compared to the era of the Warren Court, for example, legislation touches us more than Supreme Court pronouncements defining important individual rights. In this legislative age, it is the lower federal courts that are fine-tuning congressional legislation. With so many lower federal court voices interpreting so much important legislation, we need to know more about the approaches the judges are taking.

I hope to show that ours is a time distinguished by a significant number of smart, talented judges. Posner is the smartest and most talented and deserves special consideration because his contributions are unique in the same way that he is a unique figure in the law. But beyond Posner there are a half dozen or more judges—an unusually large number sitting at any one time on the lower federal benches—bringing life to the law that so affects us all. Their story and the story of judicial opinions follow.

–• 1 •–

Reporting and Publishing
Judicial Decisions

The current state of the publication of opinions of the Supreme Court and of the lower federal courts can be described easily enough. Supreme Court opinions are read from the bench in many instances and all are filed with the clerk of the court. Dissemination in one form occurs when the clerk issues the opinion the moment it is filed to those subscribing to the Court's electronic system, Project Hermes. Aside from this immediate electronic publication, the Government Printing Office publishes the opinions in slip form the day they are announced. These slip opinions are, but for typographical and other errors, the final version of an opinion. They contain, for example, the work of the reporter of decisions, who provides a syllabus of the opinion for the reader. With only the errors corrected, they are then published, along with the other opinions from the Court's Term, by the Government Printing Office in the *United States Reports*, the Court's official publication. While the slip opinions are available when the decisions are announced, the hardcover *U.S. Reports* are currently running about four years behind. That is, at the end of the 1994 Term the latest hardcover *U.S. Reports* on the law library shelves was volume 499 from the 1990 Term. Private publication ventures get the opinions into print more quickly. There are three primary private publishers of the Court's work: West Publishing Company and its *Supreme Court Reporter*; Lawyers Cooperative Publishing Company and its *Lawyer's Edition of the Supreme Court Reports*; and the National Bureau of Affairs and its *United States Law Week*. *U.S. Law Week* publishes the opinions in pamphlet form the week of issuance, while the *Supreme Court Reporter* and the *Lawyer's Edition of the Supreme Court Reports* collect two weeks' worth of opinions and publish them in softcover a few weeks after the opinions come out. Hardcover volumes compiling the Term's work appear several months later.

The various circuits of the U.S. Court of Appeals and the district courts do not have a reporter of decisions, although a specialist court such as the U.S. Tax Court does. Moreover, West Publishing is the only hardcover publisher of the opinions of the lower federal courts. The opinions of the U.S. Court of Appeals are released as slip opinions by the clerk of the court. Unlike the opinions from the Supreme Court, these slip opinions do not contain a syllabus. The case caption, the name of the district court from which the case came, the name of the lower court presiding judge, and the dates on which the case was heard and decided appear on the first page. The text of the opinion follows. Opinions to be published according to the policy of an individual circuit are then sent to West Publishing. They appear first in weekly softcover advance sheet volumes of the *Federal Reporter* several weeks later and then in hardcover volumes of the *Federal Reporter* series. West Publishing exercises no publication discretion over the opinions sent to it by the courts, publishing all of them. Opinions of the U.S. district courts are filed in typescript with the clerk and published in the *Federal Supplement*, in the same manner as are the opinions of the court of appeals, if the judge wants the decision published. Again, West Publishing publishes all opinions sent to it by the district judges.

The opinions of both the Supreme Court and the lower federal courts are made available by the courts, usually for a fee, on the Internet. In addition, they are entered into commercial computer data bases almost immediately. West Publishing's data base is WESTLAW, while Mead Data, West Publishing's major competitor, brings the decisions out on LEXIS. In addition both West Publishing and Mead Data make their data bases available in a CD-ROM format.

◆　◆

The evolution of the publication and dissemination of federal judicial opinions began with the birth of the Supreme Court, which started its work without a system for the reporting and publication of its decisions.[1] This barely mattered for the first few years, since the Court did not have any case opinions that required dissemination. But even once the court had opinions to disseminate, it did not think the obligation sufficiently important to make it official. A local Philadelphia lawyer by the name of Dallas saw a potential market for the Court's work and promoted himself to the Court as an unofficial reporter who would publish its work in the manner that he was publishing the decisions of the Pennsylvania and Delaware courts. That is, Dallas would perform the reporting duties and contract with a publisher for the actual production of the volumes.[2] The Court agreed and probably helped Dallas by providing him with written decisions to the extent that there were any. For oral decisions, Dallas had to rely on notes he or others in attendance had made. That there could be oral rather than written decisions of the Court seems unthinkable today, but for this new system the only model was that of the English, which, as I describe later, featured oral decisions with limited publication.

Dallas was not up to the job of compiling and publishing the *Reports*. His work, while pathbreaking, was beset with tardiness, incompleteness, inaccuracy, and costliness. His innovations in providing brief abstracts at the beginning of a case and in indexing both a volume's cases and the cases upon which the Court relied within those cases hardly made up for the defects in the *Reports*. He was on occasion five or six years late in reporting a Term's decisions. Sometimes he simply omitted cases from the *Reports* on the grounds that they were not important enough. And of those cases he did report, many were streaked with errors, usually the result of the incompleteness of the notes upon which he was relying. Then there was the price issue. Dallas was right in thinking that the nation wanted reports of the highest court's cases, but he failed to understand that the country was not keen to buy his *Reports*, tardy as so many of them were, for the exorbitant prices he thought he had to charge to make his venture profitable. Cause and effect chased one another, since one reason Dallas was so often late with his *Reports* was his difficulty in persuading a publisher to take a chance with them.

Dissatisfied with Dallas's eight years of reporting, the High Court was pleased that he decided not to follow the Court to Washington when it moved there in 1800. Cranch, a local judge, succeeded Dallas as the Court's unofficial reporter and produced volumes as flawed as Dallas's had been. They too were late, expensive, inaccurate, and incomplete. Cranch's only contribution was to take Dallas's supplementary material and add to it summaries of the arguments of counsel. These swollen volumes proved to be as hard to sell as Dallas's had been. After sixteen years of financial strain, Cranch's interest in easing out of reporting coincided with Henry Wheaton's desire to assume Cranch's still unofficial position.

Wheaton also saw reporting the Court's cases as a way of making money, but he too failed to attract enough buyers for his volumes, despite several improvements. Wheaton added scholarly commentary, some of it written by Justice Story of the High Court itself, in the form of marginal notes and appendix notes. He got his *Reports* out more promptly than his predecessors, but there were still delays lasting years. Wheaton also omitted some cases from his *Reports*, but his volumes were still so large and so expensive that he could not find a large enough market for them. Congress's decision to make the reporter position official in 1818 at a rate of $1,000 per year relieved some of Wheaton's financial pressure. But the salary was not all that it seemed to be since it was for his work and for 100 copies of his *Reports*. Wheaton had hoped that his name on the *Reports* would produce referrals for his law practice, but these were few and sporadic. After eleven years as reporter, Wheaton had improved the *Reports* significantly but had not made enough money to justify going on. When a minor position overseas in the State Department came up in 1827, a beleaguered Wheaton accepted and was off to Denmark.

The next reporter, Richard Peters, succeeded where Wheaton had failed in finding an audience for his *Reports*. Peters's reporting reflected business rather than scholarly interests. He eliminated the marginal and appendix notes over which Wheaton had labored and added headnotes to help the reader. As he described his innovation, "the syllabus of each case contains an abstract of all the matters ruled and adjudged by the Court, and, generally, in the language of the decision, with a reference to the page of the volume in which the particular point will be found."[3] Peters also lowered the price of the *Reports*. Here, though, Peters was responding to an amendment to the Reporter's Act in which Congress declared that the cost of individual volumes of the *Reports* was not to exceed five dollars.[4] Peters's work did not measure up to Wheaton's scholarship, but that did not matter to him.

Peters at first had as much trouble selling his *Reports* as Wheaton. But he devised two plans to increase sales. One was to convince the government that it needed to buy more copies of the *Reports* than he was obliged to provide as part of his reporter's salary. He argued that he would even be willing to give up his salary if the government committed itself to buying a thousand or so copies. Congress, however, was not persuaded. This left Peters with his second plan, which proved to be a spectacular success. He came out with a condensed version of the *Reports*, which he could sell cheaply. To reduce the volume, Peters lopped off concurring and dissenting opinions and trimmed supplementary material to a minimum. Moreover, he planned to republish the decisions prior to 1827 in the same form so that those who wanted all of the Court's decisions would be able to afford them. Peters's entrepreneurial motives intersected here with his expressed desire to provide the *Reports* for the health of the democracy.

The High Court had been making law for nearly forty years, Peters noted, but in many large districts in the country there were but few copies of the *Reports*, and "in some of those districts, it is positively averred that not a single copy of all the reports is in the possession of any one, and thus the great and overruling law of the land is almost unknown in many populous parts of the Union."[5] These sets would sell for $36.00. Not surprisingly, Peters sold them by the thousands.

Peters's success brought litigation from none other than Wheaton, who claimed that he owned the copyright to those decisions in his *Reports*. The case seems odd to us now. Here was the Court, whose members knew the litigants well and had in fact worked with them, deciding an issue that could easily have been avoided if the Court had only clarified its relationship with the reporter. But now the Court had to embark on its copyright jurisprudence and make clear what is so obvious to us today. Turning away arguments from none other than Daniel Webster for Wheaton, a unanimous Court held that "no Reporter has or can have any copyright in the written opinions delivered by this court; and that the judges thereof cannot confer on any Reporter any such right."[6]

As if spurred by *Wheaton v. Peters* to improve its organization, the Court in 1834, through an internal order, required that its opinions be filed with the clerk and thereafter be sent to the reporter. The order fell short of demanding that all decisions had to be in writing. It only required that written opinions had to be filed with the clerk. The order was probably directed at Henry Baldwin (1830–44), who on four occasions in 1832 dissented orally but refused to give the text of his opinion to the reporter.[7]

The volumes of Supreme Court reported decisions published in the early decades of the nineteenth century, as well as those volumes of reported decisions from various state courts and some lower federal courts, were reviewed in generalist journals, most notably the *North American Review*. In long, discursive essays like those of the *New York Review of Books*, in which the book under consideration occasions a general commentary, reviewers such as Daniel Webster made the case for the common law system and for the superiority of the American approach to judicial opinions. In discussing the reports themselves, the reviewers described the reporter's function, the opinion-writing process, the importance of written opinions in the scheme of common law, and the vital need that the reports be published and read.[8]

Concerned frequently with the tension between common law and statutory law, especially in light of the legislative frenzy that took place in Massachusetts in the wake of Shay's rebellion, Webster and other anonymous reviewers rejected the argument that statutory law should preeminently control the affairs of the populace. They argued that statutes at best established general principles and fell short of addressing the myriad individual circumstances calling for an application of law. Only the common law had the flexibility to meet this need. Moreover, statutory law created its own set of problems because it was often vague and ambiguous as to its application.

Rejecting the argument that the common law was too infected by the unbridled discretion of judges to serve the country's need, reviewers saw the volumes of reported decisions as proof that the judges issued principled decisions and were obligated to follow the precedents they found in the common law. For Webster, for example, the common law offered greater security and certainty. The reports became "the highest evidence of our enlightened and civilized state."[9] Another reviewer continued this theme by quoting Chancellor Kent, whose systematic treatment of American Law and its sources in the six editions of his four volume *Commentaries on American Law* influenced generations of American lawyers and jurists: "Our American reports contain an exposition of the common law as received and modified in reference to the genius of our institutions," he wrote. "By that law we are governed and protected, and it cannot but awaken a correspondent attachment."[10]

Reviewers argued that American reports were superior to those of the English. They wrote that we had passed through our phase of seriatim opinions while the English still indulged in this approach and its inherent redundancy. Equally important, American judges wrote their opinions and gave them to court reporters, ensuring accuracy, while the English delivered their opinions orally, hoping that the reporters would record their decisions accurately.

The reviewers could hardly restrain the pride they felt in the products of the American democracy. That the courts were deciding cases in this common law system was by itself proof of the democracy's success. But reviewers were quick to note that, as important as the work of the courts was, the reports had not been widely disseminated. Only a small number of law libraries carried the reports of the High Court, reviewers complained. But to say that not enough lawyers were reading the reports was to miss the point. These early cases were so important to America that, as Daniel Webster put it, "no gentleman can think he has a complete library, while he has not the judgment of the highest judicial tribunal in the country."[11]

In arguing for the value of the reports as literature in their own right, one reviewer again quoted Kent's *Commentaries*. Reports, he wrote, "are worthy of being studied even by scholars of taste and general literature, as being authentic memorials of the business and manners of the age in which they were composed. Law reports are dramatic in their plan and structure. They abound in pathetic incident, and displays of deep feeling. They are faithful records of those 'little competitions, factions, and debates at the bar,' and the elaborate opinions on the bench, delivered with the authority of oracular wisdom. They become deeply interesting, because they contain true portraits of the talents and learning of the sages of the law."[12]

One reviewer, discussing a volume of decisions from the lower federal courts of Connecticut, Vermont, and New York, went further and argued that the reports should be more widely disseminated so that they could be used as tools of legal education. He suggested that students would find reading cases in the reports far more interesting than reading the codes, digests, and elementary treatises ordinarily used for legal education. Students have difficulty comprehending the sources of law they are studying, he wrote, and if they do understand them, they cannot remember their importance for long. Law reports, on the other hand, are not only more interesting, but reading them "serve[s] as bonds of association, by which the principles interwoven with them are held together, and kept long and strongly fastened in the mind."[13]

At the same time, reviewers worried that America could have too much of a good thing if the number of volumes of reported cases was not kept in check. Webster urged reporters in future volumes to omit those cases that turned merely on evidence, while others suggested that cases should be omitted if they covered the same ground as already published cases. A different argument against the increasing number of reported decisions, oddly enough, held that too many cases on a particular point should lead to omitting some, even if the cases were not uniform in their conclusions. As one reviewer put it, "the study of these contradictory decisions will serve only to bewilder and becloud, instead of aiding and understanding."[14] For this reviewer the emphasis in the common law system was on the precedential effect of decisions, not on the reasoning of each decision and the accreting nature of the common law.

◆　　◆

Reviewers had a right to crow about America's experiment with judicial opinions. A comparison with the English experience through the first half of the nineteenth century highlights the different values Americans brought to the idea of precedent and its role, through the publication of opinions, in the judicial process. For the first three centuries of English case-law history, beginning in the twelfth century, documents known as the plea rolls recorded the results of litigation for the purpose of res judicata. Written on sheepskin, rolled and bound at the top, these plea rolls were compiled by unknown recorders and contained no discussion of judicial reasoning or even the arguments of counsel.[15] Their purpose was merely to record the decision. With the aptly named yearbooks, which began to appear in the fourteenth century, we find records of the arguments of counsel and exchanges between counsel and the bench. It seems clear, given the brevity of the yearbook cases and their failure to discuss a judge's reasoning, that the reporters did not think they were establishing precedent with their cases. Despite this, English courts looked to yearbook cases as weighty precedent.

Consider, for example, the famous case of *Rylands v. Fletcher*,[16] which established the doctrine of strict liability in the context of damage done to a property owner's land caused by water flowing onto his parcel from his neighbor's. The court relied significantly on a fifteenth-century animal trespass case, *Anon.* of 1480,[17] to support its reasoning—even though *Anon.* is only twelve lines long and contains little explanation as to why a property owner is liable for damage done by his animals in straying onto his neighbor's land. The case states, perhaps punningly, that "it behooves him to use his common so that it shall do no hurt to another man, and if the land in which has common be not inclosed, it behooves him to keep the beasts in common, and out of the land of any other."[18] We do not learn anything about the size of the parcel used for grazing, how the animals are managed on the land, what the cost of fencing would be for the landowners, or the frequency of these types of trespasses. In short, we learn nothing from the case that addresses the question of whether it makes sense to impose strict liability on animal owners for the trespasses of their animals. The facts of *Anon.*, in typical yearbook fashion, are not even recited. But of course it was not reasoning or even the facts of *Anon.* that the court in *Rylands v. Fletcher* was looking for. The court only wanted to hang its hat on an established principle of law. It referred to *Anon.* so that it could say that "the law as to them seems perfectly settled from early times; the owner must keep them in at his peril, or he will be answerable for the natural consequences of their escape."[19]

It was not until the abrupt end of the yearbooks in the mid-sixteenth century and the beginning of the law reporters that the record of a case began to reflect the judicial process. For three centuries a series of reporters kept the history of English case law with volumes of reports that varied greatly in quality. Since nearly all of the decisions were delivered orally, the reporters attempted to recreate them. Not surprisingly, they were frequently inaccurate. Some reporters, such as the father of law reporting, Plowden, were scrupulous in their attention to detail, while others were so unreliable that citations to their reports were hardly accepted in court. Moreover, the reports were spotty in that the reporters, who chose which cases to include in their accounts, reported on only a small percentage of the decisions being rendered. In addition, they went beyond reporting the decision at hand and added material from earlier cases, which, in effect, helped to create the common law. These extrajudicial commentaries were thought to have the weight of law, depending on the stature of the reporter. The common law of England, in this regard, was fashioned as much by the reporters—especially by giants such as Coke, Plowden, and Burrow—as by the judges and their decisions, as reported by the reporters. Lord Bacon said of Coke, for example, "had it not been for Sir Edward Coke's Reports (which, though they may have errors, and some peremptory and more judicial resolutions than are warranted, yet they contain infinite good decisions and rulings over of cases), the law, by this time, had been almost like a ship without ballast; for that the cases of modern experience are fled from those that are adjudged and ruled in former time."[20] "The extra-judicial opinions of Lord Coke," Justice Putnam of the Massachusetts Supreme Court noted in a nineteenth-century decision, "contain more of the common law than is to be found in the writings of any other reporter before or since his time."[21]

Law reporting reached a low point in the nineteenth century as a result of too many entries into the market. The increasing unreliability of these reports led at first to a rule giving the only official version of the reports a citation monopoly. This monopoly lasted only a few years and was followed by a quasi-official series of reports called the *Law Reports*, established in the mid-nineteenth century. Later a private competitor emerged, called the *All England Reports*, which in time supplanted the *Law Reports* in popularity. The latter, however, remains the official version of the reports, published under the aegis of the Incorporated Council of Law Reporting for England and Wales. At the time the series was established, there had been talk of giving the *Law Reports* a monopoly of citations, but the suggestion was rejected. Court stenographers were appointed to take down the oral decisions of the judges, and the judges themselves agreed to cooperate with the reporters, who remained unofficial in their jobs, to reduce inaccuracies. The reporters continued to choose which cases should be reported, and the reports remained spotty—a reflection of the English preference for a small body of precedent. For the English, a case was precedential and worth reporting only when it significantly interpreted existing law. Cases turning only on their facts or involving only slight variations of existing law were not reported. Today the English continue to follow the same approach to reporting and precedent. The *All England Reports* include all the reported decisions of the English courts in just three annual volumes. And although it has not been a frequently contested point, the general view is that the Crown retains the right, as it does with statutes, to reproduce the opinions published in these volumes.[22]

Burke was on to something when he famously noted that he could not think of English law without the English *Law Reports*. But when judged against the American experience in law reporting, their significance seems less impressive. After all, this was a system of reporting in which the reporters sometimes took it upon themselves to suppress law they did not like. "I had a drawer marked 'Bad Law,'" Lord Cambell, a former reporter, once confided, "into which I threw all the cases which seemed to me to be improperly ruled."[23]

◆ ◆

Dred Scott v. Sandford, the 1857 decision that was the ultimate debacle of the nineteenth-century Supreme Court, highlighted not only the capacity of the Court to influence American life but also the relevance and importance of its reporting and publication practices. Chief Justice Taney's opinion for the Court was an unusually weak effort, contorting itself to avoid that which could hardly be denied: that after spending three years in a free territory Scott was not a free man. Taney had read his opinion in conference and then in open court. Justice Curtis, based on what he had heard in conference, wrote a dissent that most constitutional scholars today agree completely destroys Taney's opinion. Following the reading of Taney's opinion in open court, Curtis immediately filed his dissent with the clerk of the court, as required by Court rules. Curtis then published his opinion in a Boston newspaper, on the assumption, Curtis wrote at the time, that Taney's opinion would be filed with the clerk and reprinted as well in the nation's newspapers. Taney, however, did not file his opinion with the Court. Seeing the strength of Curtis's dissent, Taney withheld his opinion and modified it to meet Curtis's arguments. This, at least, is what Curtis believed when he learned that Taney had added eighteen pages to the opinion he had read from the bench. Wanting to know what Taney had argued after the fact, Curtis wrote to the clerk for a copy of Taney's opinion. The clerk informed him that Taney had issued an order, joined by the only two Justices who were still in Washington after the end of the Term, prohibiting the clerk from releasing to anyone, including the Justices themselves, any opinion of the Court before it was published in the *U.S. Reports.*

Naturally angered by this rebuff, Curtis engaged Taney in correspondence over the new Court rule.[24] Taney denied adding anything of substance to his opinion, saying that he had only supplemented the proofs and authorities. He charged that Curtis had impugned the dignity of the Court by publishing his dissenting opinion and accused him of infringing on the reporter's statutory right to publish the Court's opinions and to make money from doing this. Taney said that he had no problem with the new order exempting members of the Court, so long as the Justice who wanted the opinion was to use it as part of the Court's work. Curtis could hardly have this in mind, he argued, and since Curtis was motivated only by partisan, political interests, he felt justified in withholding the opinion.

The story, recounted today, has an air of unreality. Aside from the dispute as to whether Curtis was entitled to a copy of the Court's opinion, which is, by itself, an extraordinary event, Taney temporarily flouted the rule that required him to file his opinion with the clerk. He eventually filed his opinion after revising it to rebut Curtis's dissent as best he could. But his order curtailing dissemination of the opinion until its publication in the *U.S. Reports* left the country in ignorance about the Court's work for several weeks. For a Chief Justice interested in letting the furor surrounding his decision die down, this order, of course, was ideal. At best, under Taney's manipulation of the reporting and publication process, only those journalists present when Taney read his original opinion could report on what the Court had decided in *Dred Scott.* Moreover, they would have been able to report only Taney's first attempt. His second, revised opinion was not to be subject to public scrutiny until it was later published in the *U.S. Reports.*

The reporting and publication issues of *Dred Scott* did not escape the notice of journalists once the decision was published. *The North American Review* began its scathing, intelligent analysis of the faulty reasoning of *Dred Scott* with a lengthy commentary worth quoting in full.

> The decisions of courts are required by law to be promulgated, printed, and published. The reasons of the decision are to be stated, to enable the court to expound the principles of law, and show their bearing on the case; as also to give assurance of the permanency of the rules of law, and of the wisdom and impartiality of their application, by reference to other decid-

ed cases. The court may thus justify its conclusions to the jurisconsult, and secure the confidence of the community, while it settles the rights of the litigants. The promulgation and publication of judicial opinions is one of the greatest safeguards of the purity of judges, and of the impartiality of the judgments. Published opinions become a part of the literature of the day. They are submitted to the criticism of the country. The law, the logic, and the morality, embodied and set forth in these carefully studied productions, are the legitimate subjects of examination and criticism. The greater the authority of the writers, the more dangerous are their errors. And the more important the public interests affected by them, the more imperative is the duty of pointing out their errors, or of vindicating their claim to confidence and respect. Moreover, the decisions of the Supreme Court of the United States are in no sense sectional, but national topics. Their validity, their mode of operation, their bearing on the civil *status* of individuals and classes of men, it is the concern of our whole people to investigate and determine. While, therefore, we have felt it our duty, in a Review intended primarily to represent the thought, sentiment, and literature of the nation, to avoid subjects of sectional controversy, this very consideration seems to force upon us the cognizance of a decision, or rather a series of opinions, emanating from a tribunal which constitutes the judicial mind and conscience of the country, taken collectively.[25]

◆　◆

Three further developments in the nineteenth century continue the story of the reporting and publication of the Court's opinions. First, by the end of the century, not only were all the cases decided with an opinion published in the *Reports,* but these opinions were in writing. Second, the Court's recognition in 1835 in *Wheaton v. Peters* that its decisions could not be copyrighted led eventually to others entering the field of Supreme Court opinion publishing. The Lawyers Cooperative Publishing Company began its *Lawyer's Edition of the Supreme Court Reports* in 1882 by republishing all of the Court's work up to that time before beginning in 1885 with its publication of current cases. West Publishing began publishing current cases in 1882 and did not republish from the beginning. *U.S. Law Week* began its publication of current opinions in 1933. Third, the government became a bigger book buyer in the second half of the nineteenth century. By the 1860s, the reporter was still obliged as part of his salary to provide copies of his *Reports* to the government for distribution at no extra charge. In 1866, for example, the number was 300. But in 1862 there is for the first time a separate appropriation for the purchase of *Reports* for the Department of State. By 1867 the government was paying the reporter only for reporting and was buying all its *Reports* from his publisher. As part of its appropriation legislation, Congress set the price for the *Reports* it would buy. In 1897 Congress appropriated $28,000 to provide sets of the *Reports* to all the courthouses where the district and circuit courts convened. In 1907 Congress appropriated money for 260 copies of the *Reports* at $2.00 per volume and for 13 copies of the *Lawyer's Edition* by the Lawyers Cooperative Publishing Company, at $5.00 per volume.

The name of the *Reports* was changed from that of the reporter to the *U.S. Reports* in 1875, but the government did not change from being a book buyer to a book publisher until 1922, when it assumed the publication of the *Reports*.[26] After this the reporter could no longer enter into a contract with a publisher to produce the *Reports* at the price set by Congress. He prepared his product and now gave it to the government for printing—under the same specifications as before—and distribution. And with this change, the government no longer had to pay for copies of its own *Reports*. The Court now controlled its own product and established, after 130 years, its own means of communication with the country.

The government did not take over the *Reports* because it wanted control over the Court's publications. Rather, the change in policy was a function of money. First, the price Congress had set for the sale of the *Reports*, which stood at $1.75 per volume in 1922, was so low, according to the floor debate in the House of Representatives over the bill to change the publication system, that the reporter was unable to renew his publishing contract with the Banks Publishing Company, nor could he interest any other legal publishers.[27] The government was, as a result, without a publisher, a condition that required prompt attention. But at the same time, Congress was disturbed by what it considered to be the excessive amount of money the reporter had been able to make by supplementing his $4,500 salary with a commission from the publishers for the copies of the *Reports* they sold. Congress thought that the reporter was technically within his rights to make additional money from the publication of the *Reports* but wanted his compensation to come only from the government, since he held an important government position. Legislation was proposed to raise the reporter's salary to $9,000 and, rather than merely prohibiting him from making additional money from the publisher of the *Reports*, to transfer the publication of the *Reports* to the government. The reporter was worth $9,000 per year, his supporters argued, because he performed highly technical work and wrote the syllabus of each case. Critics countered with the arguments that any law student or young lawyer could write the syllabus and that the Justice who had written the majority opinion himself reviewed the syllabus and made changes if needed before he approved it.[28]

Congress's action suggests that keeping the price of the *Reports* artificially low was important. But Congress could have attracted a publisher for the *Reports* if it had lifted its price control over the volumes. Moreover, it could have addressed its concern over the reporter's compensation simply by prohibiting him from having a financial interest in the contract he entered into to publish the *Reports*. Instead, after squabbling about the reporter's salary, which was set at $8,000 per year, Congress transferred the publication of the *Reports* to the Public Printer and required that they be printed, bound, and issued within eight months after the decisions had been rendered.

Congress may have decided to stay in the business of publishing the Court's opinions because, as some members argued, the quality of those reports published by the reporter in conjunction with Banks Publishing was significantly higher than those of the competitors. But Congress could hardly find fault with the accuracy and completeness of the latter since they relied on the reporter's work and merely republished all the opinions that had appeared in the slip opinions prepared by the reporter. Lawyers Cooperative Publishing had gone even further and provided the exact pagination of the *Reports* so that its users did not need to own the *Reports* to give parallel citations in their court submissions. This inspired idea led to litigation in 1909 in which the Banks Publishing Company, as a successor in interest to the reporter in publishing the opinions of the High Court, argued that Lawyers Cooperative's use of its pagination violated its copyright. The Second Circuit of the U.S. Court of Appeals ruled that since the reporter had the obligation to supply pagination for his official volumes for the orderly arrangement of the cases, the pagination could not be copyrighted.[29] With this point settled, West Publishing also began in 1919 to provide parallel citation in its *Supreme Court Reporter* versions of the High Court's cases.

Print quality rather than completeness and accuracy was the problem for at least one congressman. Raker of California complained that "some of these [competing] publications . . . publish reports that you can not read, and you might as well throw them in the wastebasket." "I think that is true," responded Congressman Walsh, the chairman of the House Judiciary Committee and author of the bill under consideration, "and a great many are thrown into the wastebasket; but of course no one would throw a volume of the Supreme Court reports into the wastebasket, and particularly if they are prepared in the manner and in a way which would appeal to a learned attorney like my distinguished friend from California."

Anyone today looking at corresponding 1922 volumes of West Publishing's *Supreme Court Reporter,* Lawyers Cooperative's *Lawyer's Edition of the Supreme Court Reports,* and the official *U.S. Reports* would be hard pressed to understand what differences in quality Walsh and Raker were talking about. It could be that the advance sheets were inferior, but the hardcover volumes are hardly distinguishable in their quality. Ironically, the *U.S. Reports* were a clearly inferior product from the important perspective of an editor's annotations. They contained only a headnote designated as a syllabus that succinctly described the nature of the case and the principles at issue. This editorial work existed by itself for that particular case. In contrast, West Publishing's *Supreme Court Reporter* was annotated in accordance with its key number digest system. The headnotes in the Lawyers Cooperative's *Lawyer's Edition* were of the sort found in the *U.S. Reports.* Only later did Lawyers Cooperative develop its own indexing system.

The key number digest system, which West Publishing had acquired when it bought Little, Brown's *United States Digest* in 1888,[30] revolutionized legal research and for many remains the quintessential research tool. Others, with access to the computer data bases of WESTLAW and LEXIS, swear by the key word research method, which searches entire data bases in seconds for matching verbal phrases. In the key number digest system, the West editors extract the legal principle, summarizing it in a one-sentence headnote paragraph based largely on the language of the opinion itself and identifying it with subject and then subissue names and numbers, which locate the principle on West's charted legal landscape made up of 220 subjects and several thousand subissue headings known as key numbers. The summarized principles of law, called headnotes, preface the opinion and follow a brief synopsis of the case written by West's editors, which details the case's procedural posture, the issues presented, and the court's conclusions. The headnotes from a particular case later appear in multivolume digests arranged by subject and subissues. The key number system has the advantage of organizing the vast legal landscape and then bringing readers to individual cases featuring the very principle they are pursuing, that is, as the principle has been used or interpreted in various factual situations.

West Publishing began annotating its *Supreme Court Reporter* with its digest key number system in 1905 with volume 26. At this stage of its development, though, the digest system had not yet advanced to key numbers, that is, the subprinciples of law that made up a digest topic that were indexed by number. These indexed subprinciples first appeared in 1908 with volume 29. The last piece in the system fell into place in 1915 in volume 36 when West Publishing began to list and number the indexed subprinciples before the beginning of the Court's opinion and then place bracketed numbers corresponding to the listed key numbers in the opinion itself at the beginning of paragraphs in which the key-numbered principle of law could be found.

◆　　◆

Developments in the reporting and publication of the decisions of the lower federal courts differed from those of the Supreme Court in emphasizing private publication. Although they are largely forgotten today, the lower courts in the nineteenth century had decisions to be reported. Throughout the century the district and circuit courts were busy trying and reviewing cases and constructing an impressive body of precedent in limited jurisdictional areas such as admiralty. The jurisdiction of the district court was expanded in 1875 to include federal matters, which made its work that much more important. The establishment of the U.S. Court of Appeals in 1891 was a relatively late development. There had been circuit judges but no circuit court of appeals before 1891, when the circuit judges, along with Supreme Court Justices riding circuit and district court judges themselves, reviewed district court decisions. This system was replaced in 1891 with an entire appellate court system staffed with circuit judges whose job it was to review lower court decisions.

Decisions coming from the federal district and circuit court benches were reported unofficially, compiled and published either by enterprising lawyers or by the judges themselves. Editors produced these volumes of reports from individual districts or particular types of cases, such as patent and admiralty cases. The result was a patchwork attempt to cover the large amount of law being created by these courts. But the coverage was so spotty that one federal judge of the time, Eli Shelby Hammond of the western district of Tennessee, called this period "the Dark Continent of American Jurisprudence."[31]

Some 327 volumes of reports from the various federal districts and circuits under the editorship of some 87 editors published the federal cases of the late eighteenth and nineteenth centuries. Reporters often published opinions that had lain dormant for decades. They explained in the prefaces to their first volumes that, since the authors of the opinions were frequently long since departed, the reports had defects in accuracies and completeness. The cases were more accurate when the authoring judge was alive and had helped with the publication of the cases. But whether the editors got their opinions from the executors of deceased judges or from the authoring judges while still alive, they noted that they published them with their permission, an odd idea in light of the Supreme Court's holding in *Wheaton v. Peters* that its cases, at least, could not be copyrighted. Perhaps the editors of the lower federal court decisions thought that the holding did not apply beyond the Supreme Court. In any event, they acted as if they needed the permission of the judges to report the cases. The reporters in their prefaces praised both the judges whose opinions they were reporting and the opinions that they wrote. They noted the need for the reports, for both the public and the practicing bar, and occasionally highlighted facts that made the reader realize the importance of their work. For example, the editor of *Bissell's Reports*, which reported Seventh Circuit cases from 1851 to 1883, noted that the volume had taken longer than expected to produce because the Chicago fire had threatened the undertaking. Typically reporters would explain that they had done little editing. Their work was limited to omitting some less important cases and to fashioning some headnotes. In general, these reported cases did not have the apparatus of summaries and miscellaneous commentary found in the earliest reported Supreme Court cases. Only rarely were the cases in the reports indexed.[32]

It was not until 1880 that order was brought to the chaos of lower federal court opinion reporting. In that year West Publishing began its series entitled the *Federal Reporter*, "devoted exclusively to the prompt and complete publication of the judicial opinions delivered in each of the United States circuit and district courts."[33] The *New York Times* was right in saying, when the series began, that it was "a publication that will be a public boon." Noting that there had been no organized or authorized system of reporting in the federal courts, that many cases had not been reported at all, and that others were not reported promptly, the *Times* continued, "if it is of prime importance to secure the prompt and accurate publication of statutes in order that the legal profession and the people may know the laws, it would seem to be hardly less important to apply the same rule to judicial decisions, for these as well as the statutes go to make up the law, and neither clients nor their lawyers can always find out what the law is unless the judicial interpretations of the law are made accessible in public print."[34] Within just a few years the *Federal Reporter* came to be recognized as the quasi-official reporter of the federal courts.

West Publishing's plan called for weekly, softcover volumes of the series for the sake of timeliness. The opinions would then be brought together in hardcover volumes later in the year, with each volume not to exceed

1,000 pages in length. The opinions were organized for reference, although the major benefit of the series was indexing. It was not until 1909, however, that West Publishing began to annotate its opinions with its digest system. Digest headnotes were numbered beginning in 1911. In 1917 bracketed numbers corresponding to the headnotes as they appeared numbered at the beginning of the opinion were placed at the beginning of those paragraphs containing the principle of law described in the headnote.

In 1894 West brought out a multivolume series designed to rescue from chaos the thousands of cases that had been reported haphazardly from the beginning of the federal courts to 1880. The thirteen volumes of *Federal Cases* represented a search through scores of volumes reporting federal decisions. They published the opinions, numbered consecutively and arranged alphabetically by title, of about thirty-one thousand cases.

With the creation of the U.S. Court of Appeals in 1891, West Publishing began to publish the opinions coming from the various circuits in the *Federal Reporter*. Not until 1933 did West Publishing separate the district court and circuit court opinions into two separate series. The circuit court opinions were published in the *Federal Reporter* and its successors, the *Federal Reporter Second* and the *Federal Reporter Third*. The decisions of the district courts around the country were published in the newly created *Federal Supplement*.

West Publishing continues to publish the circuit court and district court opinions in the *Federal Reporter* and *Federal Supplement* series respectively. The company is thought of as the official publisher for the lower federal courts, but it is not. There is no legislation nor are there rules adopted by the various circuit courts making West Publishing the official publisher of the decisions. At most, some circuits have rules specifying that opinions will be forwarded for publication only to those publishers designated by the court, of which West Publishing is one.[35] West Publishing's status as the unofficial publisher of lower federal court decisions is a function of two facts: first, that the company has virtually monopolized the private publication of these decisions; and second, that the courts themselves, aside from the slip opinions in the circuit courts and the typescripts in the district courts, have no official publication system of their own.

In two cases involving the question of whether West Publishing had an official relationship with the judiciary the courts deciding the cases explained that, despite the absence of any official connection with the courts, for all practical purposes, including that of extending immunity to West Publishing for publishing libelous decisions, the company was the official publisher of the decisions. As one court put it, "bar and Bench alike rely upon the West Reporter volumes as sources in which to find the decisions of the U.S. Courts of Appeals and of the U.S. District Courts; and we take judicial notice that an opinion of a federal circuit or district judge is considered 'not reported' until it appears in Federal Reporter or Federal Supplement."[36] Further evidence of the relationship between the federal judiciary and West Publishing is that, soon after the turn of the century, Congress appropriated money to buy sets of the *Federal Reporter* for judges, Justices, and courthouses.[37]

At least one circuit thought it had made West Publishing its official publisher. The records of the Seventh Circuit in Chicago show that in 1894 the court ordered the clerk to send to West Publishing copies of all the opinions handed down by its judges. A subsequent order in 1901 describes the appointment of West Publishing as the court's official reporter, although in this instance "reporter" should be read as "publisher," as there was no one at the court who performed duties similar to those of the Supreme Court reporter of decisions. The order went further, though, and noted that the designation of West Publishing as the court reporter was in exchange for West Publishing's reports and digests.[38]

It is not clear if West Publishing, in fact, exchanged its reports and digests for the Seventh Circuit's designation as the court's reporter. And if this exchange did exist, it is not known when the arrangement ceased. Rather than providing the federal courts with copies of its reports and digests in return for this status, West Publishing today has the government, most likely, as its biggest single customer. Each year the Administrative Office of the U.S. Courts buys nearly a thousand copies of the *Federal Reporter* for the federal judges, their law clerks, and court libraries, and the Department of Justice buys 430 copies of the Reporter series for the U.S. attorney's offices and for the offices of the attorney general.

West Publishing publishes more than ten thousand district court and circuit court opinions each year. These opinions take up approximately fifty 1,600-page volumes. As great as that figure appears, it represents only a fraction of the number of opinions rendered each year from the circuit and district courts. The company publishes those opinions provided by the district and circuits court judges, but the judges do not give West Publishing all of their opinions. In 1987 the U.S. Court of Appeals as a whole published only about 40 percent of its decisions.[39]

The nonpublication policy of the courts is a function of the growth in their workload.[40] Between 1960 and 1988, for example, there was a 55 percent increase in district court filings per judge, while there was a 336 percent increase in circuit court filings per judge in the same period.[41] This increase is related in part to population growth and the litigiousness of society at large. Equally important, Congress has in the last few decades passed a wide variety of legislation giving citizens causes of actions they did not have before. The world of today's federal judiciary is strikingly different when compared with that of 1930, for example, because of the number of statutes passed since then enabling citizens to bring claims in federal court relating to social security, employment and pension rights, environmental regulation, and civil rights, to name just a few. Today ours is a statutory rather than a common law world.

Several solutions to the workload problem have been suggested. One is to eliminate diversity jurisdiction. In 1960 diversity jurisdiction made up 21.5 percent of the judicial workload in the district courts and 26.3 percent in the court of appeals. In 1988 the district court diversity percentage was 24.0 and the court of appeals percentage was 12.0. Proponents for change contend that the original reason for diversity jurisdiction—to protect litigants from one state from being shortchanged in the forum state—does not apply in today's culture. Another solution is for Congress to add more Article 3 judges to ease the workload. Opponents of this solution argue that adding judges would dilute the quality of the federal judiciary and that judges should instead write shorter signed opinions and more per curiam opinions. A third solution is the creation of a new court to settle intercircuit disputes. Of these possible solutions, the recent Federal Courts Study Committee recommended that Congress appoint more judges and fill current vacancies. It also suggested that Congress not create a national intermediate appellate court but made no recommendations relating to opinions.[42]

The nonpublication policy that courts have adopted has been proposed as a solution to the opinion proliferation problem. Moreover, even though those looking at the problem speak in terms of "nonpublication" policies, this is something of a misnomer, since many of the nonpublished decisions make their way into computer data bases, where researchers are able to find and use them. With this qualification about language, the argument for the nonpublication policy stresses the acknowledged fact that a significant percentage of the court's cases do not contribute to the jurisprudence of the particular issue being decided and instead turn merely on the facts. Complaints about the proliferation of judicial opinions have been heard since judicial opinions were first published. Webster's review of Wheaton's Reports in the *North American Review* makes this point, for example. Undergirding the nonpublication argument is the belief that law offices are being overwhelmed by the number of volumes of judicial opinions. Where to put all those books? And, more to the point, who can afford all those books?

There are several objections to the nonpublication policy. One is a light-of-day argument, which contends that if judges know their opinions will not be published, they will take less care in making their decisions and articulating the law. This includes the notion that what the judiciary does should be open to review by all, not just by the litigants, who would be the only ones receiving copies of nonpublished opinions. A second part of this argument is the belief that judges would be more willing to let their law clerks write their opinions if they knew they would not be published. That some of the circuit courts employ full-time staff attorneys to write opinions, which are not published, supports the idea that writing will be delegated if the opinion is not to be published. Finally, this policy is at odds with the American jurisprudential approach, which is based upon precedent.

Solutions to the proliferation problem need to be understood in the context of West Publishing's virtual monopoly in the private hardcover publication of lower federal court opinions and of computer technology, such as CD-ROMs. West Publishing's hardcover monopoly is virtual rather than complete because other publishers bring out select opinions from, for instance, admiralty law or some other specialized field. But this in no way acts as an alternative to West Publishing's publication of all the district and circuit court opinions that the judges want published. In this regard West Publishing's monopoly is complete.

West Publishing's control over the publication of lower federal court opinions has been in place for so long—more than a century—that this fact alone effectively keeps competitors from entering the marketplace. The problem potential competitors face is not that West Publishing has a citation monopoly of the sort that existed briefly in England in the first part of the nineteenth century, as described above. West Publishing does not have a monopoly because judges will accept citations to decisions published by other companies such as the admiralty reporter or the labor reporter. It might be better form for a lawyer to cite authority that the judge is likely to have access to, but even the judges themselves sometimes cite reports not published by West Publishing. On occasion, when judges have done this, West Publishing has seemed to suggest that it should have a citation monopoly, going so far in one instance as to place an asterisk where the non–West Publishing citation would have been and a footnote stating "no opinion for publication." In another instance it changed the rival citation to its parallel West Publishing citation.[43]

To compete with West Publishing a newcomer would need either to access West Publishing's data base of existing opinions or to create its own. West Publishing, of course, controls permission to use its data base. The problem is not that West Publishing has a citation monopoly but that the company has a copyright interest in its citations. In the 1980s Mead Data launched an electronic competitor with its LEXIS service. The opinions of the federal courts were put into Mead Data's data base and given their own LEXIS citations. These citations were readily accepted and used by the courts. When West Publishing brought out in hardcover the same opinion that Mead Data had put on-line in LEXIS, Mead Data wanted to give the West Publishing citation to its users as well, since it was this hardcover version of the case that assumed quasi-official status. Moreover, Mead Data wanted to provide within its LEXIS opinion the pagination that corresponded to the West Publishing's hardcover version for the obvious reason that, with this parallel citation, users did not need to buy from West Publishing. Understandably, West Publishing was not happy with this turn of events.

The company sued Mead Data to keep it from using the pagination of its opinions. In an action for a preliminary injunction, West Publishing conceded that Mead Data's parallel citation at the beginning of the LEXIS version was fair use of its copyright. It argued instead that it was Mead Data's use of page breaks corresponding to West Publishing's pagination that violated its copyright. Mead Data argued that West Publishing could not copyright its pagination and cited as its authority the case of *Banks Publishing Co. v. Lawyers Cooperative Publishing Co.*, which had held that Banks Publishing, as the successor in interest to the reporter of decisions in the Supreme Court, could not copyright its pagination and that Lawyers Cooperative could place page breaks corresponding to the pagination in the *U.S. Reports*. The court in the litigation between West Publishing and Mead Data did not find *Banks Publishing* persuasive, on the grounds that Banks Publishing's interest flowed from the official obligations of the reporter to publish the *U.S. Reports*. West Publishing's publication venture, the court surprisingly concluded, was private. "West is not the official reporter for any court in this country nor is it required by statute to arrange or page its volumes. It does these things of its own initiative expending considerable labor, talent, and judgment in the process. West's page numbers and its arrangement of cases are necessarily within the scope of copyright protection."[44] The court did not seek to square its view, that West Publishing is not the official publisher of at least the inferior federal court opinions, with the development in opinion publication in the nineteenth and twentieth centuries. Ultimately, West Publishing and Mead Data settled their dispute between themselves, with Mead Data agreeing to pay West Publishing a royalty each time it used a page-break parallel citation in its opinions.

This opinion established that the decisions of the federal court cannot be copyrighted but that the pagination of a private publisher can. Therefore, any competitor to West Publishing, for retroactive comprehensiveness, would need to put all the past opinions in its data base and give them citations under a new system. This would be a project similar to what West Publishing itself undertook when it combined all the nineteenth-century federal decisions that had appeared in patchwork fashion around the country in the series known as the *Federal Cases*. The only alternative would be for a competitor to use, under some sort of licensing agreement, West Publishing's versions of those cases. This issue is important to any competitor because consumers would be loath to begin using a new citation system prospectively if they still had to have all of West Publishing's cases on hand to cover this retroactive gap in their data base.

Any competition for West Publishing's publication of federal decisions would have to be computer based. Even if a competitor wanted to give new citations to the hundreds of thousands of cases that West Publishing has published so far, hard-copy republication would not be feasible. Only in the CD-ROM world could such a project be undertaken, although even there it hardly seems likely.

In 1994 the Justice Department considered becoming a competitor of sorts when it gave thought to developing its own system for organizing the opinions of the federal courts. The system was to be public in the sense that the manner in which cases were cited would allow West Publishing's competitors to develop opinion data bases that did not rely upon West Publishing's current citation and pagination practices. The Justice Department thought better of the idea and in February 1995 informed the House Government Reform Committee that it had no plans to offer its own alternative to West Publishing: "[l]et us be very clear about this: the department has no plans to replicate the West Publishing Co. database or otherwise to develop either its own comprehensive database or alternative legal citation system."[45]

It now appears that Congress's decision, as ill reasoned as it was, to assume control of the publication of the *U.S. Reports* was wise. The federal government does buy hundreds of copies of the *Supreme Court Reporter* from West Publishing each year for use in judges' chambers, U.S. Attorneys' offices, and court libraries, but it is not compelled to do so with the availability—albeit four years late—of the *U.S. Reports*. On the other hand, the government must buy its copies of the *Federal Reporter* and *Federal Supplement* from West Publishing each year, since there is no alternative government publication. True, the court of appeals could rely only on the slip opinions that it publishes, but this is hardly feasible logistically because of distribution and indexing problems. Moreover, the district court cases have no slip opinion counterpart. Without a publication system for the lower federal courts resembling the *U.S. Reports*, the government is at the mercy of West Publishing. West Publishing, given the dynamics at work, would hardly want to be the official publisher of the opinions of the lower federal courts. If it were, it could not keep the copyright protection for its pagination. Without that protection, its empire would be threatened. More to the point, neither the legal system nor the readers of judicial opinions would want West Publishing to become the official publisher of federal decisions. That way would lie chaos if other entrants brought citation variations to what is now a simple theme.

Congress has made an implicit ongoing decision not to appoint reporters of decisions for the circuit courts of appeal in the manner of the reporter of decisions for the Supreme Court. But this decision grows increasingly questionable as the number of opinions from the lower courts increases. By providing West Publishing with opinions only, with nothing more, the various courts make themselves dependent upon an extrajudicial force to ensure that their opinions are published properly. West Publishing claims to exercise no editorial control over the judicial product it publishes. The company will correct punctuation and grammatical errors, but for corrections or changes that can affect an opinion's substance, it says that it secures the approval of the judge who has written the opinion. There is no way of knowing, without extensive investigation, if in fact West Publishing adheres to this policy. But if there were a reporter of decisions for each of the federal circuits who had jurisdiction over the opinions of the circuit court and the district courts in the circuit, then that reporter would be responsible for fashioning the opinions into their final publication form, as the reporter of decisions does for the opinions of the Supreme Court. The reporter of decisions would then distribute the final product to West Publishing, or any other publishing company, for publication, with the caveat that the opinion could be published only in its official form. Gone would be any doubt as to whether opinions appear as the judges authorized them.

The reporter of decisions would also write a short syllabus for each opinion. Although these syllabi would have no formal authority, just as the syllabi prepared by the Supreme Court's reporter of decisions do not,[46] readers would be less likely to be misled by West Publishing's occasional mistakes in the summary paragraphs it prepares for each opinion. In one recent circuit court of appeals opinion, for example, West Publishing reported that a district court decision had been affirmed when in fact the decision had been only partly affirmed. This prompted the district judge who had written the lower court opinion to note that "[t]his court cannot help but be amused by West Publishing Company's syllabus at 830 F.2d 172, which announced that this court was 'affirmed' at 818 F.2d 1537. Saying it, however, does not make it so."[47]

The amusement the court describes likely flows from West Publishing's attempted arrogation of judicial authority. If nothing else, the appointment of reporters of decisions for the circuit and district courts would break the stranglehold West Publishing has on the actual content of the opinions it publishes by interposing a facilitator acting on the court's behalf. In this way, judicial authority could not be arrogated, either in theory or in practice, placing the courts in their rightful place when it comes to the publication of their decisions.[48]

—◆ 2 ◆—

Who Writes Judicial Opinions

There is little doubt that the law clerks of the Supreme Court Justices are fully institutionalized in the opinion-writing process today and that they write most of the opinions of the Justices for whom they work. Each of the Associate Justices uses three law clerks. The Chief Justice can have four, but the current Chief Justice, Rehnquist, uses only three. The clerks prepare memoranda for the Justices on the now seven thousand cases asking to be heard by the Court each year, from which the Court will usually agree to take between 100 and 150. Once a case has been selected, argued, and decided by the Justices in conference, the Justice selected to write the opinion assigns the job in turn to one of the law clerks in his or her employ. Supreme Court Justices in the past have argued that their work load was too overwhelming for them to write all of their own opinions, although one Justice, William O. Douglas, consistently maintained that the case for the Court being overworked was a myth. He once even argued this in a dissenting opinion.[1] Today, however, with the Court deciding the fewest number of cases with opinions in decades, the complaint is not being raised as much. Instead, the Justices now need to argue that they are working as hard as before.[2]

But while there is little argument as to whether the law clerks write the opinions of the High Court, only rarely do the law clerks themselves discuss their writing roles when they leave their positions. For example, Stephen Carter of the Yale Law School, who clerked for Justice Marshall, on a recent Booknotes program on C-SPAN, begged off from answering the direct question of opinion authorship in Marshall's chambers, leaving the clear impression that, while he was protecting the illusion that Justice

Marshall wrote his own opinions, he was, at the same time with his de-murral, letting us all know that he was a Marshall ghostwriter. The Justices, as well, rarely discuss the authorship of their opinions. One exception came in 1986 when then Justice Rehnquist, in a talk at the Harvard Law School, said that his clerks wrote the first draft of his majority opinions but that he edited heavily, shortening, shortening, shortening.[3] Of Chief Justice Rehnquist's former colleagues, Justice Brennan described his opinions on the Court as "opinions that came from the Brennan chambers," noting that Bentham had said that the "law is not the work of the judge alone but of judge and company."[4] But in a 1990 *New Yorker* profile by Nat Hentoff, Justice Brennan said that he always wrote the first drafts of his opinions. Justice Lewis Powell's biographer reports that Powell's law clerks wrote the first drafts of his opinions and that when Powell did write, he dictated.[5] An earlier memoir by one of Justice Powell's first law clerks, Harvie Wilkinson, Jr., who is himself a federal judge today on the Fourth Circuit of the U.S. Court of Appeals, depicts a different opinion-writing process. Wilkinson suggested that the law clerk's role was far less important and that the Justice himself did most of the opinion writing.[6] In contrast, a recent *New Yorker* article reported that Justice Thomas not only had one of his law clerks write his opinions, but that the law clerk in question, Christopher Landau, held so much sway over the Justice that Thomas's vote on the high court was known as the Landau vote.[7] On the current Court, Justice Stevens, if the out-of-school disclosures of law clerks in a 1993 *Wall Street Journal* article are to be trusted, is the only Justice to write the first drafts of his opinion.[8] But it is also fair to speculate that the only Justice appointed after 1993, Justice Breyer, writes his own opinions, since he did so as a circuit court judge.

◆   ◆

At first the question for the Supreme Court was not who wrote the decisions but whether they were written at all. Only one original manuscript of an opinion exists from the Court's first decade, leading a prominent scholar of the period to speculate that the Justices probably did not write their opinions.[9] The Justices seemed to be following the English tradition, first, in delivering their opinions orally, and, second, in delivering them seriatim, that is, with each Justice weighing in with his view of the case, and no opinion speaking for the Court as a whole.

Beginning with the appointment of John Marshall (1801–35) as Chief Justice, two important changes took place in the production of opinions and in the opinions themselves. First, written opinions became the norm in the Marshall era. Second, Marshall, with only the rarest exceptions, did away with seriatim opinions and instituted the tradition of a Justice writing a majority opinion of the Court.[10] One Court, one voice, mostly Marshall's, as shown by the 508 opinions of the Court he wrote. Remarkably, between 1801 and 1811 Marshall wrote 147 of the Court's first 171 opinions. The only other Justice on the Marshall Court to make significant contributions was Justice Story (1811–45). This approach made the other Justices less accountable. But for Marshall, getting the work out quickly rather than accountability was the goal. Often, drafts of the Court's opinion were not even circulated to the brethren, which meant that they had no say in the reasoning of the opinion.

This uneven distribution of opinion-writing chores continued throughout the century, at least on the constitutional front. Taney wrote the majority of the important constitutional cases on his Court, although Justice Curtis (1851–57) in the handful of constitutional opinions he wrote during his brief tenure made a significant impression on the Court's jurisprudence. On the Chase Court, the ball was carried primarily by Justices Miller (1862–90), Field (1863–97), Chase (1864–73), and Strong (1870–80). Chief Justice Waite (1874–88) dominated the constitutional opinions of his Court as well, though to a lesser degree than his predecessors. He had an impressive group of colleagues in Justices Miller, Strong, Matthews (1881–89), Gray (1882–1902), and Field to help him with the constitutional problems confronting the Court.

The constitutional pen was in the hands of relatively few Justices in the nineteenth century. Many Justices contributed little or nothing to the Court's work. For example, Justice Duvall (1812–35) in twenty-three years on the Marshall Court contributed only a three-word dissenting opinion in one case.[11] This earned him the title of Most Insignificant Justice from constitutional scholar David Currie.[12] Justice McKinley (1837–52) wrote almost nothing while on the Taney Court and, in Currie's words, "left practically no trace."[13] And on the Chase Court Justices Catron (1837–65), Wayne (1835–67), Hunt (1873–82), Nelson (1845–72), Clifford (1858–81), Davis (1862–77), and Swayne (1862–81) added little. Only Justice Grier (1846–70), who was senile, had a good excuse. During the Waite years three Justices, Hunt, Swayne, and Clifford, were ill at one time, which forced the rest of the Court to take on their work. Thus, even if their competence had improved and made them better candidates for important cases, their health would have made this impossible.

The dynamics of the working environment that had contributed to the smooth running of the Marshall Court began to deteriorate under Chief

Justice Taney's leadership. By mid-century the Justices, instead of living and working together in a boarding house as they had under Marshall, worked out of their individual residences, with messengers shuttling court documents between them. As to the inner workings of the Court's operation at mid-century, we have the description of Justice McLean (1829–61). He wrote that "[b]efore any opinion is formed by the Court, the case after being argued at the Bar is thoroughly discussed in consultation. Night after night, this is done, in a case of difficulty, until the mind of every judge gives his views of the whole case, embracing every point in it. In this way the opinion of the judges is expressed, and then the Chief Justice requests a particular judge to write, not his opinion, but the opinion of the Court. And after the opinion is read, it is read to all the judges, and if it does not embrace the views of the judges, it is modified and corrected."[14]

Justice Brewer (1890–1910) provides the particulars of the Court's work habits toward the end of the century. "Five days . . . are given each week to the hearing of arguments, the court convening promptly at twelve and adjourning promptly at four, and these hours are fully occupied by arguments of counsel."[15] The Justices received printed copies of the records and briefs, which were discussed at Saturday conferences. "Each justice is expected to have made full examination of each record and the questions involved before that time, and if any one has not done so the consideration is postponed one week or until all are ready. As to the vigor and earnestness of these discussions I can only say that I have never known anything to equal them."[16] The Justices voted on the cases and were able to keep track of how their brethren voted. By Saturday night the Chief Justice or the senior member of the majority exercised his prerogative and assigned to one of the Justices the majority opinion to be written. "The duty of assigning cases," said Brewer, "is a most delicate one and could if unwisely discharged provoke no little irritation. To the great credit of the present Chief Justice be it said that no one could be more fair and wise than he in such distribution."[17] After writing his opinion, the responsible Justice would have it printed by the Court printer and then circulated. Criticisms were exchanged and changes were made to accommodate individual Justices.

The logistics but not the essence of the process have changed in this century. The practice of the Justices working out of their homes, with the government providing them a subsidy, ceased when the new Supreme Court building opened in 1935. The conferences are no longer held on Saturdays, as in Justice Brewer's time, but on Tuesdays and Thursdays. The vigor and earnestness with which Justice Brewer characterized the conferences of his day have also, from time to time, taken on a different color. Justice Douglas, for example, reported that Justice Frankfurter, who never thought highly of Chief Justice Vinson, once pushed him too far with his condescending taunts. "In a very heated argument," Douglas told an interviewer, "Fred Vinson, thinking he had been insulted . . . just got out of the chair and came around the table with a clenched fist. He would have knocked Frankfurter's teeth out if he hadn't been stopped by his colleagues."[18]

Not much has changed, however, in regard to the accommodation that is often needed to get a majority for an opinion. It still takes five Justices to make a majority, and bargaining is ultimately the only way to get some votes. But here, while the ultimate decision is advanced, the opinion supporting that decision often suffers. Justice Douglas explained the frequent consequence of accommodation on the opinion itself. "One of the reasons," he told an interviewer in 1962, "that judicial opinions are sometimes so opaque or irrational perhaps, in the sense of not being logical developments structurally, is because of the patchwork that goes into their creation, satisfying this judge, getting a majority by putting in a footnote, striking out a sentence that would have made a paragraph lucid, and it becomes opaque. This is also one of the reasons why judicial opinions, except dissents, are usually very poor literature."[19]

On the writing of opinions, Justice Brewer wrote that "the real hard work is in shaping up the opinion as it is to be written. When that is done the rest is easy. I dictate my opinions to my secretary, who takes them down in shorthand."[20] His secretary would prepare a manuscript of the opinion and Brewer would go over it with a pencil and add anything omitted in dictation. To keep up with his work, Brewer rose early and was at work on his opinions before dawn.[21] He was the only member of the Fuller Court who consistently provided the newspapers with proof copies of his opinions. In court, he would skip to the conclusion, thinking it would be too much to read the entire opinion.

It is doubtful that Brewer maintained his regimen of rising at dawn throughout his whole tenure on the Court. In full swing, the Fuller Court of which he was a member was distinguished by advancing age and physical frailty. Then President Taft's observation to Horace Lurton bluntly sums up the Fuller brethren near the end of Brewer's life. He wrote that "the condition of the Supreme Court is pitiable, and yet these old fools hold on with a tenacity that is most discouraging. Really the Chief Justice [then seventy-six] is almost senile; Harlan [also seventy-six] does no work; Brewer [only seventy-two] is so deaf that he cannot hear and has got beyond the point of commonest accuracy in writing his opinions; Brewer and

Harlan sleep through all the arguments. I don't know what can be done. It is most discouraging to the active men on the bench."[22]

Justice Oliver Wendell Holmes (1903–32) was a member of the Fuller Court, and it is with him that we get not only the first important judicial writer of the twentieth century but also, perhaps, the most interesting writer ever on the Court. Holmes wrote his opinions quickly, usually within a day or two of getting his assignment, while standing at a lectern. As he put it, "nothing conduces to brevity like a caving in of the knees."[23] Chief Justice Taft's law clerk for the 1922 Term recalled that Holmes wrote skeleton opinions in every case during oral argument on the cover of the case's record.[24] The speed of Holmes's production caused some of his colleagues distress. Justice Stone thought that Holmes's speed sacrificed thoroughness. Speaking of a case in which Holmes had written and circulated his opinion within two days of assignment, Stone noted, "this is a pretty good opinion on the point that he decides, but the old man leaves out all the troublesome facts and ignores all the tough points that worried the lower courts." "I wish," he continued, "I could make my cases sound as easy as Holmes makes his."[25]

Writing judicial opinions was Holmes's lifeblood. At the age of eighty-nine, he told Harold Laski, "I have written my first decisions of this term and expect from present appearances that they will go through. Their only merit is brevity, I hope accurate and adequate — but somehow it put new life into me to write again."[26] Holmes's correspondence is streaked with observations on his involvement with writing. He wrote to diplomat Lewis Einstein, for example: "I am in full blast and have fired off one decision which gives me pleasure although it did not quite satisfy me in point of form. One cannot be perfectly clear until the struggle of thought is over and you have got so far past the idea that it is almost a bore to state it; but decisions can't wait for that, and writers usually won't. Therefore I do not regard perfect luminosity as the highest praise. An original mind really at work is hardly likely to attain it. Those who are perfectly clear are apt to be nearer the commonplace."[27] "My pleasure in law," he wrote to Einstein on another occasion, "apart from that found in the exercise of the faculties which is the fundamental one, is just in trying to exhibit some hint of horizons, even in small details."[28] There could be no pleasure, though, until the writing process was complete. "My only serious interest when I first got here a week ago," he wrote to Einstein, "was to have my work for the term bound up in a little volume as I do each year. Until that is done the term is not closed. Then it becomes history and I can hold eight months of my life in my hand and look it over. One can put passion into anything that comes near enough to fundamental propensities. And in my fool's paradise I see a philosophy of law gradually unrolling itself as I write."[29] Even not getting the cases bound in the usual manner caused Holmes some concern. He wrote to Laski, for example, "I have my volume of opinions from the binder after anxieties due to the delay of the Post Office and am indexing it." He continued with worries about writing too quickly: "[t]he cases seem to me more interesting than those of last year's and I am rather pleased as I reread—subject to the eternal misgiving whether I have not been too speedy with them. I console myself by thinking of the immediate decisions common in England."[30]

Justice Brandeis (1915–39), Holmes's close colleague for many years, also had distinctive writing habits. He worked without a secretary or typist and wrote the drafts of his opinions in longhand. The Court printer would set each one in type and print it for him, so that he could then revise the galley proofs. The printer took the revisions, reset his type, and printed the opinion. Brandeis, in turn, would continue to revise as he worked toward his final product. Often he revised six or seven times.[31]

Brandeis was not the only methodical worker on that court. Justice Van Devanter (1911–37) was perhaps the most extreme example, polishing his opinions so extensively that he averaged only a few opinions per Term. Distinguished Court commentator Fred Rodell thought Van Devanter did little more in his opinions that crib from the lawyers' briefs.[32] But Chief Justice Taft (1921–30) considered Van DeVanter's opinions to be the best of any member of his court.[33] He also thought that Justice Stone (1924–46) had great difficulty in getting his opinions out because "he [was] quite disposed to be discursive and to write opinions as if he were writing an editorial or a comment for a legal law journal, covering as much as he can upon a general subject." Stone, however, was able to make his nearly illegible longhand into printed drafts in time to meet his deadlines.[34]

Chief Justice Hughes (1910–16, 1930–41) prepared his opinions in sections. He would write the first in longhand and give it to his secretary for transcription. Only when it was revised and then retyped would he proceed to the next section of the opinion.[35]

Hugo Black (1937–71) worked hard at learning to write judicial opinions. He said once that "the most difficult thing about coming on to the Court was learning to write."[36] Some court watchers speculated that, in his early years at least, Black relied heavily on the ghostwriting of Tom Corcoran, a suggestion Corcoran laughed off. Members of the Court themselves had reservations about the authorship of some of Black's early opinions. A few of Black's early dissents did not please Justice Stone, who wrote to Chief

Justice Hughes, "I am a good deal troubled. I see in Justice Black's dissent the handiwork of someone other than the nominal author."[37] By handiwork Stone most likely meant competence. Stone did not think highly of Black's early work and sought to tutor him by occasionally going over one of Black's opinions, showing him, as his biographer reports, where he went wrong. "He did this with very little humor," the biographer writes, "and seemed unaware that Hugo felt a certain intellectual rapport with him. As he would leave, Black, courtesy written all over him, would tell Stone what a pleasure it was to see him."[38] The biographer does not state whether Stone understood the limits of his instruction.

At least in his first years on the Court, Black wrote his own opinions in longhand on a yellow legal pad. "If you dictate," he told his son, "it's so easy to let loose too many words. Talking is the easiest thing in the world. But when you got to write it yourself, your hand and arm muscles make you practice economy with your words." Hugo Black, Jr. recalls that his father could not rest until he had finished an opinion, going through six drafts on some occasions before he had an opinion ready to circulate.[39]

Justice Black's wife described her husband's writing habits after he had been on the Court for more than twenty years. He wrote his first drafts usually at home. "He sits at his desk," she wrote, "completely oblivious to anything except working on his dissent. . . . He is a little island, completely surrounded by mountains of books, yellow pages—some of which have been crumpled up—large pieces of eraser crumbs, and many written sheets lying in more or less organized heaps. There is a little buffer or pocket of concentration that hangs over the desk like an aura—an impenetrable light of rays going out in every direction."[40] His biographer reports that he would pass the draft opinion to a law clerk, with the directions to see what he could do with it. Black would take the law clerk's revision and, with the clerk, shorten the opinion, usually by half. In his early years, Black would read the opinion aloud, with the clerk furiously trying to write down what Black would add as he read along.

Justice Wiley Rutledge (1943–49) preferred to write an opinion rather than to decide a case. His former law clerk, later Justice John Paul Stevens, wrote of his boss that "many judges find it easy to arrive at a decision but have great difficulty in preparing an opinion. For Justice Rutledge the converse was true. . . . he usually found the preparation of an opinion easy. The work was time consuming and exacting—for the most part he prepared drafts in his own hand—but not as difficult as the process of decision."[41]

Felix Frankfurter, appointed in 1939, imitated Holmes's habit of writing, standing up, at a lectern, although he was Holmes's opposite in the swiftness with which he completed his cases. Douglas, for example, complained frequently that Frankfurter "delayed or was very late in getting out his opinions."[42] Late in his career, Frankfurter not only let clerks write his opinions, he once published a piece written by a clerk in the *Harvard Law Review* under his own name.[43]

For his part, Douglas, also appointed in 1939, wrote his own opinions, secluding himself in his office, spreading his books out in front of him, and writing in longhand on yellow sheets of paper. He would then dictate what he had produced to his secretary.[44] One of Douglas's first law clerks paints a compelling picture of the Justice at work. "I see him as a man focused on his work, absolutely determined to get through and get through fast. The books would be brought down. . . . He would close the door [and work]. If you went in, you felt you were interrupting him. He would look up and seem to say, 'Why did you come in?' It wasn't put that way, but that was the feeling that was conveyed. There he was, working with the yellow sheets of paper and with the books spread out in front of him, writing everything in longhand and then he would call his secretary, Edith Waters, and he would dictate, piece by piece. But he was hard at work every moment of the time. This was not a man who took lightly the burden he had assumed getting on the Court."[45]

Douglas, like Holmes, was known for writing his opinions quickly. When asked how he was able to do this, Douglas explained: "I had never had any experience before writing for the Court, opinions of any court. I had written, of course, many briefs and so on, many law review articles and whatnot. I think, due to the fact that I was a commuter in the early years out of New York City, I learned to write with a pencil or pen on a yellow pad on my lap and that is the manner in which I have done all my work on the Court. Writing, taking briefs and records with me on airplanes, and writing opinions as I cross the country, or out in the desert in Arizona, where I try to go in the wintertime, or wherever I might be."[46]

As for law clerks, Douglas, more than thirty years into his job, wrote to Chief Justice Burger that "I will never have more than two law clerks. I think, as a matter of fact, that three are a waste of the taxpayer's money. The decisions here can be made only by one person and it is for him to do most of the work. This is no reflection on anyone else, but states my own philosophy and habits of work."[47]

Law clerks, who are so much of the writing process in today's Court, appeared on the scene in the nineteenth century, to the great relief of the Justices. Congress in 1886 provided for stenographic clerks for the Chief Justice and for each Associate Justice of the High Court, at a salary of

$1,600 per year, to help them with what was becoming a staggering case-load.[48] The Justices leaped to the offer of help. By 1888 each had a steno-graphic clerk, who in practice was more law clerk than stenographer, however. In 1919 Congress passed legislation that the Justices could hire a second assistant. There was some confusion about the title of this new assistant, but apparently the Justices understood the new position to be that of a law clerk. Some of the Justices did not want to go beyond the initial stenographic assistant. Chief Justice Hughes, who at the time was an Associate Justice, recalled that some of the brethren had argued against the idea, saying that if they had experienced law clerks, it might be thought that the clerks were writing the opinions.[49]

The Justices, whether they had one or two assistants, employed their clerks for indefinite periods, some for more than a decade. Justice Butler (1929–39) kept the same clerk for sixteen years, while Justice McKenna (1898–1925) had his first clerk for a dozen years. Only recently has the tradition developed that the clerks stay with their Justices for one- or two-year stints. The Justices also differed on the duties that they had their law clerks perform. Some gave their clerks mere secretarial duties, while others let them go so far as to write opinions. Francis Biddle, later attorney general of the United States, explained that as Justice Holmes's secretary his principal job, after summarizing the certiorari petitions, was to balance the great man's checkbook.[50] Later secretaries to Holmes spent most of their time reading to him. The clerk who worked for Justice Butler for sixteen years stated, in contrast, that he wrote the first drafts of many of the Justice's opinions, many of which were published with only few changes.[51] Other Justices did not rely on their clerks for opinion-writing help. Neither Justice McKenna nor Justice Lurton (1910–14) would let his clerks work on his opinions.[52] Holmes certainly did not use a law clerk in producing some of the most memorable language in Supreme Court opinions. Justice Jackson, his former law clerk and current Chief Justice William Rehnquist tells us, would let his law clerks write one or two opinions each term.

Frank Murphy (1940–49) depended heavily on his law clerks. After reviewing the Justice's court papers, one of Justice Murphy's biographers reports that it is doubtful that Murphy drafted a single opinion in its entirety by himself.[53] Chief Justice Vinson (1946–53) was reputed to be able to write with his hands in his pockets. His successor, Chief Justice Warren (1953–69), delegated his writing chores, usually with explicit instructions. He generally outlined to his law clerk the opinion he wanted written, summarizing the facts and the way the important points of the case should be handled. He left the particulars, the footnotes, and the research and reasoning of the opinion to his assistants.[54] His biographer writes that Warren "never pretended to be a scholar interested in research and legal minutiae. These he left to his clerks, as well as the extensive footnotes which are part of the panoply of the well-crafted judicial opinion."[55] Sherman Minton (1949–56) considered opinion writing just one aspect of his job and did not think of it as a literary exercise. Clerks would often write the first drafts of opinions. Sometimes, however, he would dictate a rough draft to his secretary and then research those points needed to support the opinion.[56] The second Justice John Harlan (1955–71) had his clerks prepare the first drafts of his opinions, which he then edited thoroughly and returned to the clerk for more revisions.[57]

There have been two major responses, at the Supreme Court level at least, to the role of law clerks in writing judicial opinions. The issue received national attention in the late 1950s. During this time the Supreme Court was at its most visible in American life as a result of both the press coverage of its rulings and the stories about the Court that grew out of the deep pockets of public dissatisfaction and resistance with the role that the Court had assumed in shaping social policy. The *New York Times* on October 14, 1957, carried an article describing the work of the law clerks for the new Supreme Court Term. It listed the names and law schools of the clerks for the various Justices, and it featured photographs of the clerks at work in conference with their Justice, at work in the library, and working at their desks. The article stressed how much the clerks did in sorting through the thousands of petitions for certiorari and in providing research assistance for their Justices in the the preparation of their judicial opinions. Within two months William Rehnquist, a former law clerk to Justice Jackson and then a practicing lawyer in Phoenix, wrote a featured article for *U.S. News & World Report* on the role of law clerks. He argued that the unconscious liberal bias of the clerks had the effect of possibly influencing the work of their Justices. In this starkly ideological piece, Rehnquist linked the influence of the clerks with the ills of the current Court. He wrote, "some of the tenets of the 'liberal' point of view which commanded the sympathy of a majority of the clerks I knew were: extreme solicitude for the claims of Communists and other criminal defendants, expansion of federal power at the expense of State power, great sympathy toward any government regulation of business—in short, the political philosophy now espoused by the Court under Chief Justice Earl Warren."[58]

The *New York Times* then ran a story on Rehnquist's article, with a summary and quotations.[59] Four months later *U.S. News & World Report* published a response by William D. Rogers, who had clerked for Justice Reed at the same time Rehnquist had clerked for Jackson.[60] Rogers argued that the clerks were not exercising the alleged liberal influence on their Justices but said nothing about law clerks writing opinions.

The controversy over law clerks prompted Senator Stennis of Mississippi to argue that they should be confirmed by the Senate, as a check on their power, and that there should be a congressional investigation of their role on the High Court. If we cannot control the Court, was the implicit argument, we can at least try to control their influential law clerks. Attempting to defuse the matter, Alexander Bickel of the Yale Law School then wrote a feature for the *New York Times* on the role of law clerks.[61] His twin themes were the valuable assistance that the clerks provided in the Court's work and the link the institutional law clerks provided between the law schools and the Justices. Bickel left unmentioned Rehnquist's admission that law clerks actually wrote at least some opinions, probably because to discuss the point would be to acknowledge the deeply troubling question of accountability.

Recently, for the first time, academic commentators have argued that there are consequences to letting law clerks write Supreme Court opinions. Most important, our discussions of who the Justices are and what their opinions mean are so falsely premised that they lose intellectual respectability. One scholar, Steven Duke, has argued that Justice Douglas's opinions in criminal cases have been especially influential because they were clearly written by Douglas himself and are bottomed on principle and policy rather than precedent. Duke then makes the more important point that Douglas's opinions "are virtually the only Supreme Court opinions in recent generations that we can be sure were written by the justice whose name they bear. Most of the opinions during Douglas's tenure, as now, are substantially written by fledgling law clerks. It is hard to understand why anyone pays much attention to the lucubrations of anonymous youngsters."[62]

Another commentator, Judge Richard A. Posner of the Seventh Circuit of the U.S. Court of Appeals, recently brought the issue of legitimate scholarship squarely into focus when he wrote of constitutional scholars and scholarship that "the truth is that constitutional lawyers know little about their real subject matter—a complex of political science, social, and economic questions. What they know is a body of decisions written by other poorly informed lawyers. Nowadays most judicial decisions, even those in the Supreme Court, are written by law clerks a year or two away from graduation. What professors of constitutional law teach and study is, to the extent I should think they would find embarrassing, the work of their recently graduated students. It is not a sustaining diet."[63]

◆　◆

Even though Congress in 1886 had authorized the Supreme Court Justices to employ stenographic clerks, it did not provide for stenographic or law clerks for the judges of the court of appeals, which it created in 1891. This was not legislated until 1930.[64] Congress provided law clerks for district court judges in 1936.[65] The need for young law school graduates to serve as stenographic or law clerks was so great that judges were already hiring top law students and paying them from their own pockets before Congress acted. Learned Hand, for example, had a small inheritance, which he used for an assistant to do legal research for him.[66]

District court judges today have two law clerks each, while court of appeals judges can have three. As is true at the Supreme Court, the law clerks of the U.S. Court of Appeals and the district courts write nearly all of the opinions coming out of their respective courts. For information on present-day authorship, we need to turn to insiders. Posner in his *The Federal Courts* devotes a chapter to the influence of law clerks on opinions coming from the federal courts.[67] He provides details of the extent of their work and states that law clerks dominate opinion writing in the inferior federal courts. And in an interview, he listed Bailey Aldrich, Stephen Breyer, and Frank Easterbrook as the only federal judges he knows who write their own opinions.[68] Justice Scalia has speculated that only four or five circuit judges wrote their own opinions. Of the group he named Breyer, Posner, and Easterbrook.[69]

Lower court judges seem to see no inconsistency between their job descriptions and their use of law clerks to write their judicial opinions. In his *On Appeal*, for example, Frank Coffin of the First Circuit openly describes the process in which law clerks write the first drafts of opinions produced in his chambers.[70] Similarly, Judge Luther Swygert of the Seventh Circuit has said that he did not think he was abdicating his judicial obligations at all in relying on his law clerks to write his opinions.[71] Judge Patricia Wald of the District of Columbia Circuit echoes this sentiment, writing that "every judge has to decide what core function she alone must perform. Personally, I feel that so long as the judge reads all the briefs (and key portions of the record), listens to oral argument and engages in face-to-face dialogue with counsel, participates in the conferences with her colleagues, and controls the formulation and expression of the ideas and analysis that go into her opinion, she has done the job. Whether the judge writes the first draft for the clerks to critique and to flesh out, or the clerk writes the first draft for the judge to revise and to challenge is not dispositive of whether the judge is still in charge."[72] The pressure of the appellate court docket compels the judge to take this approach, she argues. "Were a judge to research and write every word in every opinion," she writes, "it would mean that he or she could write only a dozen or so opinions a term." For her, the law clerk's assistance forms the core of the opinion-writing process. The judge-clerk relationship is, she says, "the most intense and mutually dependent one . . . outside of marriage, parenthood, or a love affair."[73]

Some judges, even though their name appears as the author of the opinion, explicitly acknowledge the role of the law clerk. Judge Milton Shadur of the Northern District of Illinois on occasion mentions that an opinion could not have been written without the invaluable research and writing of a law clerk, whom he usually names. Judge Lynn of the Northern District of Alabama has gone even further, several times noting both that a particular law clerk had prepared the opinion and that it is an opinion "in which the Court fully concurs."[74]

A recent survey of federal judges conducted by the Federal Judicial Center comes as close as we can get to eliciting information about writing habits from the judges themselves. The questionnaire, to which more than 80 percent of the U.S. circuit judges responded, did not ask directly whether the judges had their law clerks write their opinions. Instead the judges were requested to identify the type of work that they delegated to their law clerks. Of 113 respondents, 62 pointed to drafting judicial opinions. In a related question, 18 judges said that they "never" relied on their clerks to do work that they believed they should do themselves, 37 said that they "almost never" did this, 50 said "sometimes," 41 said "often," 9 said "usually," while 2 did not respond.[75] As high as these figures are, the authors of the working paper had doubts that the judges were being completely honest about the extent to which law clerks write their opinions, apparently because of the extent of anecdotal evidence to the contrary.[76]

The refrain from those judges providing supplemental answers was that they delegated opinion writing, including even jobs such as reviewing the record, because they were overworked. One judge, for example, wrote that "in this circuit, a judge has to turn out 150 opinions a year to stay current. It is not possible to do that without excessive reliance on the law clerks."[77] Another wrote, "keeping current with the docket has to be a high priority for any judge. I am unable to keep my work current if I read the records and do the writing and take time for thinking in those cases where it is needed. I spend time moving mail with little decisions (protecting the law clerks from being interrupted) and editing the work of clerks."[78] Short comments from two other judges give a better picture of how the work load affects a judge's work. One complained, "I am now forced to rely on my clerks for record examination and for research I would prefer to conduct myself. In the past I would draft all written materials. I now find that I am obliged to 'plug in' memoranda or research that the clerks conducted."[79] Another commented, "I use my clerks for reading and summarizing precedents that I must rely on without always having time to read the cases myself."[80]

◆   ◆

What do we know about these federal judges, and what does it suggest about their habit of delegating opinion-writing duties to their law clerks? An appointment to the federal bench, of course, does not ensure quality, either today or at an earlier time. Solicitor General Robert Jackson, for example, was probably right in writing to a friend in 1939 that he was "of the opinion that our Circuit Courts of Appeal as a whole are the weakest link in our federal judiciary."[81] Recently the quality of circuit court judges has improved, in part because of the addition of academics such as Guido Calabresi in the Second Circuit and other well-qualified judges such as Michael Boudin of the First Circuit. In fact, statistical information culled from biographical profiles of the judges of the circuit and district courts shows an increasingly academic tilt to the lower court federal judiciary. The same profiles also show differences we might expect between district court judges, whose job it is to preside over trials, and circuit court judges, whose job it is to write appellate judicial opinions.

Assuming that a relationship exists between a judge's academic and professional achievements and his or her approach to opinion writing, I have prepared biographical profiles to substantiate this. In shaping my profiles of lower court judges, I examined a judge's legal education, marks of scholastic achievement, and various aspects of a career path leading to the federal judiciary. Beyond identifying where a judge went to law school, I looked at whether the judge was a member of (1) Phi Beta Kappa, (2) the Order of the Coif (the scholastic honor society of law school), (3) the judge's law review, (4) and the law review's editorial board. In addition, I examined whether the judge held a clerkship at the federal district court, circuit court, or Supreme Court levels, whether the judge had a graduate degree, and whether the judge had an academic career prior to going onto the federal bench. I conducted this inquiry for both the district court and circuit court judges using the two principal biographical guides to the federal judiciary.[82] These guides did not have biographical summaries of all of the federal judges. Most of the omissions were of recent appointees, especially to the district courts, but there were also district and circuit court judges of some longevity who had apparently not wanted to provide their biographical information. On the circuit court side, there are 179 authorized positions, but only 164 are currently filled. Of this number 149 provided biographies. In contrast, 81 of the 82 senior circuit judges gave information. On the district court side, of the 645 authorized district judgeships, 601 are filled, and of that number 425 provided biographical information. On the senior side, 267 of the 275 senior judges provided information.

As a group, the active and senior court judges weighed in with the following statistics. Eighteen percent were members of the Order of the Coif; 14 percent were Phi Beta Kappa members; 27 percent had been members of their school's law review; 22 percent had been law review editorial board members; 13 percent held graduate degrees; 9 percent had followed academic careers; and 17 percent had held clerkships in the federal courts (5 percent at the Supreme Court, 7 percent at the circuit court, and 5 percent at the district court).

Active circuit judges, the statistics suggest, tend to be academic achievers. Twenty-two percent of the circuit court judges were members of the Order of the Coif; 18 percent were Phi Beta Kappa members. Thirty-eight percent were members of their school's law review, and 33 percent were members of the editorial staff. As for education, the five law schools graduating the highest number of circuit judges (40 percent) were Harvard, Yale, Michigan, Texas, and Virginia. Twenty percent of the active circuit judges have graduate degrees, and nearly 13 percent had been academics before taking to the bench. More than a fifth of them served as law clerks in the federal judiciary. Seven percent served at the Supreme Court as law clerks, 10 percent at circuit court, and 6 percent at the district court.

Of the 164 active circuit judges, 61 had served earlier as district court judges. Jon Newman of the Second Circuit, Cecil Poole of the Ninth, Eugene Siler of the Sixth, Michael Hawkins of the Ninth, Boyce Martin of the Sixth, Gilbert Merritt of the Sixth, Stephen Trott of the Ninth, and Samuel Alito of the Third served as U.S. attorneys. Donald Russell of the Fourth and James Buckley of the D.C. Circuit had served as U.S. senators, while Charles Wiggins of the Ninth had served as a congressman. Walter Cummings of the Seventh had been U.S. solicitor general. Frank Easterbrook of the Seventh had been deputy assistant to the solicitor general; Michael Boudin of the First was deputy assistant attorney general for the antitrust division prior to his appointment; Karen Henderson of the D.C. Circuit was deputy attorney general of the criminal division of the Department of Justice; Alvin Schall of the Federal Circuit was assistant to the U.S. attorney general; Laurence Silberman of the D.C. Circuit was deputy U.S. attorney general and ambassador to Yugoslavia; Stephen Trott of the Ninth was associate U.S. attorney general; John Walker of the Second was assistant secretary of the Treasury; William Wilkins of the Fourth was legal aide to Senator Strom Thurmond of South Carolina and is a trustee of the Thurmond Foundation; and J. Harvie Wilkinson was deputy assistant attorney general for civil rights prior to his appointment.

Danny Boggs of the Sixth Circuit was a special assistant to the president for policy development prior to his appointment; Michael Luttig of the Fourth was general counsel to the U.S. attorney general; Robert Mayer of the Federal Circuit was special assistant to Chief Justice Warren Burger; Paul Michel of the Federal Circuit was counsel to Senator Arlen Specter of Pennsylvania for the seven years prior to his appointment; Francis Murnaghan of the Fourth was the campaign chairman for Senator Paul Sarbanes of Maryland; Jon Newman of the Second was the executive assistant to HEW secretary and later senator Abraham Ribicoff of Connecticut; Randall Rader of the Federal Circuit was general counsel to the Senate Judiciary Committee; and Jane Roth of the Third is married to Senator William Roth of Delaware.

Richard Arnold of the Eighth Circuit had been the staff coordinator to Governor Dale Bumpers of Arkansas; Melvin Brunetti of the Ninth was a member of the Council of Legal Advisors to the Republican National Committee for the two years prior to his appointment; William Canby of the Ninth was an assistant to Senator Walter Mondale of Minnesota; Walter DeMoss of the Fifth held a series of high appointments in Republican campaigns; Alex Kozinski was counsel to President Reagan during his 1980 campaign; Daniel Mahoney was chairman of New York's Conservative Party; Gilbert Merritt was treasurer of the Tennessee executive committee of the Republican Party.

James Barrett of the Tenth Circuit was state attorney general from Wyoming; Proctor Hug of the Ninth was deputy attorney general of Nevada; John Moore of the Tenth was attorney general for Colorado; Ilana Rovner was deputy governor and legal counsel to Governor Jim Thompson of Illinois for seven years; Donald Russell, aside from serving as a U.S. senator from South Carolina, was governor of South Carolina and the president of the University of South Carolina.

Jose Cabranes of the Second Circuit was general counsel to Yale University; Nathaniel Jones of the Sixth was general counsel to the NAACP for the ten years prior to his appointment.

Sixteen active circuit judges had followed the academic career path for a significant portion of their careers before going onto the bench. This group includes Morris Arnold and Pasco Bowman of the Eighth Circuit; James Logan of the Sixth; Frank Easterbrook and Richard Posner of the Seventh; Harry Edwards, Daniel Ginsburg, and Stephen Williams of the D.C. Circuit; William Canby, John Noonan, and Doris Nelson of the Ninth; Deanell Tacha of the Tenth; Doris Sloviter of the Third; J. Harvie Wilkinson of the Fourth; and Guido Calabresi, Ralph Winter, and Joseph McLaughlin of the Second. Of this group seven were deans: Arnold at Indiana University, Bowman at Wake Forest, Logan at Kansas, Calabresi at Yale, McLaughlin at Fordham, Nelson at the University of South Carolina, and Tacha at the University of Kansas.

The academic judges have written several books. Three active judges, all associated with the law and economics movement, contributed significantly to legal scholarship in their academic careers. Guido Calabresi was one of the first exponents of law and economics, while Richard Posner, as I describe in chapter 6, has been its principal exponent with several books and dozens of articles. Frank Easterbrook, too, has contributed books and articles. Other academics turned circuit judges edited casebooks in their various specialties. Only a few, however, such as Harry Edwards and John Noonan, have written books on law. With only the rarest exceptions, if we put Posner to the side for a moment, these judges wrote their books while academics.

The educational backgrounds of the eighty-two senior circuit judges parallel those of the active judges. The same top five schools graduate approximately 40 percent of the senior judges. Thirteen percent were members of the Order of the Coif; 18 percent were Phi Beta Kappa members; 12 percent had been law review members; 5 percent had been members of their law review's editorial board; 1 percent had graduate degrees; 4 percent had been academics; and 7 percent had held federal court clerkships. Of those who clerked, 1 percent clerked for the Supreme Court; 4 percent for the circuit court; and 3 percent for the district court.

Of the eighty-two senior circuit judges, thirty-three served as district judges. Seven had served as U.S. attorneys: William Bauer, Harlington Wood, and Thomas Fairchild of the Seventh Circuit; Robert Krupansky of the Sixth; Edward Lumbard of the Second; Donald Ross of the Eighth; and George McKinnon of the D.C. Circuit. Three senior judges pursued academic careers. Monroe McKay of the Tenth Circuit spent only three years in the academy, while J. Dickson Phillips of the Fourth and Joseph Sneed of the Ninth became law school deans after long academic careers.

Marion Bennett of the Federal Circuit, Homer Thornberry of the Fifth, and George McKinnon of the D.C. Circuit served in Congress; Anthony Celebrezze of the Sixth was secretary of HEW prior to his appointment; Frank Coffin of the First was deputy administrator of the Agency for International Development; Elbert Tuttle of the Eleventh was general counsel to the Treasury Department; and Harlington Wood of the Seventh was associate deputy U.S. attorney general.

Thomas Meskill of the Second Circuit was governor of Connecticut; Herbert Choy of the Ninth was attorney general of the Territory of Hawaii; Thomas Fairchild of the Seventh was attorney general for Wisconsin; Floyd Gibson of the Eighth was majority leader of the Missouri legislature; Alfred Goodwin of the Ninth was on the Oregon Supreme Court; Sam Johnson of the Fifth was on the Texas Supreme Court; Robert McWilliams of the Tenth served on the Colorado Supreme Court; James Oakes of the Second was attorney general for Vermont; Wilbur Pell was deputy attorney general for Indiana; Thomas Reavley served on the Texas Supreme Court; Max Rosenn of the Third was secretary of public welfare for Pennsylvania; Robert Chapman of the Fourth was chairman of the South Carolina Republican Party; and Arthur Alacron of the Ninth was executive assistant to Governor Edmund G. Brown Sr. of California.

Comparing active circuit court judges with their district court counterparts, we find that circuit court judges are approximately three times more likely to be Phi Beta Kappa members, Order of the Coif members, and law review members and editors. Circuit judges are three times more likely to have a graduate degree, and they are six times more likely to have been an academic. Circuit judges are twice as likely to have been law clerks. They are nine times more likely to have had a Supreme Court clerkship, twice as likely to have had a circuit court clerkship, and equally likely to have had a district court clerkship as their district judge counterparts.

As for legal educations, Harvard, Yale, Texas, Michigan, and Virginia lead the way for the district judges as they do for the circuit judges. What differs is the percentages of graduates these schools have placed among their ranks. The five leading schools provided degrees for 40 percent of the senior circuit judges, nearly 40 percent of the active circuit judges, and 20 percent of the district judges.

◆　　◆

The current members of the Supreme Court, of course, have distinguished biographies. Justices Breyer and Stevens and Chief Justice Rehnquist are Order of the Coif members. Rehnquist, Stevens, and Souter are Phi Beta Kappa members. Breyer, Rehnquist, Stevens, O'Connor, Ginsburg, and Scalia were law review members. Only Ginsburg was not a law review editor. Breyer, Scalia, and Ginsburg have been academics. Rehnquist and Souter have advanced degrees, while Breyer (Goldberg), Stevens (Rutledge), and Rehnquist (Jackson) were law clerks to Supreme Court Justices. Only O'Connor did not serve as a circuit court judge before going to the Supreme Court.

◆   ◆

In contrast to the dozens of volumes of biography written about Supreme Court Justices, there have been only a few about circuit court judges. There have been some celebrated lower court judges, and from biographies and tributes from their law clerks we know something about their writing habits. Frequently mere membership on the High Court prompts the biography of a Justice. But lower court judges achieve celebrity because of their substantive work, and their biographies tend to tell us more about how they thought and wrote.

We are fortunate in knowing a good deal about three of the most important circuit court judges in the twentieth century—Learned Hand, Henry Friendly, and Richard Posner. I look at Friendly and Hand in this chapter and discuss Posner at length in chapter 6.

Hand, considered by many to be the greatest appellate judge of his generation, sat on the Southern District of New York bench from 1909 to 1924 and on the Court of Appeals for the Second Circuit from 1924 to his retirement from regular active service in 1951. His last judicial opinion came a full ten years later. He wrote every word of every opinion with a method just as idiosyncratic as Holmes's. Hand sat, with a board perched on his knee, and wrote in longhand on yellow legal pads. Harold Medina, one of Hand's colleagues on the Second Circuit, described his writing habits this way: Hand "wouldn't even let a law clerk write a sentence, not one sentence. He would let the law clerk criticize. He would hand what he had written to the law clerk and let him make all the suggestions he wanted to make. But not one word of that opinion was anybody else's but Learned Hand's."[83]

Hand wrote haltingly, looking to his law clerks for criticism either after every few paragraphs or after completed drafts.[84] He referred to his law clerks as "puny judges," which was a pun on "pusine judges," the term the English use for their trial judges. There was, however, a limit to Hand's willingness to accommodate a law clerk's criticism in his revisions. Hand's biographer, Gerald Gunther, who clerked for Hand in the early 1950s, tells of an opinion Hand had revised thirteen times in response to Gunther's criticisms. A baker's dozen was not the charm, however. Gunther writes that the latest round of criticism prompted Hand to explode into anger and to hurl a hefty paperweight at him, all the while shouting, "Damn, I can't go on forever like this! Thirteen drafts and it's still not satisfactory? Son, I get paid to decide cases. At some point, I have to get off the fence and turn out an opinion. Enough!"[85]

Hand, the great judge, was a man consumed by insecurity, low self-esteem, and melancholy. As a man who vigorously sought advancement, he was dogged throughout his judicial career by what he considered the disappointment of not getting to the Supreme Court. Apparently Hand needed external rewards for happiness and self-fulfillment. Not getting them, or not getting enough of them, led to the unhappiness. The question, of course, is why someone with his gifts would need external rewards in the first place.

Hand found at least a partial release from his self-imposed psychological pressures in his writing on the bench. Finding interesting issues to explore in small and large cases alike, he thrived on the process of taking a case apart and then putting it back together. He wrote about this judicial process as a kind of personal discovery: "when the case is all in, and the turmoil stops, and after he is left alone, things begin to take form. . . . out of the murk the pattern emerges, his pattern, the expression of what he has seen and what he has therefor made, the impress of his self upon the not-self, upon the hitherto formless material of which he was once but a part and over which he has now become the master."[86]

Hand found in judging the same kind of excitement and satisfaction had he found in mathematics as a schoolboy. Late in life he recalled his interest in mathematics: "I remember what we used to call the originals in algebra and geometry. I can to this day [remember] the pleasure that came when I felt, 'Go, I've got the forms; I've devised the form that fits this thing!' "[87] With only the slightest modification, this description could equally describe Hand's application of reasoning to legal problems.

An oral history interview that he gave in 1957, in which he answered questions with remarkable candor and extended responses, helps explain much about Hand the man and Hand the opinion writer.[88] Here he gives us the clearest description of the insecurity and low self-esteem that plagued him. In response to the question of whether he knew Brandeis well, for example, Hand says "yes, I suppose I did," and then launches into an extraordinary answer that addresses alcohol, melancholy, and insecurity. Without prompting he says:

> Did I ever tell you the strange alternations I had with Brandeis. Well, I'd go and see him and a strange thing, I never particularly liked him but I'd have this strange sense of deference for him. I'd say to myself, "Here you are, what do you do? You sit around and talk a good deal, haven't any very definite convictions. You're not spending your life trying to leave the world better for being in it. You like to drink too much." In those days it was true to say also our feelings about women were not always very nice at all. And here was this man whose life was dedicated to virtue. If he has a moment he lapses into reading interstate commerce reports. Of course, you never converse with Brandeis. You listen. But it was awfully impressive, you know and there was always a kind of atmosphere of infallibility. I used to leave him feeling, "you are a self-indulgent, inadequate person." About three days afterwards I'd say, "Look here, why do you prostrate yourself before that fellow? You know he's a colossal egoist. He lives for adulation. He just gets the atmosphere that will bring it. Stand up, be a man." But when I was with him again, my crest would fall. Now, maybe I was wrong. . . . I think he had an overbearing will. I didn't like him.[89]

In other passages from the oral history interview Hand gives us significant insight into his writer's sensibility. Consider for example what he says about Jackson, Holmes, and Frankfurter as writers. Hand says of Jackson that he wrote the best opinions on the Court. "Oh, he had style, that fellow. He had real style, and he could strike the jugular in an opinion."[90] Of Frankfurter he says:

> [h]e's too discursive. If you're very discursive people get lost. You must deliver punches more, and he hasn't that faculty. That was the great thing about Bob Jackson. He would give you something that would just throw you back on your heels and you'd remember it. That was true of Brandeis, although he had indefinite particularity, you know, detail. He didn't write very long ones . . . but of course [Frankfurter] didn't have the Master's touch of Holmes, of selection. Well, nobody has that. He could say a thing in five pages. The rest of us lumber around in twenty pages, and when you're done "what the hell are you trying to say?" That's the feeling. That was the reason I think he was the great master. The words seem to troop in his mind. You've seen his copy, haven't you? There's hardly any erasures or interlineation.[91]

Hand's most telling comments relate as well to Frankfurter. We can assess his personal and intellectual values by considering what he found as flaws in Frankfurter's personality. A man fully conversant with Shake-speare, his comments echoed, perhaps unintentionally, Caesar's on Cassius in his "sleek-headed men" speech, in which he says he fears Cassius in part because he loves no plays and hears no music.[92] The interviewer is Louis Henkin of the Columbia University Law School.

Interviewer: I have a feeling from what I've heard that Brandeis succeeding in limiting himself more, in confining himself more within his job, much more so than Frankfurter has been able to do. Frankfurter, it is said, makes a more charming companion.

Hand: Why, he doesn't have many outside interests, does he?

Interviewer: Not in the sense of activity, but in the sense of reading and people.

Hand: Does he? Is he widely read?

Interviewer: Oh, yes.

Hand: Well, I didn't know that.

Interviewer: Tremendously—he reads all the periodicals, and—

Hand: He doesn't give you a sense of being widely acquainted with letters.

Interviewer: No, that's true. He isn't acquainted in the classics. He's a brilliant political and social analyst, very much aware of and interested in what's going on today all over the world.

Hand: That is true. He has very—I was going to say discordant interests, but that isn't it. His periphery, and the angles of receptivity, are too large, really. That is true. And yet he never seems to be acquainted—I don't think he has any care for beauty. I never saw it.

Interviewer: He listens to music.

Hand: Well, does he enjoy it?

Interviewer: I think so.

Hand: I don't think he has any eye whatever, has he? I never saw it.

Interviewer: He has a lovely wife.

Hand: That's really irrelevant. But I never saw him show any sensitivity to the arts, to the plastic arts. Did you? Or to the dramatic arts. I never heard him mention a play. Nor does he ever to me give any evidence of interest in literature.

Interviewer: It's spotty, perhaps.

Hand: Well, I didn't even find the spots.

Interviewer: His chief interest is in human beings. He's got a genius for friendship, and for knowing what goes on in the world.

Hand: Makes some good enemies, too.

Interviewer: Yes, there's no doubt.

Hand: No, I've come more and more to respect him and have affection for him. But he's contentious, too. Now, this comes to me—I hadn't thought of it before—it's hard to leave a matter in balance with him,

without a little residuum of feeling. That I miss a good deal. If you disagree—well, you must take a positive position, for or against. Well, that
interferes with intimacy, doesn't it?

Interviewer: Perhaps he spreads himself out. For a man who does that, he
does very remarkably, but still he's spreading himself out.

Hand: Do you know—well, I wasn't thinking just of this. I was thinking
that in his intercourse with people, things are brought too much to a
conclusion, one way or the other. Marian is said to have said: "Do you
realize what it is to live with a man who's never tired." Is he never tired?

Interviewer: Never tired. We had a dinner the other night, and at 2:00
o'clock in the morning, most of us wanted to go home, but we had to
take him home. He was ready to go on.

Hand: I never saw him really drunk, or anything like it. I've seen him when
the liquor hit him some, but not really.

Interviewer: I don't think he has any real interest in that.

Hand: Well, does that do anything to him. I thought it did.

Interviewer: He doesn't really care about it.

Hand: Well, it changes him somewhat. I don't think it lifts, I don't think
he has a load of melancholy, or has he?

Interviewer: Not that I know of.[93]

Henry Friendly's career on the Second Circuit began in 1959 and continued until 1985. Like Hand, he is considered the greatest appellate judge
of his generation. Friendly, who had achieved the highest grades in the
history of the Harvard Law School, with an eighty-three three-year average in an academic world in which seventy-five was an A,[94] was, as Paul
Freund put it, "not merely a legend in his own time, he had become one
in his mid-twenties."[95] Felix Frankfurter did his best to steer him into teaching, but he opted for practice, twenty-seven years of it, before going onto
the federal bench in 1959, where he stayed until his death in 1985. Once
a judge, he wrote to Frankfurter that "looking back on my own career, I
can see that I stayed too long in private practice—as, of course, you told
me."[96]

In an insightful tribute to Friendly in the *Harvard Law Review,* Bruce
Ackerman, who clerked for Friendly during the 1967–68 year, elaborates on
his theme that "Henry Friendly did his own work" and provides details into
Friendly's writing process.[97] When Friendly was working on the mammoth
Penn Central merger case, four days after the oral argument, Ackerman
wandered into Friendly's office looking for a volume of the *U.S. Reports.*
He sees that Friendly "has begun to write his opinion, longhand, on white
sheets neatly stacked in the corner of his small work desk. On the fifth day,
a typed opinion appears in my office—beginning with 'Friendly, J.,' and

proceeding for 227 pages to 'Affirmed.' The working draft has wide margins and is triple spaced: still, 227 pages in four days seems a bit much for a six-ty-four-year-old who regularly leaves his office before five in the afternoon."[98] Ackerman goes on to describe Friendly's willingness to change parts of his opinion when Ackerman makes a good point, even scuttling 55 of the original 227 pages. Although this acknowledgment of Friendly's open mind is important in understanding how he worked, two points dominate Ackerman's portrait of Friendly: Henry Friendly did his own work, and he did it with blinding speed.

An exploration of the ways in which Learned Hand and Henry Friendly wrote their opinions should not overshadow their respective contributions to the law. With nearly fifteen hundred signed majority opinions,[99] Learned Hand's work on the bench continues to influence courts today, most notably in the areas of copyright, admiralty, statutory interpretation, and procedure. The stylistic excellence of Hand's opinions certainly has something to do with their currency today, but equally important is the significance of the ideas they contain. Hand's was a global vision that understood cases in their particulars and their greater implications.

Like Hand's, Friendly's opinions continue to have influence today. His most notable work was in procedure, statutory interpretation, habeas corpus, and commercial cases. His writing style has had less of an impact on the ongoing significance of his opinions, however. Friendly's tenure on the bench took place in our distinctly modern age of legislative dominance, and in that sense he has more in common with today's law than did Hand. Hand mastered the jurisprudence of his age and added to it. Friendly mastered the jurisprudence of his age—a significant achievement in its own right—and was able to add to an even more complex body of jurisprudence. That both Friendly and Hand were gifted writers who labored over their opinions, in the end, was not a coincidence.

—• 3 •—

Style and Substance
in Supreme Court Opinions

The Supreme Court of the United States sits atop the federal judiciary pyramid and has authority over state judiciaries when they interpret issues of federal law. An average of seven thousand cases each year are now filed with the Court, but the Court gives an opinion on barely more than a hundred of these. All but the last vestiges of the Court's mandatory jurisdiction were swept away with legislation in 1988, which made the Court the master of its own docket.[1] It hears what it does only because it wants to. Exercising this discretion, the Court in the representative 1992 Term reviewed thirty-four cases to resolve conflicts between the courts of appeal or, in a few instances, to resolve issues that had divided both the courts of appeal and state supreme courts. In other cases involving the First Amendment and handbills,[2] the adjusted basis of depreciable mining costs,[3] preference hiring in the construction industry,[4] and Haitian refugees,[5] the Court noted that it had reviewed each because of the importance of the issue presented. One hundred seven cases were decided with signed opinions. The Court reviewed eleven habeas corpus cases; eight civil rights cases; four cases involving monopolies and antitrust; eight tax cases; three reapportionment cases; three forfeiture cases; three immigration cases; three bankruptcy cases; three pension cases; one Fourth Amendment case; one patent case; two Indian cases; one securities case; five criminal cases, including two cases involving the Sentencing Guidelines; three labor cases; three church and state cases; thirteen cases on jurisdiction; procedure, both civil and criminal; and ten constitutional cases.

Not surprisingly, no common law cases were reviewed by the Court, although the common law did play an important role in cases involving qualified privilege for court reporters,[6] the competency standard for standing trial and pleading guilty,[7] and double jeopardy.[8] In one form or another, except for cases calling for constitutional interpretation, all of the cases decided involved statutory interpretation. The Court interpreted a wide array of statutes, including the Civil Rights Act, the Employee Retirement Income Security Act, the Longshore Harbor Workers' Compensation Act, the Sherman Act, the Interstate Agreement of Detainers, the Voting Rights Act, the Kansas Act, the Comprehensive Drug Abuse Prevention and Control Act of 1970, the Federal Tort Claims Act, the National Labor Relations Act, the Interstate Commerce Act, the Sovereign Immunities Act, the Soldiers' and Sailors' Civil Relief Act, the Debt Collection Act, the Age Discrimination in Employment Act, the Federal Railroad Safety Act, the McCarran-Ferguson Act, the United States Housing Act, the Fair Labor Standards Act, the Federal Freedom of Information Act, the Indian Health Care Improvement Act, the Securities and Exchange Act of 1934, the Cable Communications Policy Act of 1984, the Multiemployer Pension Plan Amendments Act, the Flood Control and Cheyenne River Acts, the Immigration Reform and Control Act, the Administrative Procedures Act, the Immigration and Nationality Act, and the Clayton Act. On the constitutional front, the Court interpreted the establishment of religion, due process, equal protection, impeach and trial, commerce, import-export, supremacy, double jeopardy, free speech, and search and seizure clauses. The Court also reviewed the ripeness, mootness, and standing doctrines relating to its jurisdiction as set out in the constitution.

In other words, the Court considered many varied issues, such as whether Kentucky's persistent felony offender statute was constitutional,[9] whether the challenged portions of Arizona's and Texas's death penalty statutes were constitutional,[10] whether having someone's mobile home physically torn from its moorings qualified as a "seizure" within the meaning of the Fourth Amendment to state a cause of action under section 1983 of the Civil Rights Act,[11] the test that should be applied to determine whether an office in a taxpayer's home qualifies as his "principal place of business,"[12] whether the Senate has the sole discretion to choose impeachment procedures in the impeachment of a federal judge,[13] whether a claim of innocence based on newly discovered evidence can be a basis for federal habeas corpus relief,[14] whether Tennessee's tax on cargo container leases is constitutional,[15] and the extent to which accountants in Florida can solicit business.[16]

The majority opinions of the 1992 Term averaged sixteen pages in the U.S. Reports and approximately eight pages in the Supreme Court Reporter and contained, on average, nine footnotes per opinion. The majority opinions were uniformly unremarkable in style and language. The issues were stated, the procedural history of the case detailed, the contrasting arguments presented, the prevailing argument explained, and the result announced. The statutory analysis that made its way into almost all of the cases also followed predictable patterns. The words of the statute were parsed, and the canons of statutory construction applied if needed. If there was ambiguity the Court looked to statutory history and the internal logical coherence of the statute to make its pick of contrasting interpretations.

◆   ◆

Readers of the *U.S. Reports* cannot help noticing that, with only a few exceptions, all of the opinion writers in the 1992 Term seem to write and sound alike. This is even more true for the opinions in the *Federal Supplement* and the *Federal Reporter*. Even though divers hands write these opinions, they all tend to sound and look the same because the law clerks who write them are almost always drawn from the ranks of recently graduated law review editors. Their prose is law reviewese, which means that it is colorless, scholarly in the sense of citing many cases as precedent for each and every principle of law, and extensively footnoted. Clerk-written opinions, to use Randall Jarrell's savage observation about bad poetry, are opinions written on a typewriter by a typewriter. Law clerks approach opinions timidly, as well they should given their judicial experience, and write as narrowly as possible. Every step in establishing either the standard of review or the analysis itself is taken gingerly. For every step precedent is cited. Given the author's experience and knowledge of law, this is how it should be. We can find this approach at all three federal levels, as well as at the appellate levels of state courts, but of course there are exceptions. It cannot be denied, however, that the days of judges or justices doing all of their own work, which of course was the only way they could operate before the rise of the law clerk in the twentieth century, has been long gone.

This is not to say that a law clerk's opinion is not a well-written opinion. Those that the reader finds in the pages of the *U.S. Reports*, as well as those in the *Federal Reporter* and the *Federal Supplement*, are all exceedingly well done. The complaints listed above involve the expressiveness and the breadth of the law clerk's knowledge. But beyond the excessive citation and sometimes rigid adherence to structure, clerk opinions are often models of clarity and organization. Writing a judicial opinion at any level, but especially at the federal level, is not an easy job. The issues need to be identified, and the clerks often have to supplement the research of the lawyers, depending on the quality of the briefs. Research has to be done just to verify that the counsel are correctly stating the principles of the cases they cite. Finally, clerks have to fashion persuasive arguments, often reconciling various points of view, a heady job for someone just out of law school. A judge who takes an active role as an editor certainly makes the clerk's job easier, but it is the task of fashioning that first draft that is, by itself, an imposing and difficult one for the writer, whether a law clerk or a judge.

The only relief from the tedium of the Court's prose in the 1992 Term came from an occasional concurring or dissenting opinion. Justice Scalia provided the highpoint of the year in language and style in a church and state case, *Lamb's Chapel v. Center Moriches School District*,[17] in which he railed against the three-part test articulated in *Lemon v. Kurtzman*,[18] which is routinely applied by the Court in such cases. He concurred only in the judgment. The issue presented to the Court was whether denying the church access to school premises to exhibit films violated the Freedom of Speech Clause. Invoking movie metaphors, Scalia playfully inveighs,

[a]s to the Court's invocation of the *Lemon* test: Like some ghoul in a late-night horror movie that repeatedly sits up in its grave and shuffles abroad, after being repeatedly killed and buried, *Lemon* stalks our Establishment Clause jurisprudence once again, frightening the little children and school attorneys of Center Moriches Union Free School District. Its most recent burial, only last Term, was to be sure, not fully six feet under: our decision in *Lee v. Wiseman* conspicuously avoided using the supposed "test" but also declined the invitation to repudiate it. Over the years, however, no fewer than five of the currently sitting Justices have, in their own opinions, personally driven pencils through the creature's heart (the author of today's opinion [Justice White] repeatedly), and a sixth has joined an opinion doing so. The secret of the *Lemon* test's survival, I think, is that it is so easy to kill. It is there to scare us (and our audience) when we wish to do so, but we can command it to return to the tomb at will. When we wish to strike down a practice it forbids, we invoke it. Sometimes, we take a middle course, calling its three prongs "no more than helpful signposts." Such a docile and useful monster is worth keeping around, at least in the somnolent state; one never knows when one might need him. For my part, I agree with the long list of constitutional scholars who have criticized *Lemon* and bemoaned the strange Establishment Clause geometry of crooked lines and wavering shapes its intermittent use has produced. I will decline to apply *Lemon*—whether it validates or invalidates the government action in question—and therefore cannot join the opinion of the Court today.

58

◆   ◆

The evolution of the Supreme Court opinion as we know it today began in the eighteenth century when the Court, staffed with its initial complement of six Justices, for several years found itself with almost nothing to do. First in New York and then in Philadelphia, the Supreme Court decided only eleven cases with opinions. The Court had difficulty in keeping its Justices from quitting, either because of better offers or fatigue brought on by constant circuit riding. Its opinions also suggested a shaky future, not just because the Court's most important case, *Chisholm v. Georgia*,[19] was reversed by Congress with the passage of the Eleventh Amendment, which immunized states from suit without their consent. With the Justices straining to get the most out of the first principles they were applying, the opinions read like the essay examination answers of college students. To make matters worse for the reader and for the opinion's precedential value, the Justices of the early Court followed the English seriatim approach of opinion writing. Each Justice delivered his opinion on the matter, regardless of whether his view was the same as another Justice's. The Justices hardly sought to distinguish themselves or their opinions. Only Wilson, who served for eight years before financial problems forced him to leave the Court and seek cover, unsuccessfully, from pursuing creditors, brought dash to his opinions. He was the first to use figurative language when he wrote in *Chisholm:* "For in an instrument well drawn, as in a poem well composed, silence is sometimes most expressive."

Marshall imposed his style on judicial opinions in the same way he imposed reforms on the Court to speed the production of opinions. His was a magisterial style that declared more than it explained. Obfuscation was not without its place, though. His famous opinion in *Marbury v. Madison*[20] establishes the fundamental principle of judicial review, although neophytes reading it would swear that he smuggled the principle in without detection. The public, fortunately, did not have to contend with Marshall's tortuous judicial exercise. The case was widely noticed in newspapers of the day, but rather than the opinion itself, the newspapers ran summaries of the decision. Constitutional scholar Currie says of Marshall's opinions that they featured "rhetorical flourish, bare assertion, plentiful dicta, multiple holdings, inattention to favorable precedent, and emphasis on the undesirable consequences of an interpretation at variance with his own."[21] He was more magisterial in the first decade of his service and more willing thereafter to provide explanations as to the authority, if any, upon which he based his conclusions.

Justice Joseph Story's was the only other important voice that Chief Justice Marshall used to help establish his Court's fundamental constitutional doctrines in the areas of judicial review, sovereign immunity, comity, the implied powers of the constitution, the commerce clause, and the contract clause. Story's opinions frequently displayed what he termed his calm but "ambitious self-possession." His opinions were usually didactic, self-consciously displaying his deep learning. In *Charles River Bridge v. Warren Bridge*,[22] for example, he wrote fifty-seven pages in dissent, reciting the wide-ranging legal authority supporting his position. According to his biographer Kent Newmyer, Story followed a scholarly approach, writing architectonically structured opinions that approached law comprehensively, resorting frequently to black letter law.[23] The author of important treatises and commentaries, Story searched for the organizing principles of a case. This was the essence of legal science for him. He taught for many years at the Harvard Law School while also sitting on the High Court bench, and the scientific method that he brought to his teaching influenced his opinions, which, Newmyer notes, instruct and lecture.[24]

Chief Justice Roger Taney (1836–64) dominated his court as much as Marshall had dominated his. He was not the equal of Marshall at his most eloquent and magisterial, but he wrote competently, if not forcefully. Benjamin Curtis, his sometime rival on the Court, possessed great skills as a lawyer and a writer, which he illustrated to great effect in his dissent in *Dred Scott*. If anyone could match Marshall's authoritative style, it was Curtis. During the balance of the century, only Samuel Miller could rival Curtis and Marshall as the best writer on the Court.

Brevity was not a value much honored in those times. One opinion written by Chief Justice Waite, for example, takes up an entire volume of the *U.S. Reports*.[25] The tendency of some Justices to quote at length and generally to write extended opinions tested the patience of others. In 1878 the Court established a three Justice committee to consider the possibility of producing condensed reports of their opinions, which in large part meant producing shorter opinions. The committee could reach no satisfactory remedy, an exasperated Justice Miller reported, because Chief Justice Waite had neither the firmness nor courage to take the lead in moving the Court toward shorter opinions.[26] "It is probably the last effort I shall make for any serious reform in the body," he wrote. "My interest in it fades rapidly and if I could leave it tomorrow I would gladly do so."[27]

Most nineteenth-century Supreme Court opinions are nearly unreadable to us today. Style and substance mix here for the impenetrable effect. The Court spent most of its time dealing with issues, such as ejectment and land titles, that are alien to us today. Its docket for most of the nineteenth century got much of its work from the twenty-fifth section of the Judiciary Act of 1787, which gave litigants a right to appeal their cases to the Supreme Court if they involved property interests that had been affected by any federal law, legislation, or treaty. Constitutional cases made up only a small fraction of the Court's work, which explains why so much of the Court's nineteenth-century jurisprudence is largely forgotten. Equally important, the Justices were not engaged in judging in the Grand Style as described by Llewellyn in *The Common Law Tradition*. But state court judges throughout the country were judging in this style, moving through the doctrinal problems confronting the growing nation in a disciplined, reasoned manner.[28]

As if the alien language and principles of the Court's nineteenth-century jurisprudence were not enough, most of the Court's nineteenth-century Justices were indifferent writers. They felt no particular need to state the nature of the case and the issues to be considered. Rather, the Justices launched into long recitations of facts, rarely explaining why these were important. Only the lawyers involved in the cases could follow what the Justices were saying. Moreover, the Justices wrote with an indifference toward style and the principles of effective composition. The dominant impression is that they were compelled to engage in the exercise known as the judicial opinion and brought to it as little effort and interest in creating a readable document as possible.

These nineteenth-century documents show a connection between a Justice's effective writing style and his contribution to constitutional jurisprudence. It is perhaps fortunate that the Chief Justices who assumed the responsibility for writing the majority of the constitutional cases in their tenures, such as Marshall, Taney, and Waite, were good writers. Those other Justices who contributed most to nineteenth-century constitutional jurisprudence also tended to be the better writers of the century. On the flip side, the worst writers—such as Henry Baldwin (1830–44) and Nathan Clifford (1858)—tended to contribute the least, primarily because they were not assigned to write the important constitutional cases.

The Court's struggle to interpret the constitution consistently was a direct result of the inability of many of the Justices to write competent constitutional opinions. Living as we do in an age of expected judicial competence, it surprises us that the challenges in constitutional jurisprudence should have so often taken the measure of the Justices of the nineteenth century. Yet the legal world of the nineteenth century was quite different from ours. The Justices came to the Court with widely varying abilities and backgrounds. Legal educations as we know them today were nearly unheard of, which made it more difficult for those appointing the Justices to employ satisfactory measures of competence. The Justices, at the same time, were working in relative isolation. Their opinions had little dissemination and received even less critical commentary to guide them. Academic lawyers, who exist in part to comment on the work of courts and to produce scholarly writing to help them, did not appear until the latter part of the nineteenth century, and when they did arrive, did not much resemble the academic lawyers of today. Perhaps equally important, it was not until the end of the nineteenth century, with the first use of law clerks, that a connection was forged between the legal academics and the judiciary. The inconsistency and incompetence that so often characterized the work of the Supreme Court could never happen in our time because the Court's work is scrutinized too carefully and because the Justices have far more resources —the law clerks, to name the most important—to compensate for whatever inadequacies they might have as legal thinkers and competent opinion writers.

The Court's calendar had something to do with the quality of its opinions. In the nineteenth century, the Supreme Court continued to have a light docket until the end of the Civil War. From 1856 to 1865 the Court decided an average of 70 cases per term by opinion, while in the decade after the war the average rose to more than 150 cases per term. The Court's docket continued to grow more crowded in the following decades. From 1876 to 1895 the average number of cases decided each term by opinion rose to more than two hundred. During the next decade the average rose even more, to 250 per term.

Footnotes in Supreme Court opinions appeared for the first time after the Civil War. Occasionally the Justices put citations to authority below the text but used an asterisk or other symbol to designate them. The first numbered footnote appeared in a Justice Gray opinion in 1887.[29] The rare early twentieth-century footnotes almost always set out statutes or other material in the margin. On only a few occasions did they seek to explain a point made in the text, and then it was only to show how a calculation of some sort was made. In 1894 Justice Harlan became the first to put a string citation in a footnote.[30]

Congress seemed to be of two minds on the issue of the Court's work load. It had first added to the problem in 1875 by giving state court litigants the right to remove their case to federal court, if there was a federal jurisdictional basis. This enlarged the class of cases that could make their way to the High Court. But then, in 1891, Congress created the courts of appeals in nine circuits around the country. The court of appeals' decision was to be the final word on a variety of cases, such as admiralty, diversity, and many commercial cases, thus relieving pressure on the Supreme Court. The innovation did not work as well as hoped, which required the Congress to act again in 1925, this time effectively, with the Judge's Bill. This enabled the Court to make its review function largely discretionary. Cases decided by opinion had continued to average more than two hundred per term, but once the legislation took effect, the number of cases decided each term by opinion dipped to approximately 150.

During this time, Justice Holmes served as a transitional figure in the development of judicial opinions. Throughout his career Holmes wrote brief opinions, almost as a matter of pride. His opinions as a member of the Fuller Court, from his appointment in 1902 until Fuller's death in 1910, were the shortest, averaging 3.54 pages of the *U.S. Reports* per opinion. Justice Gray wrote the longest opinions, averaging 12.24 pages per opinion. The Court's average was 8.93 pages per opinion.[31] During the same period, Holmes cited the greatest number of cases per page. The Court's average was 1.91 cases cited per page. Justice Peckham was low Justice with 1.34 cases cited per page, while Holmes led with 3.35 cases cited per page.[32]

Twenty years after the Fuller Court, with Justices such as Brandeis, Roberts, and Stone on the Hughes Court, Holmes's opinions were by far the shortest and, in addition, now contained the fewest number of cases cited per page. In one four-page opinion from 1921, for example, Holmes did not cite a single case.[33] On the Fuller Court Holmes had not been particularly conspicuous for not writing footnotes, since so few of the Justices did, but by the time of the Hughes Court, all the Justices, save Holmes, used them, and they used them in great numbers.

Not just in brevity but also in style Holmes was exceptional. The prose of his judicial opinions is lively, imagistic, lucid, prone to epigram or aphorism, and, above all, brimming with self-confidence. It is also marked by decisiveness, which Edmund Wilson thought came from Holmes's wartime experiences of being wounded three times during the Civil War.[34] Then there's the Olympian quality that permeates the prose. Consider Holmes's opinion in *Grant Timber and Mfg. Co. v. Gray.*[35] The case questioned whether the Fourteenth Amendment was violated by a Louisiana statute prohibiting a petitory action for property to be brought by a defendant in a possessory action until after the judgment in that action. In an extraordinary tour de force summarizing the law spanning a period of a thousand years, Holmes undauntedly writes that "from the exceptio spolii of Pseudo-Isidore, the Canon Law, and Bracton, to the assize of novel disseisin, the principle was of very wide application that a wrongful disturbance of possession must be righted before a claim of title would be listened to . . . and from Kant to Ihering there has been much philosophizing as to the grounds."[36]

The self-assurance that allows Holmes to scan with ease this vast legal landscape informs the figurative language of the law that he is perhaps best known for. Thus, we have Holmes the aphorist writing that "three generations of imbeciles are enough."[37] Such casual indifference gives way to Olympian sensibility when Holmes writes that "the power to tax is not the power to destroy while this Court sits"[38] and that "the common law is not a brooding omnipresence in the sky but the articulable voice of some sovereign or quasi-sovereign that can be identified."[39] With great simplicity he writes that "taxes are what we pay for civilized society,"[40] and that "great cases like hard cases make bad law."[41]

Holmes could write with such aplomb in part because he had no fears as a writer. He had complete self-confidence as to his social and intellectual status, tracing his lineage to three important New England families. Moreover, his father was a respected man of both science and letters, whose influence helped open doors for him, here and abroad. It is with these advantages that Holmes's career developed. Intellectually, he considered only Laski and Pollock his equals, and he might even have had doubts about Pollock when he failed to grasp Holmes's meaning in their correspondence. Holmes, simply put, was an intellectual snob. About Will Durant, for example, he wrote Laski, "how could anyone who calls himself Will write anything on philosophy that I should care to hear."[42]

Though Holmes is the best-known writer of his time on the Supreme Court, his friend and longtime colleague Justice Brandeis had a greater effect in the evolution of judicial opinion writing. The changes he helped bring about actually began before he went onto the High Court, when he was an advocate and progenitor of what came to be known as the Brandeis Brief. This was a richly documented argument that relied more on the social sciences than law to make its arguments. The most notable example of this type of brief writing came in *Muller v. Oregon*,[43] which looked specifically to law in only 3 of its 113 footnote-studded pages. Not surprisingly, Brandeis brought the same approach to opinion writing as a Justice as he had to brief writing as an advocate. And in the same way that he had imitators in brief writing, he had imitators in judicial opinion writing. Brandeis's approach of relying on extrajudicial authority found in the social sciences passed after a few decades, but the movement toward longer, more richly documented, and more heavily footnoted opinions has continued unabated to the present time, with only the exception of Justice O'Connor and her near moratorium in footnote use. As part of his belief in the importance of extrajudicial authority, Brandeis was also the first Justice to cite law review articles in his opinions.

As much as anything else, Justice Brandeis's attitude toward footnotes has most influenced judicial opinion writing today. Although he once famously noted that the High Court was so respected because its Justices did their own work,[44] Brandeis in fact did not, at least not all of it. He, like Justice Stone, let his law clerks loose to write the footnotes. Noting in 1957 that the Justices seemed to write textbooks as marginal annotations of their opinions, Dean Acheson, one of Brandeis's clerks, revealed with some pride that his were the Mount Everest of footnotes. He had written the greatest footnotes, he said, fifteen pages of them in the case of *Ruppert v. Caffey*.[45]

Brandeis arranged to select his law clerks from the Harvard Law School. In time other Justices made similar arrangements with professors at various law schools who would screen law clerk possibilities and select the best candidates. Coming from the most elite law schools in the country, these law clerks, who contributed so importantly to the Court's work, brought with them the imprint of their legal educations. Their twentieth-century legal educations were not what they would have been in the nineteenth century, in large part due to the legal texts read at law schools and the new way law was being understood.

Treatises had dominated legal writing and legal education in the nineteenth century.[46] Treatise writers believed that they could make sense of the law by systematically examining the principles undergirding individual areas of the law, such as bailments or replevin. They concentrated on the tracing and exposition of legal doctrine. The scientific method made its way into the law school by the close of the nineteenth century. Its chief proponent, Christopher Columbus Langdell of Harvard, contended that students should examine individual cases, edited and collected in casebooks, and be led to a micro-understanding of the law by the Socratic method. The emphasis was still on doctrine, but now it was inverted. Instructors, rather than displaying the scope and application of the law by a broad canvass of cases, sought to extract and illustrate doctrine from individual cases.

A second major change at this time was the rise of student-run law reviews. In these, law students contributed to legal literature by editing the lead articles of professors and by writing their own case notes, in which they brought to bear exhaustive legal research for their conclusions. Law reviews as an institution grew to impose a particular type of bland, overly documented legal writing on both professors and students. Fred Rodell, the anti-academic Yale Law School professor who wrote frequently for general audiences about the Court, claimed that there were only two things wrong with law review writing, style and content,[47] but his criticisms had little effect on the institutional habits, which were by now entrenched.

Changes in legal education and the rise of law reviews were significant in the development of opinion writing. Law clerks brought the values of their institutions to their clerking chores. When Justices such as Brandeis and Stone let their law clerks write their footnotes, the impulse was toward the exhaustive and the pedantic. In later years, when this new type of law clerk was writing an opinion for his Justice, he wrote it, not surprisingly, as he would write a law review article or a student note. That, after all, was the training he had in writing. The approach and values these law clerks expressed in their work, both in opinions as a whole and in footnotes, set a standard in opinion writing that remains in place today.

With the institutionalization of law clerks in the Supreme Court, the complaints about the competence of the Justices, which had thrived in the nineteenth and early twentieth centuries, died out. The rise of legal education also brought with it legal academics to the Supreme Court, which in turn helped solidify the technical competence of the Court's work. Chief Justices Taft, Hughes, and Stone had been legal academics at various times in their careers. In 1943 there were five former academics on the Court: Stone, Roberts, Frankfurter, Rutledge, and Douglas. This Court was the last to have Justices who had not graduated from law school — Justices Reed and Jackson, both former solicitors general — but no complaints were heard about the quality of their work.

Brandeis lengthened opinions and slowed them down with footnotes, but he also brought occasional flights of eloquence to his work. He could write, for example, that "men born to freedom are naturally alert to repel invasion of their liberty by evil minded rulers. The greatest dangers to liberty lurk in insidious encroachment by men of zeal, well meaning but without understanding." "If the government becomes a lawbreaker," he continued, "it breeds contempt for law; it invites every man to become a law unto himself; it invites anarchy. To declare that in the administration of criminal law the end justifies the means — to declare that the government may commit crimes in order to secure the conviction of a private criminal — would bring terrible retribution. Against that pernicious doctrine this court should resolutely set its face."[48]

66

Despite his occasional eloquence, Brandeis was not a particularly grace-ful writer. Holmes wrote with an elegance that was most unusual among the Justices of the time. The next writer of comparable skill was Cardozo. His place in the evolution of judicial opinions is important because he brought legitimacy to a brand of opinion that impressed as much with style as with substance. To write with style, before Cardozo, was to risk credi-bility. Robert Jackson, before he himself went on to the High Court and became one of the best writers ever to sit there, described the problem in a letter to Irving Dilliard. "Until Cardozo's time," he wrote, "there was a suspicion among lawyers of any lawyer who wrote too well. It was almost believed that a good literary style was evidence of poor legal craftsman-ship. Cardozo shattered that tradition, and while some of the imitators of his style have made pretty pathetic exhibits, I think his influence on the whole has been a marked improvement in the style of legal writing."[49] Ironically, Cardozo's writing was not admired by the doyen of style, Holmes himself. "I am sorry to say that I do not admire Cardozo's style as much as I would like to," Holmes confessed in the last years of his life.[50] Nor was Jerome Frank, himself a fine writer from the Second Circuit of the U.S. Court of Appeals, fond of Cardozo's eloquence. He wrote an anonymous essay for the Virginia Law Review attacking the style.[51]

Cardozo's literary talent on the High Court was followed and surpassed by that of a quartet of Roosevelt appointees, Hugo Black, William O. Douglas, Felix Frankfurter, and Robert Jackson. The Court has never seen such a talented assembly of writers or a such a feuding group of Justices. Conservatives Jackson and Frankfurter battled relentlessly against liberals Douglas and Black. All used their impressive writing skills to persuade the other members of the Court, but they also had broader aims and used their stylistic talents to bring their cases to the public. Douglas had political ambitions; Black, following the revelations of his Ku Klux Klan member-ship, wanted to dispel the suspicion that he was a racist; Jackson wanted to be Chief Justice; and Frankfurter wanted to shape the Court in his image.

Frankfurter was so keen on wanting to influence the Court that in one of his earliest cases he argued for the resurrection of the seriatim approach to opinion writing.[52] He proposed that when a Court with new personnel announced a major shift in constitutional law, as it was doing in the case at hand, each of the Justices should weigh in with his own belief. No doubt Frankfurter believed that, when judged against the rest, his voice would sound sweetest. In practical terms, Frankfurter was seeking to usurp the Chief Justice's opinion assignment prerogative and to eliminate the vastly inferior precedential value attaching to concurring opinions as compared to the precedential value of the majority opinion. The opinion, for Frankfurter, would become a powerful weapon in his conquest of the Court's legal landscape.

Frankfurter believed that as a student of the Court and as a constitutional scholar he was better trained to be a Justice than any before him. An academic to a fault, Frankfurter in conference subjected his brethren to lengthy lectures supporting his position. These conference lectures tended to last an hour, the length of the law school class Frankfurter was used to teaching. More than an academic, Frankfurter was to most of his colleagues a pedant. This pedantry became his greatest weakness as an opinion writer. While he could write gracefully and eloquently, too often for his colleagues' taste he wrote with the stilted manner that is a pedant's crutch. Even friends were put off by this style. A mock Frankfurter opinion rewriting the Gettysburg Address, found in the papers of Jerome Frank, highlights Frankfurter's pedantic style with great humor. It reads in part,

> [a] semi-centennial, three decades and seven winter solstices preceding the present, our paternal progenitors gestated and regurgitated upon the western hemisphere (49 degrees longitude 38 degrees latitude) a pristine commonwealth, political, social, and economic, of our glorious and heterogeneous population proclaiming the universal hypothesis, proposition and thesis, that all male issue are politically and economically liberated and equal, pari-passu per capita and not per stirpes. Engaged now we are in a collosal bellis civilis (cf. Slaughter House Cases 9 Wall—construing "civil war" to mean "War Between the States" in Alabama) for the purpose of determining qualitatively and quantitatively in perpetuity the tensile strength and viscosity of a government, including its interstices and lacunae, with this ontogeny.[53]

Douglas's approach differed dramatically. He often dashed off opinions and demonstrated no real interest in accommodating the interests of other Justices in an attempt to get or maintain a majority. He went his own way judicially, just as he did literally when the Term ended each summer, often not even telling his colleagues that he was leaving. As a writer, Douglas shared Holmes's fondness for trenchant observation and pungent brevity.

Justice Black brought distinctive stylistic and substantive approaches to his opinions. Substantively, Justice Black recognized the importance of history and frequently incorporated historical digressions into his opinions. Stylistically, he eschewed the use of metaphorical language, complaining that it lacked the precision he sought, but he invoked it for some of his most powerful expressions of feeling and thought. The "[f]reedom to speak and write about public questions is as important to the life of the government as is the heart to the human body," he wrote. "In fact, this privilege is the heart of our government. If that heart be weakened, the result is debilitation; if it be stilled, the result is death."[54]

More than the other Justices, Jackson would unleash his formidable writing skills — in prose that had a jaguar's power, swiftness, and agility — and go after brethren he wanted to wound or tweak. Justice Douglas once noted that Jackson "was a lone wolf on the court, having no close friend except Frankfurter. He loved to write essays and publish them as opinions, not necessarily to illuminate a problem but to embarrass or harass a colleague."[55] Justice Jackson had a natural gift for writing. With him, style was the measure of the man. As Justice Stewart put it, "because [Jackson] was able to express what he had to say with such singular clarity and force, he never left any doubt where he stood on any issue, and why. And because of that extraordinary gift, there shines through the pages of his writing not just his intellect, but the whole power of his personality."[56] Jackson coupled his gift with a deep appreciation of the power of language and the force of literature. Consider *Edwards v. California*,[57] in which the Court struck down California's anti-Okie law, which made it a crime to bring indigent persons into the state, adding to the state's financial burden. The case turned on whether the defendant Edwards could be prosecuted for bringing his friend Duncan into the state when he knew that Duncan had no money. In a concurring opinion Jackson dazzles the reader by invoking the most apt literary reference, Shakespeare on broken promises and paupers. "Rich or penniless," Jackson wrote, "Duncan's citizenship under the Constitution pledges his strength to the defense of California as part of the United States, and his right to migrate to any part of the land he must defend is something she must respect under the same instrument. Unless this Court is willing to say that citizenship of the United States means at least this much to the citizen, then our heritage of constitutional privileges and immunities is only a promise to the ear to be broken to the hope, a teasing illusion like a munificent bequest in a pauper's will."

◆   ◆

With the exception of the years of World War II and its aftermath, press coverage of the Supreme Court rose dramatically beginning in the mid-thirties. This is demonstrated not only in the number of front-page stories in the *New York Times* but also in the number of occasions that the paper and national news magazines reprinted excerpts or entire opinions of the High Court. Between 1930 and 1934, for example, the *Times* ran an average of five front-page stories per year on High Court decisions. The average jumped to ten until the beginning of the war. For the next five years the average was four front-page stories per year. For the next ten years, beginning in 1947, the average rose to nearly ten. From 1957 to 1966, there was an even more dramatic rise, from ten to twenty-five front-page stories per year.

The number of occasions in which the *New York Times* reprinted opinions of the High Court, either completely or in part, shows a similar pattern. For the years 1930–34, there were four opinions reprinted; for the years 1935–41, twenty; for the years 1942–46, one; for the years 1947–56, eighteen; for the years 1957–66, forty-one. Not all of the important cases involving social and personal liberty issues were reprinted. For example, the second flag salute case was not. But many of the Court's most important cases were, such as *Brown v. Board of Education, Jencks v. United States, Mapp v. Ohio, Gideon v. Wainwright, Griswold v. Connecticut, Loving v. Virginia,* and *Miranda v. Arizona.*

The decisions that the *New York Times* reprinted in full or in part chart the movement of the High Court's major concerns from the business, governmental, and regulatory interests of the thirties—with the Court first resisting and then embracing the legislative initiatives of Roosevelt's New Deal—to the social and individual liberty issues relating to matters such as desegregation, privacy, speech, religion, and criminal procedure.

That Justices Jackson, Black, Frankfurter, and Douglas had a higher degree of public recognition, due to their individual personalities and their much reported feuds, probably had some impact on the reporting of the Court's cases. Headlines frequently noted that one of them had written the majority opinion or that one or more of them had dissented. But because the reprinted opinions usually did not contain memorable passages, it seems clear that the decision to reprint an opinion turned on its legal importance, not its literary value.

The connection between the medium and the message in the Supreme Court's work was especially clear in the fifties and sixties. Opinions resolving issues of important individual rights tended to be shorter than the usual opinion and were more directly aimed at the average reader. In particular, Chief Justice Earl Warren understood that the more a case affects the general public, the more it must be written for that audience. For *Brown v. Board of Education* he prepared the outline of the opinion, wrote the opinion's most important sentence, and gave his law clerks specific instructions, his judicial biographer tells us, to write the opinion so that it could be understood by the general public.[58] It has neither the length—at only fourteen paragraphs—nor the density that one would expect in an opinion on such an important problem. It places the issue in a historical and social context, moving away from legal arguments to sociological ones. Form has responded to function, which is to communicate to a nation on the dilemma of fairness.

The Court by the mid-seventies had seen three important changes. First, it was deciding fewer cases involving important individual rights; second, Justice Douglas, the last of the quartet that had dominated the Court with personally identifiable opinions during the fifties and sixties, finally retired; and third, the reins of the Court passed from Chief Justice Warren to Chief Justice Burger. The Court's opinions, as a result, became more homogenized in voice and approach, growing longer and more heavily footnoted. By 1975 the average signed majority opinion was 8.21 *Supreme Court Reporter* pages (or approximately 17 *U.S. Reports* pages) long and contained 17.44 footnotes. The Court with its elaborate research and exegeses seemed to reinvent every jurisprudential wheel.

The opinions continued along in their bloated, voiceless way until the ideological divisions within the Court, coupled with the advancing age of some of the most liberal Justices, brought a number of stinging dissents in the late 1980s. These suggest an old order giving way, grudgingly, to the current membership and dynamics of the Court. In their dissenting opinions the Justices squarely confront the majority, at times assaulting each other, not just on ideological and jurisprudential grounds but also on personal grounds. In 1986 then Justice Rehnquist acknowledged that there was a certain shrillness in the opinions of the recent Supreme Court, but he understated the problem when he argued that "it may reflect conflict among law clerks rather than acerbity or lack of civility among the justices."[59]

Frequent dissents, in themselves, do not raise the issue of collegiality in the Court of the late eighties. Rather, it is the shrillness to which then Justice Rehnquist referred. Dissents have always been important. In addition to suggesting that legal doctrine must not be pressed too far, dissents have demonstrated that opinions are not perfunctory or that the Justices are not infallible. Sometimes, of course, a dissenting position becomes a majority position over time. As Chief Justice Warren put it, "we do not always agree. I hope the Court will never agree on all things. If it ever agrees on all things, I am sure its virility will have been sapped because it is composed of nine independent men who have no one to be responsible to except to their own consciences."[60] Holmes, for one, liked the freedom of the dissent. He said that "one of the advantages of a dissent is that one can say what one thinks without having to blunt the edges and cut off the corners to suit someone else."[61] His dissents could not be personal attacks because he often wrote them before reading the majority's opinion. He was concerned with principles of law, nothing else.

Consider a few of the stinging dissents of the 1989 Term. The most strongly asserted view was Justice Blackmun's dissent in *Webster v. Reproductive Health Services,*[62] in which the majority, through Chief Justice Rehnquist, held that restrictions on the use of public employees and facilities for the performance or assistance of nontherapeutic abortions did not violate due process rights. With Justices Brennan and Marshall joining him, Justice Blackmun wrote:

> I fear for the future. I fear for the liberty and equality of the millions of women who have lived and come of age in the 16 years since *Roe* was decided. I fear for the integrity of, and public esteem for, this Court . . . I dissent. . . . By refusing to explain or to justify its proposed revolutionary revision in the law of abortion, and by refusing to abide not only by our precedents, but also by our canons for reconsidering those precedents, the plurality invites charges of cowardice and illegitimacy to our door. I cannot say that these would be undeserved. . . . For today, at least, the law of abortion stands undisturbed. For today, the women of this Nation still retain the liberty to control their destinies. But the signs are evident and very ominous, and a chill wind blows. I dissent.[63]

The power and eloquence of language displayed by Justice Blackmun is taken yet further by Justice Brennan in *Florida v. Riley.*[64] Writing on the Fourth Amendment, Justice Brennan finds the most powerful literary allusion available to make a compelling dissent in a case in which the plurality held that aerial observations by police officers in a helicopter above a defendant's greenhouse was not a search for which a warrant was required. He writes:

> The issue in this case is, ultimately, "how tightly the Fourth Amendment permits people to be driven back into the recesses of their lives by the risk of surveillance." . . . I hope it will be a matter of concern to my colleagues that the police surveillance methods they would sanction were among those described forty years ago in George Orwell's dread vision of life in the 1980's: "The black-mustachio'd face gazed down from every commanding corner. There was one on the house front immediately opposite. BIG BROTHER IS WATCHING YOU, the captain said. . . . In the far distance a helicopter skimmed down between the roofs, hovered for an instant like a bluebottle, and darted away again with a curving flight. It was the Police

Patrol, snooping into people's windows." G. Orwell, *Nineteen Eighty-Four* 4 (1949). Who can read this passage without a shudder, and without the instinctive reaction that it depicts life in some country other than ours? I respectfully dissent.[65]

The movement toward impassioned dissents is taken to its extreme in Justice Blackmun's statement in *DeShaney v. Winnebago County DSS*.[66] Here the majority, through Chief Justice Rehnquist, held that a state had no constitutional duty to protect a child from abuse after receiving reports of such abuse.

Today, the Court purports to be the dispassionate oracle of the law, unmoved by "natural sympathy," [citation omitted]. But, in this pretense, the Court itself retreats into a sterile formalism which prevents it from recognizing either the facts of the case before it or the legal norms that should apply to those facts. As Justice Brennan demonstrates, the facts here involve not mere passivity, but active state intervention in the life of Joshua DeShaney—intervention that triggered a fundamental duty to aid the boy once the State learned of the severe danger to which he was exposed.

The Court fails to recognize this duty because it attempts to draw a sharp and rigid line between action and inaction. But such formalistic reasoning has no place in the interpretation of the broad and stirring clauses of the Fourteenth Amendment. Indeed, I submit that these clauses were designed, at least in part, to undo the formalistic legal reasoning that infected antebellum jurisprudence, which the late Robert Cover analyzed so effectively in his significant work entitled *Justice Accused*.

Like the antebellum judges who denied relief to fugitive slaves . . . the Court today claims that its decision, however harsh, is compelled by existing legal doctrine. On the contrary, the question presented by this case is an open one, and our Fourteenth Amendment precedents may be read more broadly or narrowly depending upon how one chooses to read them.

Poor Joshua! Victim of repeated attacks by an irresponsible, bullying, cowardly, and intemperate father, and abandoned by respondents who placed him in a dangerous predicament and who knew or learned what was going on, and yet did essentially nothing except, as the Court revealingly observes, ante, at 1001, "dutifully recorded these incidents in their files." It is a sad commentary upon American life, and constitutional principles—so full of late of patriotic fervor and proud proclamations about "liberty and justice for all," that this child Joshua DeShaney, now is assigned to live out the remainder of his life profoundly retarded. Joshua and his mother—as petitioners here, deserve—but are now denied by this court—the opportunity to have the facts of their case considered in the light of constitutional protection that 42 USC 1983 is meant to provide.[67]

There is power in Blackmun's dissent, but at the same time the level of personal involvement that he brings to it highlights its subjective nature, which in turn undermines its effectiveness. The weaknesses inherent in this subjective, emotional approach are similar to those in the more vitriolic dissents of the eighties. In both, language and vision are not adequately paired. Whether the current bland style continues to dominate, or whether we will see a return to the emotional or the vitriolic is, of course, a function of the evolving Court's membership. It is possible that there will be in the future great writers on the bench to rival giants such as Jackson and Black, who were able to combine vision and language. The chances, though, are that we will not see their likes again.

—• 4 •—

The Canon

Constructing the canon of judicial opinions, that is, a list of the greatest and most important, prompts important questions concerning the function of judicial opinions and what distinguishes those that are effective. What we mean by the greatest or the most important opinions becomes clear when we recognize that we are thinking about opinions that have important consequences for the public. For example, we would tend to exclude opinions from courts other than the U.S. Supreme Court because of their limited applicability. This would be true even for those cases that ultimately make their way to the Supreme Court and are transformed into an important or great opinion. Until they reach the national stage, their applicability is limited, on the state court level, to a particular state or, on the federal level, to a particular circuit court of the U.S. Court of Appeals.

But to restrict the canon to opinions from the Supreme Court adds only a necessary condition. The question of importance and greatness, after all, depends on interest and audience. The measure can hardly be technical proficiency, as only aficionados of judicial opinions would think that important. That audience would honor technical virtuosity and judge proficiency by how well the opinion writer followed the five-part opinion structure advocated by handbooks on judicial opinion writing. According to them, the opinion writer must describe the nature of the case and how it got to the court, state the issue to be considered, detail the essential facts, provide a determination of the issue, and declare the disposition of the case.[1] Aficionados as well could look to the way authority is marshalled. Here perfect citation form is a must, but beyond that, citing the seminal case for each principle invoked would count. Those who write judicial opinions can tell the difference in citation form and the authorities invoked and value these aspects of form accordingly, but for most readers these considerations are secondary.

Canons reflecting other values are possible in such areas as economic history, social history, and political history. There could be a canon of opinions in the development of constitutional jurisprudence. David Currie does this in passing in his two-volume treatise on Supreme Court constitutional jurisprudence.[2] He applies traditional doctrinal analysis, testing the Court's work for consistency, thoroughness, and an honest confrontation with the issues with which the Court is grappling. There could be a canon for subclasses of constitutional jurisprudence. A constitutional scholar could well put together a list of the greatest or most important cases in areas such as the Court's interpretation of the commerce clause, the due process clause, and the privilege and immunities clause. And there could be a canon for opinions that establish constitutional doctrines, both substantive and procedural.

There could also be a canon for an audience looking at opinions as literature. The two hundred years of Supreme Court cases are sprinkled with eloquent, moving, and literate passages. But the great language tends to come in spurts, with the balance of the opinion lagging behind as a judicial exercise, that is, as expository prose in which the authoring Justice, in standard fashion, distinguishes and reconciles precedents and sets out the line of legal reasoning supporting the opinion's conclusion. Moreover, an eloquent opinion that does not establish or reassert an important right seems to be little more than a literary exercise. Opinions in a literary canon must go beyond this and deliver substance as well as style.

Traditionally a canon represents the required reading in a field. This leads us to the domain of the Supreme Court. As the highest judicial tribunal charged with the task of ultimately resolving constitutional questions, the Court, with its judicial opinions so rightly characterized by Judge Wyzanski as a "text unto the people," is charged with nothing less than interpreting the American democracy. A canon illustrating the discharge of this responsibility would need to feature opinions articulating fundamental aspects of that democracy. Many, although not all, opinions would relate directly to the individual citizen. Opinions articulating the role of the federal government on issues such as the separation of powers would need to be included. The role of government is further defined by those opinions detailing individual rights or liberties. Here the relationship is not between the branches of government, for example, but between the government and the individual citizen.

In constructing my canon I have used the following criteria: the judicial opinion (1) comes from the United States Supreme Court, (2) establishes or acts as a harbinger of (3) an important rule (4) affecting a fundamental aspect (5) of the American democracy or the American way of life (6) with clarity, conviction, or eloquence. I have chosen eleven opinions: *McCullough v. Maryland,*[3] Justice Holmes's dissent in *Abrams v. U.S.,*[4] *Chambers v. Florida,*[5] *The Steel Seizure Case,*[6] *Brown v. Board of Education,*[7] *Miranda v. Arizona,*[8] *West Virginia State Board of Education v. Barnett,*[9] *Gideon v. Wainwright,*[10] *Loving v. Virginia,*[11] *Skinner v. Oklahoma,*[12] and *Roe v. Wade.*[13]

Stating the significance of these cases by detailing their holdings, that is, the rule controlling the particular case, would be accurate. But, shrouded in legal language, it would not capture the true significance for the average citizen. It is one thing, for example, to say that *Gideon* makes the Sixth Amendment right to counsel applicable to the states through the Fourteenth Amendment. It is something else to say that *Gideon* guarantees us that if we are thrown into the machinery of the criminal justice system, we have the right to a lawyer's help. When we state only what these decisions have done for our average citizen, we recognize how much these cases have shaped the way we live now. *Roe v. Wade* guarantees to women the right to have an abortion; *Barnett* guarantees that the state cannot compel schoolchildren to make affirmations relating to the state if they do not believe them; *Loving* protects the fundamental right to marry, regardless of the race of your beloved; *Brown* guarantees schoolchildren the right to an integrated public education; *Miranda* guarantees criminal suspects the right to be warned that what they say may be used against them and that they can have a lawyer appointed to help them before they say anything to the police; *Chambers* ensures fundamental fairness in criminal proceedings; and *Skinner* guarantees procreative rights that the state cannot take away for some penal convictions but not others. The other three cases affect more abstract rights in the sense that they establish or further define pivotal relationships within the constitution. *McCulloch* declares that deference must be given to the federal government when the "necessary and proper" clause of the Constitution is interpreted; the *Steel Seizure* case makes clear that the president's power is limited to executing and recommending laws and that it does not extend to declaring laws; and *Abrams*, the only dissent in the group, presages the protection later cases would give surrounding the fundamental right of freedom of speech.

We can sketch the nature of the judicial opinion when we consider the way the opinions in these canon cases are constructed. Most important, the approaches the Justices take vary, depending on their needs. In each instance the Justice writing the opinion makes the genre of the judicial opinion his own and shapes it accordingly. Put another way, in the opinions of the canon we see what happens when we take Justices, give them important cases to decide, and perforce make them writers. We see that these Justices acquit themselves as fine, forceful, and frequently eloquent writers communicating on the business of the American civilization.

Consider the case of *West Virginia v. Barnett*, in which the question was whether public schoolchildren could be compelled to salute the flag. The Court had, just three Terms earlier, found a similar compulsory oath constitutional in *Minersville School District v. Gobbitis*.[14] Now, with different personnel on the Court, and with Justices Black and Douglas changing their minds and their votes, the Court went the other way. Writing for the majority, Justice Jackson sets out the facts of the case and then carefully isolates the precise issue so as to charge it with universal significance. He writes that "to sustain the compulsory flag salute we are required to say that a Bill of Rights which guards the individual's right to speak his own mind, left it open to public authorities to compel him to utter what is not on his mind." He then details and rebuts the specific grounds on which *Gobbitis* was decided, using compact, powerful language to expose the fallacy of each argument, saving his most eloquent response for the end. To appreciate *Barnett* we need to recognize that in *Gobbitis* the majority, through Justice Frankfurter, had argued in part that "national unity is the basis of national security," that the authorities have "the right to select appropriate means for its attainment," and that, hence, compulsory measures toward national unity were constitutional. To this Jackson responds with irrefutable eloquence that

> struggles to coerce uniformity of sentiment in support of some end thought to be essential to their time and country have been waged by many good men as well as by evil men. Nationalism is a relatively recent phenomenon but at other times and places the ends have been racial or territorial security, support of a dynasty or regime, and particular plans for saving souls. As first moderate methods to attain unity have failed, those bent on its accomplishment must resort to an ever-increasing severity. As governmental pressure toward unity becomes greater, so strife becomes more bitter as to whose unity it shall be. Probably no deeper division of our people could proceed from any provocation than from finding it necessary to choose what doctrine and whose program public educational officials shall compel youth to unite in embracing. Ultimate futility of such attempts to compel coherence is the lesson of every such effort from the Roman drive

to stamp out Christianity as a disturber of its pagan unity, the Inquisition, as a means to religious and dynastic unity, the Siberian exiles as a means to Russian unity, down to the fast failing efforts of our present totalitarian enemies. Those who begin coercive elimination of dissent soon find themselves exterminating dissenters. Compulsory unification of opinion achieves only the unanimity of the graveyard.[15]

Jackson's closing rhetorical strategy takes him from the specific to the general to build on overwhelming, unquestioned analogous authority. This clinches his argument and stamps his opinion as an enduring declaration of fundamental freedoms. With a flourish, he concludes, "if there is any fixed star in our constitutional constellation, it is that no official, high or petty, can prescribe what shall be orthodox in politics, nationalism, religion, or other matters of opinion or force citizens to confess by word or act their faith therein. If there are any circumstances which permit an exception they do not now occur to us."[16]

The significance of the rights under discussion in *Barnett* is stressed at the conclusion. But in many of the fundamental rights cases, the authoring Justices declare the right's importance at the beginning of the opinion. In *Skinner*, for example, in which the right to procreate is at issue, Justice Douglas begins, "this case touches a sensitive and important area of human rights. Oklahoma deprives certain individuals of a right which is basic to the perpetuation of the race—the right to have offspring."[17] In *Chambers*, Justice Black begins, "the grave question presented by the petition for certiorari, granted in forma pauperis, is whether proceedings in which confessions were utilized, and which culminated in sentences of death upon four young negro men in the State of Florida, failed to afford the safeguard of that due process clause guaranteed by the Fourteenth Amendment."[18] And in *Miranda*, Chief Justice Warren begins, "[t]he cases before us raise questions which go to the roots of our concept of American criminal jurisprudence: the restraints society must observe consistent with the Federal Constitution in prosecuting individuals for crime."[19]

In *Skinner* Douglas needed only to explain the violation of the equal protection clause. Under the sterilization statue in question, embezzlers would be exempt from the law while mere thieves stealing the same amount of money would not. He goes further, though, and, as Jackson would do in *Barnett*, links the minor to the major, making effective use of occasional flights of figurative language.

We are dealing here with legislation which involves one of the basic civil rights of man. Marriage and procreation are fundamental to the very existence and survival of the race. The power to sterilize, if exercised, may have subtle, far-reaching and devastating effects. In evil or reckless times it can cause races of types which are inimical to the dominant group to wither and disappear. There is no redemption for the individual whom the law touches. Any experiment which the State conducts is to his irreparable injury. He is forever deprived of a basic liberty. We mention these matters not to reexamine the scope of the police power of the States. We advert to them merely in emphasis of our view that strict scrutiny of the classification which a State makes in a sterilization law is essential, lest unwittingly or otherwise invidious discriminations are made against groups or types of individuals in violation of the constitutional guaranty of just and equal laws. The guaranty of "equal protection of the laws is a pledge of the protection of equal law." When the law lays an unequal hand on those who have committed intrinsically the same quality of offense and sterilizes one and not the other, it has made as an invidious a discrimination as if it had selected a particular race or nationality for oppressive treatment. Sterilization of those who have thrice committed grand larceny with immunity for those who are embezzlers is a clear, pointed, unmistakable discrimination. . . . The equal protection clause would indeed be a formula of empty words if such conspicuous artificial lines could be drawn.[20]

In *Chambers* Justice Black begins with a declaration that his opinion concerns grave issues. He then gives a cogent recitation of the facts, detailing not only how the four defendants were interrogated but the words themselves that the interrogators used in trying to break them down. The opinion sketches a compelling drama with which the reader can identify. The technical point is that the Fifth and Fourteenth Amendments have been understood to protect against convictions based on such interrogations. But this is overshadowed by Black's eloquent conclusion. After recreating the scene of oppression, he then casts the Court, to the relief of the reader identifying with the defendants, in the role of protector:

We are not impressed by any argument that law enforcement methods such as those under review are necessary to uphold our laws. The Constitution proscribes such lawless means irrespective of the end. And this argument flouts the basic principle that all people must stand on an equality before the bar of justice in every American court. Today, as in ages past, we are not without tragic proof that the exalted power of some governments to punish manufactured crime dictatorially is the handmaid of tyranny. Under our constitutional system, courts stand against any winds that blow as havens of refuge for those who might otherwise suffer because they are helpless, weak, outnumbered, or because they are non-conforming victims of prejudice and public excitement. Due process of law, preserved for all by our Constitution, commands that no such practice as that disclosed by this record shall send any accused to his death. No higher duty, no more solemn responsibility, rests upon this Court, than that of translating into living law and maintaining this constitutional shield deliberately planned and inscribed for the benefit of every human being subject to our Constitution—of whatever race, creed or persuasion.[21]

In *Loving* Chief Justice Warren declares the seriousness of the issue under consideration at the beginning. But in addition he adds weight to the opinion by stating the Court's conclusion in his opening remarks: "This case presents a constitutional question never addressed by this Court: whether a statutory scheme adopted by the State of Virginia to prevent marriages between persons solely on the basis of racial classifications violates the Equal Protection and Due Process Clauses of the Fourteenth Amendment. For reasons which seem to us to reflect the central meaning of those constitutional commands, we conclude that these statutes cannot stand consistently with the Fourteenth Amendment."[22] Warren states the arguments made by Virginia and quickly and easily dispatches them, setting up his conclusion. He stresses the illogic of tying race to a fundamental right. He too follows a rhetorical strategy that builds to a crescendo. The final paragraph is written within the context of a due process argument, but the argument builds, seemingly breaking the limits of the Fourteenth Amendment, and looks to universal significance.

> The freedom to marry has long been recognized as one of the vital personal rights essential to the orderly pursuit of happiness by free men. Marriage is one of the "basic civil rights of man" fundamental to our very existence and survival. To deny this fundamental freedom on so unsupportable a basis as the racial classifications embodied in these statutes, classifications so directly subversive of the principle of equality at the heart of the Fourteenth Amendment, is surely to deprive all the State's citizens of liberty without due process of law. The Fourteenth Amendment requires that the freedom of choice to marry not be restricted by invidious racial discriminations. Under our Constitution, the freedom to marry or not marry, a person of another race resides with the individual and cannot be infringed by the State. These convictions must be reversed.[23]

In *Brown v. Board of Education* Chief Justice Warren, in an opinion of only fourteen paragraphs, is two-thirds through before he frames the issue to be decided. He does so in a way that strongly suggests the resolution of the issue, which he then explicitly states in the sentence following the description of the problem. "Does segregation of children in public schools solely on the basis of race, even though the physical facilities and other 'tangible' factors may be equal, deprive the children of the minority group of educational opportunities? We believe that it does."[24] In the first nine paragraphs the Chief Justice recounts the procedural history of the case, discusses Fourteenth Amendment jurisprudence in the context of segregation, and then states that the "so-called" doctrine of "separate but equal" spawned in the *Plessy v. Ferguson* case had not been reexamined since its inception. He then sweeps away the precedent of *Plessy* by announcing that a contemporary perspective must be brought to such important institutions as state and local governments and public education. "In approaching this problem," he writes, "we cannot turn the clock back to 1868 when the [Fourteenth] Amendment was adopted, or even to 1896 when *Plessy v. Ferguson* was written. We must consider public education in the light of its full development and its present place in American life throughout the Nation. Only in this way can it be determined if segregation in public schools deprives these plaintiffs of the equal protection of the laws."[25]

The Chief Justice needed only to look to a lower court opinion in the case—in which the segregation was nonetheless upheld—for evidence, which he quotes, that segregation has a detrimental effect on black children. A footnote supplements the lower court finding with sociological studies leading to the same conclusion. He is then able to conclude, only two paragraphs after stating the issue in the case, that "in the field of public education the doctrine of 'separate but equal' has no place. Separate educational facilities are inherently unequal. Therefore, we hold that the plaintiffs and others similarly situated for whom the actions have been brought are, by reason of the segregation complained of, deprived of the equal protection of the laws guaranteed by the Fourteenth Amendment."[26]

Few cases have affected as many people as *Brown*. The Chief Justice was speaking in a technical sense when he wrote of "others similarly situated." The reference is to the class of litigants in the companion cases to *Brown*. But of course the case had implications far beyond the members of the class for whom suit had been brought. In its practical effect—though it would take many years, if it has in fact happened completely—all children in segregated school systems across the country would be affected by the decision. In dealing with *Plessy* as he did, the Chief Justice was saying, paradoxically, that the case was more about the reality of contemporary culture than it was about legal precedents. His approach, ultimately, seems designed to persuade a nation rather than just lawyers or litigants.

In *Brown* Chief Justice Warren centers his opinion on the certainty of the contemporary importance of education and the state's role in providing it. In *Roe v. Wade*, however, an opinion that rivals *Brown* in its impact,

Justice Blackmun centers his opinion on the uncertainty about the beginning of life, within the context of modern medicine. But as in *Brown*, the approach suggests that the issue is not one that can be decided by resorting to legal science alone. Acknowledging the "sensitive and emotional nature of the abortion controversy,"[27] Blackmun uses his introduction to advance the theme of tolerance. He then relies on historical expositions of medical, theological, and legal attitudes toward abortion and the protectible rights of prenatal children. The opinion establishes the right to privacy quickly. Then the state's interest in prohibiting abortions is balanced against the privacy right, in light of the historical digressions. It is not enough that the state has based its opposition to abortion on the notion that protectible life begins at conception, the argument runs. The opinion offers a compromise: abortion is permitted for the first trimester; the state's interest in protecting prenatal children supersedes the woman's privacy interest thereafter.

A case rivaling *Roe* and *Brown* in its effect on the general population is *Miranda v. Arizona*. As in *Brown* Chief Justice Warren examined the current state of events and drew conclusions from it. In *Brown* this approach had enabled the Chief Justice to eliminate the relevance of *Plessy v. Ferguson*. In *Miranda*, though, there is no difficult precedent that the Chief Justice has to overcome to reach his conclusion. The admissibility of coerced confessions had been decided years earlier. The Chief Justice has something else in mind. He wants to give concrete constitutional guidelines to law enforcement agencies. As a way of rejecting current practices, he cites police department manuals to illustrate that a favored strategy is to get the suspect to talk under a variety of ruses. The Court justifies establishing procedural policies for police departments and law enforcement agencies because it is convinced that there is a pervasive disregard for the rights of suspects being interrogated. Having exposed a catalog of abuse, Chief Justice Warren changes gears and writes that "we sometimes forget how long it has taken to establish the privilege against self-incrimination, the sources from which it came and the fervor with which it was defended. Its roots go back into ancient times."[28] We know, therefore, that the Court is concerned with a fundamental right it believes is in jeopardy. Warren continues, "[a]ccordingly we hold that an individual held for interrogation must be clearly informed that he has the right to consult with a lawyer and to have a lawyer with him during interrogation under the system for protecting the privilege we delineate today. As with the warnings of the right to remain silent and that anything can be used in evidence against him, this warning is an absolute prerequisite to interrogation. No amount of circumstantial evidence that the person may have been aware of this right will suffice to stand in its stead. Only through such a warning is there ascertainable assurance that the accused was aware of this right."[29] The Miranda warning that we are all now so familiar with is taken almost verbatim from the case of the same name, putting, in literal terms, the words of the Supreme Court into the mouths of the police.

Justice Black takes a different approach in his opinion in *Gideon v. Wainwright*. The case turns on whether every person brought to book is entitled to be represented by a lawyer. Without stating the issue of its resolution, Black implicitly declares what must be the obvious answer by giving the essential facts of the case—that Gideon was charged with a felony, that he had appeared in court without funds and without a lawyer, and that he asked the court to appoint counsel for him. Black then quotes the colloquy between Gideon and the court in which the court first turns down Gideon's request because he can appoint a lawyer only in capital crimes. Gideon presents the issue when he declares that the United States Supreme Court says that he is entitled to be represented by counsel. The effect of this opening is to put the reader in Gideon's shoes and make him understand the fundamental disadvantage that a pro se defendant faces. With this established, Justice Black needs only to get around the precedent of *Betts v. Brady*, which on strikingly similar facts twenty-one years earlier had held that the Fourteenth Amendment did not make the assistance of counsel provision of the Sixth Amendment binding on the states. Yet an even earlier case, *Powell v. Alabama*, had established, in the context of a capital crime, that the right to counsel was fundamental. *Betts* had gone wrong, Justice Black concludes, by not following the holding of *Powell*. Once it is accepted that the right to counsel is fundamental, it follows naturally that this provision applies to the states. "In returning to these old precedents, sounder we believe than the new, we but restore constitutional principles established to achieve a fair system of justice."[30] Arguing that the conclusion goes beyond the technical niceties of the law, Justice Black continues. "Not only these precedents but also reason and reflection require us to recognize that in our adversary system of criminal justice, any person haled into court, who is too poor to hire a lawyer, cannot be assured a fair trial unless counsel is provided for him."[31] The argument then is that this conclusion is inevitable. "This seems to us an obvious truth," Justice Black writes. "Governments, both state and federal, quite properly spend vast sums of money to establish machinery to try defendants accused of crime. Lawyers to prosecute are everywhere deemed essential to protect the public's interest in an orderly society. Similarly, there are few defendants charged with crime, few indeed, who fail to hire the best lawyers they can to prepare and present their defenses. That government hires lawyers to prosecute and defendants who have money hire lawyers to defend are the strongest indications of the wide-spread belief that lawyers in criminal courts are necessities, not luxuries. The right of one charged with crime to counsel may not be deemed fundamental and essential in some countries, but it is in ours."[32]

Not all of the cases of the canon address individual rights. In the *Steel Seizure* case, the Court looks to the powers of the president. Rather than moving away from the strict application of legal doctrine, as often happens in personal liberty issues, the Court through Justice Black sticks to the facts, the applicable legal authority, and the reasoning to be applied. He treats the issue somberly and briefly in an approach that seems designed to reinforce the correctness of the Court's ruling. He underlines the legitimacy of the Court's role in settling a dispute of this sort in the first sentence, writing, "we are asked to decide whether the President was acting within his constitutional power when he issued an order directing the Secretary of Commerce to take possession of and operate most of the Nation's steel mills."[33] In only a few pages, Justice Black applies the test of whether there is any authority in legislation, statute, or the Constitution for the president's order and concludes that there is none. The central passage makes clear that the president's power is limited because he is not a lawmaker. "In the framework of our Constitution, the President's power to see that the laws are faithfully executed refutes the idea that he is to be a lawmaker. The Constitution limits his functions in the lawmaking process to the recommending of laws he thinks wise and the vetoing of laws he thinks bad. And the Constitution is neither silent nor equivocal about who shall make laws which the President is to execute."[34] He concludes by drawing back from the immediate issue to articulate the grand scheme. "The Founders of this Nation entrusted the law making power to the Congress alone in both good times and bad times. It would do no good to recall the historical events, the fears of power and the hopes for freedom that lay behind their choice. Such a review would but confirm our holding that this seizure cannot stand."[35]

There is a hint of the magisterial style at the end of the *Steel Seizure* case. It is used, however, not as a weapon but as a brief flourish. Chief Justice John Marshall, on the other hand, employs a magisterial style throughout *McCulloch v. Maryland* to emphasize his panoramic view of constitutional interpretation. To make his point that the "necessary and proper" clause of the Constitution permits the federal government to charter a bank, Marshall delivers a précis on the constitution. His rhetorical strategy is to provide analogous examples of the unquestioned unenumerated powers of Congress under the "necessary and proper" clause. When the authority to charter a bank is compared with these examples, the reasoning goes, it can hardly be doubted that Congress has this power. The reasoning of the decision seems less important, however, than the authoritative tone of the opinion. While willing to explain himself, Marshall at the same time sets himself up as a lawgiver. Sounding biblical, he declares, "let the end be legitimate, let it be within the scope of the constitution, and all means which are appropriate, which are plainly adapted to that end, which are not prohibited, but consist with the letter and spirit of the constitution, are constitutional."[36] Similarly, Marshall's handling of the taxation issue falls into place once the constitutionality of the bank is established. Marshall epigrammatically declares that the "power to tax involves the power to destroy"[37] and concludes that "the court has bestowed on this subject its most deliberate consideration. The result is a conviction that states have no power, by taxation or otherwise, to retard, impede, burden, or in any manner control the operations of the constitutional laws enacted by Congress to carry into execution the powers vested in the general government. This is, we think, the unavoidable consequence of that supremacy which the constitution has declared."[38]

Holmes's rhetorical strategy in *Abrams v. United States*, in part because he was writing in dissent, and in part because he had unsurpassed writing gifts, turned on sheer eloquence. The accused and several other Russian emigrants had thrown some political leaflets into the wind from a loft in the garment district in New York City. They were prosecuted under the Espionage Act amid the jingoistic atmosphere of World War I. Making, according to Max Lerner, "the greatest utterance on intellectual freedom by an American, ranking in the English tongue with Milton and Mill,"[39] Holmes wrote in dissent that

> persecution for the expression of opinions seems to me perfectly logical. If you have no doubt of your premises or your power and want a certain result with all your heart you naturally express your wishes in law and sweep away all opposition. To allow opposition by speech seems to indicate that you think the speech impotent, as when a man says he has squared the circle, or that you do not care whole-heartedly for the result, or that you doubt either your power or your premises. But when men have realized that time has upset many fighting faiths, they may come to believe even more than they believe the very foundations of their own conduct that the ultimate good desired is better reached by free trade in ideas, that the best test

of truth is the power of thought to get itself accepted in the competition of the market, and that truth is the only ground upon which their wishes safely can be carried out. That at any rate is the theory of our Constitution. It is an experiment, as all life is an experiment. Every year if not every day we have to wager our salvation upon some prophecy based upon imperfect knowledge. While that experiment is part of our system I think that we should be eternally vigilant against attempts to check the expression of opinions that we loathe and believe to be fraught with death, unless they so imminently threaten immediate interference with the lawful and pressing purposes of the law that an immediate check is required to save the country.[40]

Holmes's dissent is notable not only for its eloquence but for its absence of legal authority. He cites neither cases nor legal authority of any kind, except for the Constitution. Critics might fault Holmes's exclusive reliance on rhetoric here and elsewhere, but that weakness hardly undermines the opinion.[41] Other cases in the canon have been criticized for a variety of deficiencies. The liability is potentially even greater for them because they are majority opinions. (A dissenter such as Holmes in *Abrams* is not making law; he is merely dissenting.) *Roe v. Wade*, for example, has been attacked for the simplistic and sometimes erroneous historical excursions upon which it relies.[42] Other opinions have been criticized because they do not hold up well to traditional doctrinal scrutiny or other critical analyses. That is, the opinions do not always trace and reconcile controlling precedents or even directly confront the issues before them. These weaknesses do not necessarily lessen a case's status as great or important, however. The flawed execution of an opinion, such as that of *Roe v. Wade*, may well be counterbalanced by its contribution to American life. Put differently, many of the opinions seize a moment in judicial history and in American history generally and go beyond what the doctrinal analysis compels as a conclusion. This is certainly true in *Brown v. Board of Education*, in which Chief Justice Warren inters *Plessy v. Ferguson* by saying that it is no longer culturally relevant. Though it is judicial activism at its best, few, if any, would argue that *Brown* was wrongly decided. But, at the same time, an otherwise important case can be kept off the canon because it is so badly reasoned. This is true for *Griswold v. Connecticut*, in which a fundamental right to privacy, as it relates to contraception, is fashioned from expansive and perhaps untenable readings of precedent.[43]

Going beyond doctrinal weakness, readers keen on detecting inconsistencies, discrepancies, and ambiguities—lawyers, for example—will notice that not all of the cases of the canon meet all of the criteria I set out earlier. *McCullough v. Maryland, Roe v. Wade,* and *Miranda v. Arizona* are not particularly brief, for example. Moreover, some of the cases lack flights of eloquent language. A more serious criticism is that not all of the cases fit the categories of "most important" or "great." Cases that do not establish or significantly reaffirm an important constitutional right could hardly claim to be among the most important, which could well be those found in a good constitutional law casebook. But at the same time the most important cases might not include the greatest cases. Ultimately, any choice for inclusion in the canon is subjective. Why should the *Steel Seizure* case be included and *United States v. Nixon*[44] be excluded, for example? Why *Abrams* on free speech and not *New York Times v. Sullivan*[45] on the freedom of speech as it relates to the press? After all, *New York Times v. Sullivan* is so important that the Australian High Court has recently adopted it point for point. What about the voting apportionment cases, such as *Reynolds v. Sims,*[46] which gave meaning to the "one person, one vote" principle? What about the cases establishing core Fourth Amendment values? Or, for that matter, what about the cases establishing basic Fifth, Sixth, and Eighth Amendment values? How, for example, can the cases prohibiting and then reviving the death penalty be excluded? The answer to all of these questions, which could be multiplied manyfold, is that some of the choices in the canon could indeed be replaced. Only a small group would appear on everyone's list.

The usefulness of the canon is that it provides a better understanding of the nature of the judicial opinion. Those included in my canon suggest that the opinion, when used effectively, is a vehicle of communication between the Court and the people. In other words, the Justices see the people as their audience. Although Marshall in *McCulloch v. Maryland* and Holmes in *Abrams* write more for history than for the people, they are exceptions. The majority of the opinions in the canon were written with the average reader in mind. Their rhetorical strategies stress the importance of the issues being considered by highlighting their universality and by making them human rather than legal.

Simple justice, the canon suggests, calls for simple eloquence. Figurative language, when it is used, fits the occasion and does not soar above the opinion. In making their profound points about fundamental freedoms, the Justices, such as Jackson in *Barnett,* invoke concrete imagery with a readily recognizable common denominator: "[c]ompulsory unification of opinion achieves only the unanimity of the graveyard."[47]

The majority of the opinions in the canon are brief, especially compared with today's standards. *Chambers v. Florida, Brown v. Board of Education,*

Loving v. Virginia, West Virginia State Board of Education v. Barnett, Skinner v. Oklahoma, Gideon v. Wainwright and the *Steel Seizure* case are all between four and eight pages long. Even the longer opinions do not seem verbose because the Justices use footnotes to flesh out technical points and to elaborate on the legal and nonlegal authority upon which the opinion relies. With the fine points of law kept below the page, and with the goal of reaching a broader audience, the opinions read like essays.

The opinions of the canon, ultimately, are discussions of fundamental rights of principles in the constitutional order occasioned by controversies brought to the Court by litigants. In their essays, the Justices are writing not just for the litigants but for all those who are to be affected by the rights and principles they are resolving and declaring. They are writing for the People writ large and they adopt strategies to reach them.

—• 5 •—

Style and Substance in
Lower Federal Court Opinions

The bland, homogeneous style that dominates the judicial opinions of the High Court today also dominates the opinions of the lower federal courts. At the same time, however, lower federal court judges are seeking to distinguish themselves and their opinions with a variety of stylistic approaches. These draw upon and expand the approaches that federal judges in earlier decades had used. The difference, however, is in the significantly greater number of judges who are writing distinctive opinions and in the frequency with which they write them. The opinions of the lower federal courts, as a result, are now defined by what had been the exception in earlier times. The reader, of course, benefits from the variations in style. The readers of current Supreme Court opinions wade through bland prose. But readers of the lower federal court opinions, while they too encounter blandness, frequently find prose that, more than merely amusing or lively, draws the legal issues and the judiciary's response to them into sharper focus. To tell the story of developments in lower federal court opinions, we need first to recognize the role these courts play. We need as well to understand the historical evolution of the distinctive approaches that the lower court federal judges have taken to judicial opinions.

◆   ◆

The lower federal courts are where the action is. The federal district courts have original jurisdiction of all civil actions arising under the constitution, laws, and treaties of the United States; cases of admiralty or maritime jurisdiction; civil cases against a foreign state; and civil cases between citizens of different states or between the citizens of a state and subjects of a foreign state when the amount in controversy exceeds fifty thousand dollars. In 1989, 45,995 criminal cases were filed. On the civil side, there were 233,529 cases filed nationwide in the district courts. Of these, 61,906 involved the United States as a party. Of the private civil cases, 103,768 were premised on federal questions, while 67,247 invoked diversity jurisdiction. The appellate counterpart to the district courts, the U.S. Court of Appeals, was established by Congress in 1891 and now has thirteen circuits. There is the U.S. Court of Appeals for the District of Columbia, eleven other regional circuit courts throughout the country, and the Federal Circuit Court of Appeals, which is a national court. It hears appeals in patent, copyright, and trademark cases from any U.S. district court, all appeals from the Court of Federal Claims, the U.S. Court of International Trade, and the Merit System Protection Board. The twelve regional courts of appeal have original jurisdiction to review and enforce orders of many federal administrative agencies, such as the Securities and Exchange Commission and the National Labor Relations Board. They also have appellate jurisdiction over the review of all final judgments and certain interlocutory decisions of the U.S. district courts. This means that the courts of appeal review decisions from the lower district court relating to federal legislation, cases arising under the constitution, and diversity jurisdiction in which the court applies state law. In 1989, 39,734 appeals were filed in the eleven circuit courts of appeal and the D.C. Court of Appeals. Of this number, 8,020 were criminal cases, 26,975 were civil cases, and 4,739 were either bankruptcy, administrative agency, or other original proceedings cases. Of the 26,975 civil filings, 9,559 were prisoner petitions, 4,284 involved the United States as a party, and 13,132 were private civil suits.

As a consequence of the federal legislative explosion of recent decades, federal judges have become the interpreters of vast areas of the law. I illustrate this development with a partial catalog of federal legislation culled from Judge Posner's opinions during his first ten years on the Seventh Circuit bench. Even this partial catalog is extensive: the Social Security Act; the Hobbs Act; the 1980 Staggers Rail Acts; the Sherman Antitrust Act; the Age Discrimination in Employment Act; the Securities Exchange Act of 1934; the Longshoremen's and Harbor Workers' Compensation Act; the Federal Coal Miners Health and Safety Act of 1969; the Fair Labor Standards Act; the Federal Deposit Insurance Act; the Privacy Act; the Federal Trade Commission Act; the Administrative Procedure Act; the Commodity Exchange Act; the Labor Management Relations Act of 1947; the Interstate Commerce Act; the Civil Rights Attorney Fees Award Act;

the Federal Tort Claims Act; the Milwaukee Railroad Restructuring Act; the Suits in Admiralty Act; the United States Arbitration Act; the Federal Reserve Act; the Black Lung Benefits Act; the Speedy Trial Act; the Bankruptcy Reform Act; the Equal Access to Justice Act; the Racketeer Influenced and Corrupt Organizations Act; the Jury Selection and Service Act; the Clean Air Act; the Federal Anti-Head Tax Act; the Federal Aviation Act of 1958; the Futures Trading Act; the Taft-Hartley Act; the Medical Care Recovery Act; the Amateur Sports Act of 1978; the Rehabilitation Act of 1973; the Trade Secrets Act; the Education of the Handicapped Act; the Bail Reform Act; the National Housing Act; the Natural Gas Act; the National Environmental Policy Act of 1969; the Communications Act of 1934; the Petroleum Marketing Practice Act; the Lanham Trade-Mark Act; the Railway Labor Act; the Railroad Unemployment Insurance Act; the Railroad Retirement Act of 1974; the Federal Omnibus Crime Control and Safe Streets Act of 1968; the Civil Service Reform Act; the Copyright Act of 1976; the Clayton Act; the Occupational Safety and Health Administration Act; the National Labor Relations Act; the Civil Rights Act of 1964; the Labor Management Reporting and Disclosure Act; the Federal Employers' Liability Act; the Employment Retirement Income Security Act of 1974; and the Admiralty Jurisdiction Extension Act. Some of this legislation created and codified criminal acts, but not listed here are all of the federal criminal offenses that are tried in the district court.

The litigation in the district courts and circuit courts translates into a staggering flow of judicial opinions and legal language. The courts together publish more than ten thousand cases in the *Federal Supplement* and the *Federal Reporter* each year. In the fifty or so combined volumes of the *Federal Supplement* and the *Federal Reporter* the West Publishing Company produces approximately eighty thousand pages of opinions from the district and circuit courts annually. Each volume has about sixteen hundred pages, and approximately twenty five of each series come out in a year. Each page of either series contains approximately 750 words. Put differently, West Publishing publishes approximately 60 million words of judicial opinions from lower federal courts each year.

With so much happening in the lower federal courts, the weekly advance sheet volumes of the *Federal Supplement* and the *Federal Reporter* are the most illuminating record of what is happening on the jurisprudential front. For those who look through them each week they become something of an observation deck onto the federal legal landscape. Browsing through the volumes and noting the types of cases and issues presented we see, for example, litigation trends in areas such as the savings and loan crisis, asbestos and other mass torts, and the Sentencing Guidelines. And for those interested in the offbeat, the controversial, or the juicy, we find them in mass quantities. We read in recent advance sheet volumes of patent and copyright cases involving penile implants,[1] artificial sweeteners,[2] analgesic products using the suffix "PM,"[3] and computer programs.[4] We learn the details of Wayne Newton's mobster friendships.[5] We learn that when Attorney General Richard Thornburgh tried to avoid responsibility for a senate campaign debt, the judge trying the case found that he was not a credible witness.[6] We learn that Gordon Lish's ego was so great that he wrote his own dust jacket blurbs in which he proclaimed himself the most important living writer.[7] We see federal judges gallingly make the claim that they are immune from social security taxes because of the constitutional prohibition against diminishing their salaries.[8] We learn the details of the last words spoken by the ill-fated Challenger crew.[9] We see Richard Nixon's claim that he should be compensated for his Watergate tapes;[10] we see an underage college student, ironically named Booker, get drunk at a party and then sue his university for letting him get that way,[11] and we see lawyers fighting over the telephone number Call-INJURY.[12]

Not many readers would associate humor with the advance sheets, but it is there to be found. On occasion the West Publishing editors point the way with their case synopses or key number squibs at the beginning of the opinion. One irresistible synopsis reads, "defendant was convicted of bank robbery and unlawfully using a firearm during the commission of a violent crime. Court of appeals held that trial court did not abuse its discretion in refusing to order a second competency examination for defendant after he became disruptive, exposed himself, and began to urinate in the courtroom."[13] An equally irresistible key number squib states, "conduct of counsel in dancing, prancing, grimacing and gesturing before the jury while court announced ruling supported adjudication of contempt."[14] Then there is the headnote that reads, "[d]olphin lacked standing to maintain action alleging that his transfer from aquarium to the Department of the Navy without permission authorizing transfer violated the Marine Mammal Protection Act."[15] In one more worth noting we find "[c]rew member acting as caretaker on towboat in drydock filed Jones Act suit against ship's owner, seeking to recover for injuries sustained when he was overcome by mercury vapors when he attempted to transform mercury into gold by baking it inside potato."[16]

Sometimes the best humor is coincidental and has nothing to do with the opinion writer. In *U.S. v. Van Boom*,[17] for example, the defendant, as if compelled by his name, "developed an elaborate plan by which he might obtain money from a bank by pretending to have control of explosive devices he would detonate if his demands were not met." And in *U.S. v. Hash*,[18] the aptly named defendant was convicted of manufacturing and cultivating marijuana. In *U.S. v. Funmaker*,[19] the defendant did anything but provide fun, convicted as he was of damaging by fire a building involved in interstate commerce and using a destructive device in connection with a crime of violence. Then there is the case in which commercial farmers named Worm sued a herbicide producer for damage to their crops.[20]

Once we turn from the peripheral amusements of the *Federal Supplement* and the *Federal Reporter* to the opinions themselves, we see that district and circuit court judges frequently write opinions quite unlike those of Supreme Court Justices, even though the prose style of law clerks dominates these opinions in the same way that it dominates those of the Supreme Court. When the latter takes a case, either from the federal system or from the state courts, it does so to review only one or two issues. That is, the Court does not sit to review general claims of error. But this is what the courts of appeal do throughout the country when they review cases from the district courts or administrative agencies. A case can present as many issues as the lawyers want to raise. This does not mean that the court of appeals will review each one with equal regard. The appellant, however, is not limited in what he can present. In a similar way, district judges can address any number of issues in their opinions. These are usually occasioned by dispositive motions, such as motions to dismiss or for summary judgment, but in theory and in practice dozens of procedural and substantive issues prompt the district judge to write an opinion that makes its way to the *Federal Supplement*. The district judge is on the front line of litigation and the court of appeals is present to review all that the district judge has done. Thus, these two layers of the judiciary have a greater intimacy with the litigation process than does the Supreme Court, which takes on only bits of the process. This intimacy is reflected in the way the district court and circuit court judges approach their opinions.

The other major difference between opinions from the Supreme Court and from the lower federal courts is in the dynamics of the opinion-writing process. There are nine Justices at the Supreme Court who can have a hand in what is ultimately written. With a group dynamic made up of nine opinionated Justices, there is a special need for accommodation. At the court of appeals level, on the other hand, only three judges are involved. Therefore, the judge who writes the opinion has more opportunity to write the opinion as he or she wants. Certainly there can be calls for accommodation from the other members of the panel, but they will be fewer. Only when the circuit court sits en banc—as a complete group of all the circuit's active judges—does the circuit court judge face the group dynamic pressures that the Supreme Court Justice faces. District judges do not have this pressure, since they, as the only ones hearing the case, write only for themselves. Their freedom in writing is naturally the greatest.

The inherent differences between the Supreme Court and the lower federal courts, however, only partially explain the differences in their respective opinions. A second explanation lies in the historical evolution of the opinions of the lower federal courts and in a series of notable judges who advanced the genre of the judicial opinion. I want to examine this historical evolution with a series of snapshots of the *Federal Reporter* series, looking at individual volumes at intervals of a hundred or sometimes fifty volumes.

◆   ◆

The first volume of the *Federal Reporter*, published in 1880, reported cases from both the district courts and the then circuit court. The district court's jurisdiction from its founding and through most of the nineteenth century was limited for the most part to admiralty, patent, and bankruptcy cases. Its jurisdiction was expanded in 1875 and extended to all federal questions and significantly more criminal matters. At the time of the first volume of the *Federal Reporter*, however, the circuit court continued to have original jurisdiction in limited criminal and civil matters and appellate jurisdiction over decisions of the district court. Volume 1 reported 330 cases. Approximately 10 percent were admiralty cases, 10 percent were bankruptcy cases, and 10 percent were patent cases. There were only a handful of criminal cases.

The opinions of West's debut volume dealt with patents, bankruptcy, admiralty, common carrier, and criminal matters. Many of the opinions were oral rather than written. To us today they seem to move through their issues with almost no discussion of standards when it comes to the assessment of facts and the application of law. Appellate cases scarcely seem to be reviewing a lower court case. They work through all of the evidence, never identifying particular issues on which the case turns, concluding that the lower court was right or wrong. In admiralty cases in particular the courts sort through all of the evidence, making their own credibility assessments by looking at corroborating and contradictory evidence. The opinions, both at the trial and appellate level, cite few cases, and none uniformly. When citation occurs, it is to one of the ad hoc volumes that reporters in the various circuits were variously producing. The opinions have no footnotes and only an occasional concluding note citing authority. Sometimes judges stack up citations at the conclusion of a case, like a compound German sentence with the verbs at the end. Judges generally rely on treatises more than case law to make their decisions. They look to *Benedict's Admiralty, Dunlap's Admiralty, Angel on Corporations, Angel on Insurance, Kess on Injunctions, Story on Equity, Herman on Executions,* and *Freeman on Executions.*

Between the appearance of volume 1 in 1880 and volume 100 in 1900, Congress, to break the log jam at the federal courts, established the circuit court of appeals as we know it today. The 1891 legislation creating the court of appeals, known as the Evarts Act, established nine circuits, with appellate jurisdiction over cases from the district courts in their circuit. Though stripped of their appellate jurisdiction, the old circuit courts continued until 1911 and maintained their original jurisdiction in limited matters, but for all practical purposes the district courts became the courts of original jurisdiction. There were 350 cases decided with an opinion from the new U.S. Court of Appeals in volume 100. Unlike volume 1, there were also sixty-four cases decided by brief memoranda. But, as was true with the first volume, patent, bankruptcy, and admiralty cases led the way, with each making up approximately 10 percent of the opinions.

Opinions were often prefaced by long statements of the case in smaller print. It seems that the judge usually prepared this statement. Judges cited on average four cases per opinion for the 350 cases, using citations to the *Federal Reporter.* They cited fewer treatises. Only one judge in one case used a footnote. The facts, with relatively few principles of law, continued to dominate the cases in volume 100. Judges continued to summarize evidence as their principal decision-making technique. Commentary of any sort continued to be shunned. In only one instance did a judge comment on a case. In *In re Smith,*[21] Judge Speer began his opinion, "I think this is an exceedingly plain [bankruptcy] case."

Opinions in volume 100 are distinguished by exceedingly long paragraphs. Then Judge Taft of the Fourth Circuit, for example, frequently wrote paragraphs of fifteen hundred words. Judge Jackson of the District Court of West Virginia wrote even longer paragraphs, some exceeding three thousand words. To dull the reader even further, judges frequently incorporated lengthy documents, such as contracts and treaties, into their opinions. Nor did they help the reader understand the issues, writing amorphous opinions of the sort written in 1880. Standards, for example, were not articulated to any greater extent. Frequently, when the courts did talk about a principle of law and its application, there seemed to be no separate appellate standard of review. The court in *Ulman v. Clark*[22] states the trial court standard for granting a motion for a new trial and simply applies the same standard at the appellate level, with no discussion of how facts found at trial should be reviewed by the appellate court.

Volume 200, published in 1913, brought few changes. Patent, bankruptcy, and admiralty cases each continued to make up approximately 10 percent of the volume's cases. There were significantly more criminal cases, though. The judges gave slightly fewer citations, down to 3.37 cases per opinion. One significant event in volume 250 of the *Federal Reporter* is the appearance of Learned Hand in *In re Keep Shirt Co.*,[23] a bankruptcy case with an issue of first impression. Hand's opinion, set against the backdrop of what had gone before him and what was going on around him in the *Federal Reporter*, jumps off the page for the reader.

◆   ◆

In tight prose that crisply summarizes the facts in the manner of a newspaper reporter, Hand changes the genre of the opinion by giving the reader more than just discrete aspects of the case. With his mastery of the facts and law at issue, he is able to present a comprehensive review. After establishing the case as an individual factual and legal event, he raises the questions behind the claims of the litigants to show us how the case works. Hand would continue this approach throughout his career, using each case to throw light onto the entire jurisprudential landscape. As Henry Friendly, one of his greatest admirers, explained, with the aid of his own dazzling metaphor, "repeatedly he would make the tiniest glowworm illumine a whole field."[24]

Hand's opinions are dotted not only with Latin tags but with allusions to the great literary and historical giants of western civilization. No federal judge until Hand wrote this way, but these allusions should hardly surprise us given Hand's understanding of the judge's job. In an extrajudicial essay, he once wrote that "it is as important to a judge called upon to pass on a question of constitutional law, to have at least a bowing acquaintance with Acton and Maitland, with Thucydides, Gibbon and Carlyle, with Homer, Dante, Shakespeare and Milton, with Machiavelli, Montaigne, and Rabelais, with Plato, Bacon, Hume and Kant, as with books which have been specifically written on the subject." He then goes further and argues, "for in such matters everything turns upon the spirit in which he approaches the questions before him. The words he must construe are empty vessels into which he can pour nearly anything he will. Men do not gather figs of thistles, nor supply institutions from judges whose outlook is limited by parish or class. They must be aware that there are before them more than verbal problems; more than final solutions cast in generalizations of universal applicability. They must be aware of the changing social tensions in every society which make it an organism; which demand new schemata of adaption; which will disturb it, if rigidly confined."[25]

Hand's gift as a judicial writer was to get to the heart of the matter. As Friendly said, in his own inimitable language, "all [of Hand's opinions] exhibit the same ability to frame a lambent phrase that will strip every shred of covering from a fallacy or drive a point home to one's very marrow. No other judge within my ken has had the same gift of doing this, and of doing it not once or twice but again and again."[26]

Proof that Hand got to the heart of an issue appears each time he formulated a principle of law. He is the circuit judge most often cited or quoted by name (more than nine hundred times by circuit court judges), which means that his quoted phrases have become landmarks on the judicial landscape. In criminal law, courts repeatedly refer to his definition of aiding and abetting, which is that the alleged aider and abettor "in some sort associate himself with the venture, that he participate in it as in something that he wishes to bring about, that he seek by his action to make it succeed."[27] Circuit court judges alone have used the definition in more than 150 cases.

Hand had the gift of felicitous phrasing. His description of the charge of conspiracy as "the darling of the modern prosecutor's nursery,"[28] for example, has been used fourteen times by circuit court judges while his description of an idea as "in the womb of time but whose birth is distant"[29] has been used twenty-nine times. Apt expression merges with insight to produce the memorable. In the area of statutory construction, to name just one, Hand wrote that "statutes should be construed, not as theorems of Euclid, but with some imagination of the purposes which lie behind them"[30] (six times); that we should look first to the words of the statute, "not to make a fortress out of the dictionary; but to remember that statutes always have some purpose or object to accomplish, whose sympathetic and imaginative discovery is the surest guide to their meaning"[31] (forty-three times); and that "words are not pebbles in alien juxtaposition; they have only a communal existence; and not only does the meaning of each interpenetrate the other, but all in their aggregate take their purport from the setting in which they are used"[32] (thirteen times). In nearly all the fields in which he worked, Hand left us language and principles that we still employ today.

◆ ◆

Changes in the types of cases distinguish the district and circuit court opinions reported in volume 250, which appeared in 1918. Admiralty, patent, and bankruptcy cases still dominated, but there were more criminal cases, more cases interpreting statutes, more diversity jurisdiction cases. Footnotes were scattered here and there, and in one instance Judge Hough of the Second Circuit used several in one case. The first woman on the federal bench, Beverly D. Evans of the Southern District of Georgia, appears for the first time in the *Federal Reporter.* Learned Hand tangles with the meaning of "despoiled" in *Daeche v. U.S.*;[33] draft cases from World War I begin to appear; one judge looks to the English to define "domicile"; and for the first time judges question and reject the asserted basis of jurisdiction. While applicable law is still amorphously stated and applied, a few judges have begun to state the law and the standard of review, albeit awkwardly. We see as well for the first time judicial complaints at the beginning of an opinion, such as "our work has been too heavy since the submission of this case a few weeks ago to permit an extended analysis to be made by the court before vacation."[34]

Volume 250 also furnishes the first general introduction to a case, which displays the particular issues against a broader backdrop. In a labor relations case concerning the granting of a temporary injunction, we read,

> [t]he right of wage-earners to organize themselves into unions for the purpose of bettering their conditions is a right which no one can question. There can be no doubt that, but for these organizations, the conditions of wage earners would have been much less endurable than they are at the present time. The law recognizes them, and has never questioned their right to exist. Nor can any one question the right of any employees to quit their employment, whether they do it singly or collectively, whether it is done for a good reason or without any cause, and no court can compel any man to work against his will. But it is a right which may cause great injury, injury to the wage-earners in the loss of their wages, injury to their employers in the loss of their business, and generally the greatest loss falls upon those who are least responsible for it, the innocent public. For this reason, it is a weapon that should never be used, unless all efforts of conciliation have failed.[35]

As in the past bankruptcy, patent, and admiralty cases formed the core of volume 300, published in 1925. The sharpest increases came in tax (11) and criminal cases (15). Prohibition produced both criminal and forfeiture cases. The number of opinions interpreting federal statutes continued to increase. The Jones Act, the National Prohibition Act, the Merchant Marine Act, and the Revenue Act of 1921 were but a few of the statutes construed. In this volume we find the first cases resolving, as subissues in criminal cases, search and seizure issues, which invariably arise in the context of illegal alcohol and forfeiture cases. We also find the case giving rise to the notorious Ponzi scheme.

Judges in volume 300 make few changes in the way opinions are written. Footnotes appear in six cases, and for the first time judges use parallel citations to the *U.S. Reports*, the *Supreme Court Reporter*, and the *Lawyer's Edition*. In only one case does a judge gratuitously comment on the case before him. Judge Rose of the Fourth Circuit, near the end of a long opinion, remarks on "the history of this litigation, as we have given it in perhaps wearisome detail."[36]

The *Federal Reporter* ended with volume 300 and was followed in 1925 by the *Federal Reporter, Second Series*. With this change, opinions were reported in double columns, which allowed West Publishing to produce more opinions per volume. Volume 50, for example, contained 840 cases with full opinions. Statutory interpretation and tax cases were strong gainers at this time. The National Prohibition Act and its companion criminal statutes produced more criminal and forfeiture cases. Judges continued to shun footnotes and to be vague about the standards of review they were applying.

At the same time, judges continued to pay little attention to jurisdiction. There were, however, several cases in which they began to question this issue. More important, judges occasionally began their opinions by detailing the nature of the case's jurisdiction. For example, "[t]his is an appeal from a decree in a suit instituted in the court below under Section 60b of the Bankruptcy Act, 11 USCA s 96b";[37] or "[t]his is a suit to quiet title brought by plaintiff under the provisions of section 4 of the Pueblo Lands Act."[38] The general absence of references to procedural rules is highlighted by a case from the Southern District of New York in which the defendant seeks to strike paragraphs of the complaint. What strikes us is that the motion is made under the New York Rules of Civil Practice.[39] All of this changes with the adoption of the Federal Rules of Civil Procedure in 1938, which spawned an ever increasing jurisprudence of procedure.

Volume 101, published in 1939, brought impressive changes in the use of footnotes. Not only are many of the judges regularly using footnotes, several liberally douse their opinions with them. It was not uncommon for then Judge Vinson of the D.C. Circuit or his colleague Judge Miller to use twenty or thirty footnotes in a seven- or eight-page opinion, establishing from the beginning the D.C. Circuit's preeminence in footnote use. Some of these opinions contained *"see"* citations, but generally the judges put their citations below the page in footnotes. Statutes were also set out in footnotes.

The opinions in Volume 150, published in 1945, indicate that the use of footnotes was now the standard. In addition it was now the norm to identify the nature of the action and the issue to be considered at the beginning, suggesting that this too would become the standard in opinion writing. Some judges, however, preferred to launch dramatically into the facts to set the tone of the opinion.

Jerome Frank, who had been appointed to the Second Circuit in 1941, appears for the first time in volume 150, the same year as his appointment. A former law professor and spokesman for the legal realism movement, Frank incorporated as best he could elements of this legal philosophy, which held that law is what judges say it is. An apt vehicle for this approach was the judicial opinion not constrained by the traditional values in opinion writing. Frank asserted that the certainty with which opinions were written revealed the frailty or, going further, the disingenuousness of the process, which implicitly proved the validity of the legal realism thesis. As he wrote in one dissent, "a legal system is not what it says but what it does."[40] Applying this skepticism to the way judges justify their conclusions, Frank wrote in a dissent that "the conventions of judicial opinion-writing — the uncolloquial vocabulary, the use of phrases carrying with them an air of finality, the parade of precedents, the display of seemingly rigorous logic bedecked with 'therefores' and 'must-be-trues' — give an impression of certainty (which often hypnotizes the opinion writer) concealing the uncertainties inherent in the judging process. On close examination, our legal concepts often resemble the necks of flamingos in Alice in Wonderland which failed to remain sufficiently rigid to be used effectively as mallets by the croquet-players."[41] As a judicial activist imbued with legal realism, Frank wanted judges to "peer behind the mere verbal articulation of a legal rule or concept to observe the policy it embodies, whenever a logical application of that rule or concept as previously articulated, will yield socially disvaluable results."[42]

Frank, however, wrote many opinions in the style of the traditional values of opinion writing he sometimes inveighed against. That is, he frequently sounded like the other judges. But at the same time Frank brought an individual approach to opinions that featured the discursive, the essayistic. "My aims," he wrote to Felix Frankfurter, so far as I can articulate them, in writing opinions, when they are "essayistic," are these: (a) To stimulate the bar into some reflective thinking about the history of legal doctrines, so that they will go beyond the Citator perspective of doctrinal evolution; (b) To induce them to reflect on the techniques of legal reasoning, (e.g., to consider the nature and value of stare decisis, or the use and value and limitations on the proper employment of fictions); (c) To recognize that the judicial process is inescapably human, necessarily never flawless, but capable of improvement; (d) To perceive the divers "forces" operative in the decision-making, and the limited function of the courts as part of government.

And, underlying it all, is a strong desire, not easily curbed, to be pedagogic — not in a didactic manner but in a way that will provoke intelligent questioning as to the worth of accepted practices in the interest of bettering these practices. The Holmes approach was, of course, differently motivated. He wrote for the few. If what he said was over the heads of the many, he didn't care — or, rather he preferred it that way. Don't misunderstand: I don't mean that I'm a Holmes, or that I can compete with him. I do aim to teach; he did not.[43]

Volume 200, published in 1953, contained 196 cases decided with an opinion. There were 34 criminal cases, 37 tax cases, 17 labor relations cases, 11 bankruptcy cases, 5 habeas corpus cases, 4 illegal liquor cases, and 1 shipping case. Only one case involved search and seizure issues, that important criminal law area in which the individual's rights most visibly collide with the interests of the state. An increasing number of cases in this volume interpreted federal statutes. Several dozen cases interpreted statutes ranging from the more common, such as the Federal Employee Liability Act, the Longshore Harbor Workers' Compensation Act, and the Federal Tort Claims Act, to less often invoked statutes, such as the Universal Military Training and Service Act, the War Contracts Hardship Claims Act, the Taylor Grazing Act, the Marihuana Tax Act, the Housing and Rent Act of 1947, the Agriculture Adjustment Act, the Federal Drug and Cosmetics Act, the Federal Home Loan Bank Act, the Defense Production Act of 1950, and the Contract Settlement Act of 1944. The cases take up some 713 double column pages. The average case is 3.63 pages long and contains 1.98 footnotes. In regard to style, three judges added slight color to their opinions with introductions that either set a faintly dramatic mood or reflected the irritation with which the judge approached the case.

There was a significant increase in footnote use in volume 300, published in 1962. Cases in this volume average 3.43 pages and 3.38 footnotes, nearly one footnote per page. The volume contained 27 criminal cases, only 2 of which involved search and seizure issues. There were 23 tax cases, 4 habeas corpus cases, 4 bankruptcy cases, 22 labor relations cases, 1 shipping case, and only 1 civil rights case. The habeas corpus cases include perhaps the most famous, *U.S. v. Fay*,[44] which, when it got to the Supreme Court, was renamed *Fay v. Noia*. For the reader, however, the only other notable event is the first appearance of Henry Friendly.

As a judicial writer, Friendly tried to practice what he found and admired in Hand's approach to the problems that a case presents. While he had a tendency to write too expansively, he, like Hand, used the opinion to work through a problem to find a thoroughly satisfying solution. As for style, Friendly seemed to be of two minds. Sometimes he seemed to be writing for insiders, that is, for lawyers and other judges, using the terms that are the tools of the trade. At other times he seemed to be writing for a general audience, explaining more than detailing.[45] Hand, it should be added, did not shrink from the jargon of the profession and, to the extent that he used it, limited the applicability of his opinions to a wider audience.

Volume 400, published in 1969, showed developments on several fronts. The volume contained 198 cases. The number of criminal cases increased to 51, with 4 involving search and seizure issues. There was an increase in habeas corpus cases to 12 and civil rights cases to 4. That civil rights cases were on the rise is made clear with Judge John R. Brown's introduction to a civil rights case in which he says, "[t]his is another of those now frequently coming to us under Title VII of the Civil Rights Act, 42 U.S.C. s 2000e, forbidding discrimination in employment by reason of race, color, religion, sex, or national origin."[46] There were also 19 labor relations cases, 23 tax cases, 1 shipping case, and 3 bankruptcy cases.

Footnote use increased. There are 784 pages of opinions and 936 footnotes, for an average of 3.95 pages per case, 4.73 footnotes per case, and 1.19 footnotes per page. As for style, volume 400 included Irving Goldberg of the Fifth Circuit, who brought to the court a penchant for thoughtful introductions that set a case's issues against a broader backdrop. In a labor relations case, for example, Judge Goldberg writes, "[i]n our assessment of another industrial drama, we again turn to the rise and decline of a local union: its birth and early struggles, its frustrations in failing to maintain momentum, and its eventual exhaustion of power. As always we must search for the source of the decline. Was union evanescence the result of its own fatal flaws, or was its strength sapped by management's unfair use of industrial weaponry?"[47] There were, as well, several wry introductions. In one, we find that "[i]n the breast of the litigant who has suffered an adverse factual decision by an administrative body, hope springs eternal that he can persuade a reviewing court to overrule it."[48]

Civil rights, criminal, and search and seizure cases exploded in volume 500, published in 1975. Civil rights cases rose to 14, criminal cases to 92, and search and seizure cases to 19. Habeas corpus cases rose to 12, and labor relations cases to 5. Equally important, opinions began to be structured differently. Following an opening paragraph that described the nature of the case and stated the nature of the appellant's claims, judges began to address an appellant's arguments point by point and to use these points and their responses to construct the opinion. It continues to be the structure of choice today for opinion writers. The most significant consequence of this change is that by writing responsively, judges are more likely to understand the essential nature of the opinion not as an occasion to engage in the law but merely as a way of moving toward a conclusion that supports a decision.

Footnote use, as part of this new approach, increased as well. There were 240 opinions in the volume, with an average of 4 pages per opinion and 5.38 footnotes per case. A curious footnote in one case, written by Judge John R. Brown of the Fifth Circuit, suggested that within the judiciary there were doubts about whether opinions were adequately performing their obligations. In a civil rights case, which involved the testimony of a physician, Judge Brown noted that "like legal and judicial opinions the doctor's opinion . . . really stated the problem, not an answer to it."[49]

In volume 600, published in 1979, there were 87 criminal cases, 6 habeas corpus cases, and 12 search and seizure cases. Civil rights cases rose to 17. Cases averaged 4.44 pages and 7.70 footnotes. Judge Goldberg of the Fifth Circuit added a different stylistic touch to the judicial opinion with an extensive allusion to a William Faulkner short story. In a social security fraud case, in which the issue was whether the government had met its burden of proof, the government argued that the defendant's failure to respond to several Social Security Administration letters revealed his criminal intent. Goldberg quoted several paragraphs of Faulkner's "A Rose for Emily" to illustrate that the defendant was guilty of nothing worse than insisting that the government know its place.[50]

The numbers continued to rise in volume 700, published in 1983. Of the 184 cases in the volume, there were 58 criminal cases, 11 search and seizure cases, 13 civil rights cases, 6 habeas corpus cases, and 31 labor relations cases. Cases interpreting federal statutes rose as well. In a case involving the ERISA statute, one judge offered an explanation for this phenomenon, noting that in the past decade Congress had enacted nearly 100 statutes granting additional jurisdiction to the federal court.[51]

Opinions continued to get longer and have more footnotes. The 184 opinions of volume 700 average 5.53 pages and 6.14 footnotes, with footnotes exceeding one per page for the first time. The volume as a whole is a showcase of some of the most talented judges to sit on the circuit court. We find opinions from Richard Arnold of the Eighth Circuit, Richard Posner of the Seventh, Antonin Scalia of the D.C. Circuit, Jon Newman and Henry Friendly of the Second Circuit, and Stephen Breyer of the First Circuit.

By the time that volume 800 was published in 1986, a pattern had been set in the proportions of case types. There were 3 criminal cases, 10 search and seizure cases, 12 habeas corpus cases, 12 labor relations cases, and 18 civil rights cases. Opinions, however, were shorter at 4.37 pages and 3.82 footnotes for each. Two judges were consciously using fewer footnotes. Abner Mikva of the D.C. Circuit swore them off altogether, while Amalya Kearse of the Second Circuit frequently wrote opinions without them.

A recent addition to the list of the circuit court's most distinguished judges is Alex Kozinski, of the Ninth Circuit, whose work appears for the first time in volume 800. In one of his first opinions, in a case involving the nude photographs of Elizabeth Ray, the distinctly unskilled secretary of a U.S. congressman, Judge Kozinski serves notice that he enjoys writing with style. He begins, "[e]ncrypted in this story about nude photographs, shoddy business ethics, politics and unexpected riches lies a question about the calculation of damages for copyright infringement. Both facts and law make for fascinating reading."[52] That style matters to Kozinski is confirmed only a few volumes later when he writes an opinion involving the motion picture industry and subtly includes references to 207 movie titles.[53]

Two striking changes appeared in volume 900, published in 1990. There was an increase in criminal cases to 58, 27 of which raised sentencing guidelines issues. Ten of these cases also involved search and seizure. The other dramatic increase was in the area of civil rights, which produced 27 cases in the volume. Opinion length rose to 4.37 pages per opinion, as did footnote use, to 3.82 footnotes per opinion.

Frank Easterbrook of the Seventh Circuit and Bruce Selya of the First Circuit, two judges whose prose compels notice, appear for the first time in volume 900. Easterbrook is the more penetrating thinker and is considered by many to be one of the two or three most gifted judges on the current circuit court bench. Selya, a formidable judge in his own right, has a more dramatic prose style.[54] Ironically, for someone with significant writing gifts, Selya's weakness as a writer is his propensity for flashiness that too often betrays even that questionable objective and creeps into cuteness. The dominant impression Selya's prose creates is that he wants it to be noticed. He consistently and frequently uses obscure diction, for no other apparent reason than to show off. Using words such as "pleonastic,"[55] "perscrution,"[56] "concinnous,"[57] "neoteric,"[58] and "concatenation,"[59] for example, cannot be understood in any other way. Other examples from volume 900 include a clever opening: "[t]he appeal before us represents yet another march in a litigatory trek of unusual length and complexity. We recount the case's by-now-familiar itinerary and thereafter proceed to blaze what few new trails remain";[60] a clever closing: "[t]his long safari of a case may at last be brought to a conclusion";[61] and an epigram: "[w]hile we eschew the imposition of rigid guidelines for the trials in this circumstance-specific area of law, the judge should take pains neither to use an elephant gun to slay a mouse nor to wield a cardboard sword if a dragon looms."[62] Here we also find Selya's penchant for dismissing, sometimes flippantly, a litigant's position. In one case he notes that "the district court concluded that appellants were several bricks short of the required load"[63] and later observes that "we understand the lyrics, but the music is off key."[64]

◆ ◆

The *Federal Reporter, Second Series* ended with volume 999 and was followed with the *Federal Reporter, Third Series.* The most recent volume of the *Federal Reporter, Third Series* available for review, volume 14, is similar in style and content to the *Federal Reporter, Second Series,* volume 900. Opinions in volume 14 average 6.5 pages per opinion, with slightly more than 6 footnotes per page. Moreover, they involve approximately the same number of civil rights, criminal, sentencing guidelines, and search and seizure cases.

Turning from this chronological survey of opinions, we can now consider the approaches in opinion writing current in the lower federal courts. For this last stage in the evolution of inferior federal court opinions, I look at the last 100 volumes of the *Second Series* and then the first 14 volumes of the *Third Series.* In addition I survey the last hundred volumes of the *Federal Supplement.* It is not surprising that the contents of these recent volumes reflect the developments of their predecessors. Without the voices of earlier judges, we could not have the voices of today's judges. On the level of reader satisfaction, of course, it does not matter whether the judge is writing the opinion or merely exercising varying levels of editorial control over the law clerk's work. Seizing the moment is what matters, which law clerks are able to do with the help of their judges.

Introductions are the means of choice for judges interested in distinguishing their opinions. They use dramatic introductions, apt or poignant introductions, angry introductions, and humorous introductions. An example of a dramatic introduction is, "[a] broken iron, a shattered vodka bottle, pictures of the lifeless naked body of [the victim] covered with blood and bruises, a warning note left for a friend—these trial exhibits relate to the nightmarish facts of the case before us."[65] Another example comes from civil litigation against the City of Milwaukee spawned by the killing and cannibalism spree of Jeffrey Dahmer. The court begins: "'I'm on 25th and State, and there is this young man. He's buck naked. He has been beaten up. . . . He is really hurt. . . . He needs some help.' With these words, a caller asked a Milwaukee Emergency 911 operator to send help to a person in need of assistance. When the call was made, on May 27, 1991, the name Jeffrey Dahmer was largely unknown. Today, everyone knows the story of the 31–year-old chocolate factory worker, a killing machine who committed the most appalling string of homicides in this city's history."[66]

Apt or poignant introductions characterize not only the judge's view of the case but also the essence of the matter at hand. In a tax protestor case, for example, the court begins, "[l]ike moths to a flame, some people find themselves irresistibly drawn to the tax protestor movement's illusory claim that there is no legal requirement to pay federal income tax. And, like the moths, these people sometimes get burned."[67] In a case involving a scam operation in which promoters promised hapless investors that through the control of money and real estate they could become financially independent, the court begins with a quotation from one of the scam's operators, that "the movement of money creates wealth. What we believe is that if you organize people and get money moving, it can actually create wealth." The judge then adds his own opening quotation from Gertrude Stein, that "money is always there but the pockets change."[68] In another, the court captures the irony of a case in which a property owner could well have lost his property for failing to pay a negligible amount of tax. The court begins, "'[f]or want of a nail the shoe is lost, for want of a shoe the horse is lost, for want of a horse the rider is lost.' And for want of $84, a homesite was lost. Specifically, for allegedly failing to pay $84.43 in back taxes, Elmer and Helen Ritter may have permanently lost thirty-eight acres in Rock County, Wisconsin."[69] Another case involved the principals of an insurance company who expected to get favorable treatment from their handpicked candidate, aptly named Green, for commissioner of insurance. Because of a series of false loans, the candidate, rather than being elected, was charged with mail fraud. This prompted the court to begin by quoting Euripides, "They say the gods themselves / Are moved by gifts, and gold does more with men than words."[70]

Turning to the Bible for an appropriate quotation, one judge in an age discrimination case opens with "the psalmist wrote: 'Cast me not off in the time of old age.'"[71] In a case involving the alleged wrongful termination of a minister by his church, in which the issue was whether the free exercise clause of the First Amendment prohibits the court from exercising jurisdiction in the case, another court begins, "but if it be a question of words, and of your law, look ye to it; for I will be no judge of such matters."[72]

The more impressive and useful introductions are thoughtful essays in which the judges identify the issue to be resolved in broader historical and philosophical legal contexts. In one case, for example, federal taxpayers brought suit against a federal agency alleging violation of establishment clause through the appropriation and expenditure of public funds for construction, maintenance, and operation of religious schools. This prompts the court to write that "Aristotle once observed that to give money away is an easy matter and in any man's power, but to decide to whom to give it, for what purpose and how, is neither in every man's power nor an easy matter. The observation remains true to this day, as this case illustrates."[73] In an antitrust case, the court begins,

> We have before us on this appeal a claimed violation of the Sherman Antitrust Act. Certainly one strand of the philosophical underpinning leading to the passage of the Act is derived from the thinking of John Stuart Mill, who, in his influential essay "On Liberty," observed: "trade is a social act. Whoever undertakes to sell any description of goods to the public, does what affects the interest of other persons, and of society in general; and thus his conduct, in principle, comes within the jurisdiction of society." Plainly, not all competitive conduct that injures another allows resort of laws regulating trade. Antitrust law is not intended to be available as an over-the-counter cold remedy, because were its heavy power brought into play too readily it would not safeguard competition, but destroy it. Determining whether conduct allegedly in restraint of trade violates the Sherman Act requires careful analysis and fine discernment between those actions that generally tend to inhibit competition and those that either tend to promote it or at least injure it. Such an analysis is our task on the present appeal.[74]

And in a case in which groups representing urban areas and minorities filed an action against the Department of Commerce and its officials administering 1990 census in an attempt to enjoin the census, the court puts

Two exasperated judges let their feelings be known from the beginning. In the first, a dog owner sought a preliminary injunction to prevent destruction of the animal. To this the court writes, "federal courts used to be viewed as austere, even learned tribunals, normally charged with such duties as the interpretation of statutes enacted by Congress; once in a while we are asked to consider one of the cherished clauses of our Constitution; and for the rest we would on occasion ponder over lofty—and legally difficult—questions which may even on occasion attract the attention of the highest court in the land. Not any more. Thanks to the expansion of civil rights jurisprudence, this is now a 'doggie' court. Indeed this case is an animal 'doubleheader' since it involves both dogs and llamas!"[82] In the second instance, in which the defendants in an antitrust action moved to disqualify the plaintiff's lead counsel on the ground that the defendants intended to call him as a witness, the judge, apparently overworked, begins, "[a]ntitrust case—17 plaintiffs—11 defendants—69 lawyers—and literally a half ton of pleadings."[83]

Not all introductions are successful in drawing the audience into the discussion of an opinion. Some strain for effect. For example, when a tomato seller sued a tomato purchaser for breach of contract, the court works hard at getting a literary reference into his opinion. He writes, "underlying this litigation is an alleged delay in a shipment of $24,000 worth of tomatoes. Delay is serious in the tomato business because what is today a marketable commodity becomes tomorrow spoiled and unmarketable garbage. In common parlance tomatoes are vegetables, as the Supreme Court observed long ago, . . . although botanically speaking they are actually a fruit. . . . Regardless of classification, people have been enjoying tomatoes for centuries, even Mr. Pickwick, as Dickens relates, ate his chops in 'tomata' sauce."[84] In a case in which the subject is chickens, the court, aware of the long history of chicken opinions, especially Friendly's famous opening in his chicken case,[85] "what is a chicken," the court labors to distinguish itself, turning to Chaucer and pedantry, writing, "this is an appeal from the district court's grant of summary judgment rejecting the Secretary of Agriculture's interpretation of a critical inspection standard contained in the Poultry Products Inspection Act (PPIA). Like Pertelote, we heed Chanticleer's clarion call to resolve the central issue of this most recent in a long line of illustrious line of gallinaceous litigation: whether the interpretation of poultry importation standards by the Defendant-Appellant Secretary of Agriculture (the Secretary) is entitled to deference [under the controlling Supreme Court precedent]."[86]

The impulse to seem erudite also pushes judges to strain for effect. In reviewing a district judge's summary judgment ruling, which was made, unusually, sua sponte, the court begins: "[o]ver twenty-four centuries ago, a Greek philosopher warned that 'haste in every business brings failures.' VII Herodotus, *Histories*, ch. 10. This appeal illustrates that courts are no exception to the rule."[87] In another, in which the appellant had only limited success, the court writes that "Plutarch, the great biographer, recounts the battle between the foot soldiers of Pyrrhus, king of Epirus, and the Romans at Asculum in 280 B.C. Six thousand Romans were felled but Pyrrhus lost three thousand of his own troops. According to Plutarch, when advised that he had won the battle, Pyrrhus reportedly replied, 'Another such victory and I am undone.' In this case, history will recount that, like Pyrrhus, plaintiffs won a battle, but lost the war."[88]

The only introductions less successful than these are the introductions that make no sense. They seem born out of the opinion writer's urge to state something personal, with little regard for the relationship between the personal recollection and the case. In one example the court begins "[t]his case resembles one of those 1920's automobiles that sometimes, even when my father was driving, would become stuck on a high center on a slightly improved road in east central Texas following a wet early spring. It seems to defy all efforts of both the district and circuit courts to bring about a final disposition."[89] In another example, a building owner filed action in state court, seeking to recover the cost of an asbestos abatement program. Apparently making the point that the asbestos had been installed many years earlier, the court opens the opinion with "[m]any years ago, when Hank Aaron was the hero of every teenage boy in Georgia and James Earl Carter, Jr. was still a farmer in Plains, the Trust Company Bank secured a contractor to erect a building in downtown Atlanta."[90]

Judges striving for humor in their opinions seem unable to resist subject matter puns that, unfortunately, produce more groans than chuckles. This has been the case for birds,[91] spices,[92] peanuts,[93] and beans,[94] as in "this spicy case finds its origins in several shipments of Jamaican sweet peppers."[95]

Equally deliberate but vastly more entertaining are the decidedly unjudicial subheadings of some opinions. For example, in a trademark infringement action concerning the registered mark "pig sandwich," the court moves into humorous high gear after the opening paragraph with subheadings reading, *This Little Piggy Went to Market, This Little Piggy Went to See His Lawyer, Piggish Stands, Collateral Estoppel—Does the Pork Stop Here?, A Pig Is a Pig Is a Pig—Or Is It?, Fraud in the Registra-*

tion—Did a Greased Pig Slip Past the PTO?, Unjust Enrichment—Did [defendant] Bring Home the Bacon?, Award of Attorney Fees—Did the Trial Court Go Hog Wild?, D-D-Dt D-D-Dt That's All, Folks."[96] In another case involving a failed bank, the court combines FIRREA, the Financial Institutions Reform, Recovery and Enforcement Act of 1989, 12 U.S.C. section 1821(d), the *Twin Peaks* television series, and the movie *Fire Walk with Me*. Subheadings include *Who Killed Southeast Bank?, Twin Peeks, FIRREA Walk With Me*, and *Entering the Black Lodge.*[97]

Humor sometimes comes at the expense of the litigants or their lawyers. In one case, an irritated judge mocks counsel's innovative attempts at drawing unnecessary attention in their briefs to aspects of their argument: "We do not (except in the caption) follow the appellant's interesting practice of writing the names of the people in CAPITAL LETTERS. Neither do we follow the appellee's counsel's practice of writing appellant's name in **BOLD-FACED CAPITAL LETTERS.** Nor do we intend to write all numbers both as text and numerals, as in 'eleven (11) loose teeth, two (2) of which were shattered. . . .' Appellee's Brief at 7. Finally, we will also not
'set off important text'
by putting it on
'separate lines'
and enclosing it in
'quotation marks.'
While we realize that counsel had only our welfare in mind in engaging in these creative practices, we assure them that we would have paid no less attention to their briefs had they been more conventionally written."[98] Taking aim at the litigants in an action brought by a dentist against an attorney for the creditor's committee formed during the course of the dentist's Chapter 11 bankruptcy and the individual members of the committee, purporting to allege state law tort claim for tortious interference with contract, the court succinctly begins, "[b]asically, this is a cat fight between two dentists over the aborted sale of a dental practice, and an attorney for the Creditors' Committee of one of the bankrupt dentists . . . gets in the middle of it."[99]

Judges use various forms of figurative language throughout their opinions to attract an audience. One such device is the epigram. Judge Easterbrook is especially epigrammatical. Complaining about the work that some lawyers demand of judges, he writes that "judges are not like pigs, hunting for truffles buried in briefs."[100] And complaining of inadequate explanation in an NLRB decision, Easterbrook says, "fiat does not support a decision. Tough nuts must be cracked open before the court swallows."[101] Easterbrook uses the full array of figurative language. He is fond of hyperbole, for example. In holding that a defendant was not entitled to be represented by a jailhouse lawyer [by the name of Deutsch] attempting to pass himself off as a lawyer admitted elsewhere, he writes, "Deutsch is a con man, a fraud, a phony, a humbug, a mountebank—in short, an imposter."[102]

Another type of figurative language that appears in opinions is the extended metaphor. In an action brought against a railroad by the administrators of the estate of a motorist killed at a train crossing, the court writes, "[t]his appeal unlooses a legal dinosaur, which, once out, tramples twentieth century negligence law and then lumbers back to its dark cave to await another victim. The jurisprudential fossils it leaves behind are truly daunting as this case illustrates. However, absent any contra-indication from the Oklahoma Supreme Court, the dinosaur prevails. At issue in this diversity action is Oklahoma's 'occupied crossing rule' which governs the relationship between individuals traveling upon public roads that cross railroad tracks and railroads whose moving or stationary trains occupy grade crossings."[103]

In the world of literary allusion we find, among others, quotations ranging from Melville's "Bartleby the Scrivener" on the subject of unwillingness,[104] Samuel Johnson on avarice,[105] Kafka on the nature of legal process,[106] Virgil on the lust for gold,[107] G. K. Chesterton on wine and water,[108] Bacon on opportunity and thievery,[109] Wittgenstein on philosophy,[110] Marvell on vast deserts of eternity,[111] Byron on ruined temples,[112] Carroll's Humpty Dumpty on the meaning of language,[113] and detective novelist E. Stewart on murder most sweet.[114]

Then there is Shakespeare.[115] He might head the hit list of the political correctness police and canon reformers who find him an inappropriate influence on our culture, but he is by far the dead white male of choice for those judges looking to add sparkle, substance, and wit to their opinions. Consider three representative Shakespeare references that appeared in a recent volume of the *Federal Reporter*. One judge invokes "what's in a name" to embellish his consideration of whether it matters if a rule regulating a lawyer's professional conduct is called a rule of conduct or a rule of procedure,[116] while another seals his substantive point with an apt reference from *Henry VI, Part Two*. In the context of the need for maintaining attorney-client confidentiality, he writes, "[the interest at issue] recognizes that in the adversary system, the professional's strategy, individually, or in concert with others, is irrevealable. The command is, 'Seal up your lips and give no word but mum: / The business asketh silent secrecy.'"[117]

A third judge, Richard Posner of the Seventh Circuit, seeks the same decisive effect in a civil rights case when he rejects the plaintiff's false imprisonment claim on the grounds that, while the plaintiff could not leave his home state, he was nevertheless not deprived of his liberty in a constitutional sense: "He was, it is true, 'confined' to Illinois; and if Denmark was a dungeon to Hamlet (as the latter claimed), we suppose Illinois could be a prison to [the plaintiff] . . . but constitutional torts do not follow the exact contours of their common law counterparts."[118]

◆ ◆

It is not that judges have just discovered Shakespeare. Nor is it that the stylistic and rhetorical approaches some judges use to distinguish themselves are new to the judiciary, although it is true that judges have never sought to distinguish themselves as often as they do today. Two points are important here. First, the judicial opinions of the inferior federal courts are but the latest step in the evolution of the federal judicial opinion. In the way they use introductions, humor, wit, and sarcasm, for example, judges today are developing in fuller form the approaches others before them had taken at various times. Second, it is significant that judges use stylistic and rhetorical devices today with greater frequency. True, the percentage of opinions featuring these approaches is still slight—my estimate is 5 percent—but that percentage increasingly exceeds the percentages of earlier decades as we move back through the century. As compared to those of the Supreme Court, the dimensions for lower court opinions are more flexible and judges take advantage of this. The inferior courts are adventurous where the Supreme Court is staid.

It is clear, when the evolution of the inferior federal court judicial opinions is examined, that judges today write to make their work more accessible and comprehendible. In short, to bring life to the law. But, of course, there are limits to the contributions of style to substance. To bring the evolution of the judicial opinion to its fullest development, we need to merge style with a global vision of the legal landscape and an approach that features exposition. In short we need to turn to the work of Judge Richard Posner.

Closing the Circle

Judge Richard A. Posner and the Exploration
of the Judicial Opinion

To understand the judicial opinion as a genre of legal literature and of literature generally, we have examined opinions as they are written today and have explored the historical evolution of both Supreme Court and lower federal court opinions. Finally we consider extensively the work of one judge, Richard Posner of the Seventh Circuit of the U.S. Court of Appeals. The connections between Posner and his work and what has gone on before him—especially the work of Holmes, Hand, and Friendly—run deep. By examining his judicial work and by considering what others are saying about him and his work, we better understand how Posner has influenced the judicial opinion and how the judicial opinion has influenced him. This last point is especially significant because it goes to the quintessential nature of the opinion as a form of literature. To appreciate the extent to which Posner has influenced judicial opinions as a genre, we need to understand his work both on and off the bench as well. As a working intellectual he wrote nine books and ninety-three articles in twelve years before going onto the bench and thirteen books and ninety-five articles since becoming a judge in 1982. More specifically, we need to understand his work in the field of law and economics, which has defined his scholarly work and has influenced, albeit in surprising ways, his work on the bench.

Law and Economics

Even though Richard Posner the federal judge cannot be cabined by his interest in law and economics, the first stop in charting his career as a legal figure—which brings together his roles as an academic, judge, and intellectual—must begin with this interdisciplinary approach to law, which had been simmering during the fifties and sixties and which boiled over with Posner's work in the seventies.

Once a scholarly approach on the fringe, law and economics is now part of the mainstream. Bruce Ackerman of the Yale Law School thinks that "law and economics is profoundly changing the way we look at law." "It is," he says, "the most important thing that has happened in legal thought since the New Deal. It's the most important thing in legal education since the birth of the Harvard Law School."[1]

Posner's work in law and economics falls within the field of applied economics. The importance of this field was recognized recently when Ronald Coase, of the University of Chicago, was awarded the Nobel prize for his law and economics work. University of Chicago professor Gary Becker, who won the Nobel prize in economics in 1992, thinks Posner "has been the most important contributor to the field of law and economics." "Posner," he says, "built on the work of people like Guido Calabresi and Ronald Coase, but he didn't simply mimic it. He built on it and greatly extended it in numerous directions."[2]

Posner's creative and original applications of law and economics have been an important contribution to the field of economics, according to Becker, and on that basis he considers Posner a serious candidate for the Nobel prize in economics. "Maybe not next year or the year after," Becker says, "but within the not too distant future." Ackerman, on the other hand, thinks that if Posner wins the Nobel, "it would be the politicization of the prize rather than anything else."[3]

Although law and economics in academic literature has been extended to areas such as free speech and the Fourth Amendment, judicial implementation of law and economics has generally been restricted to areas traditionally understood in economic terms, such as antitrust and bankruptcy. Consulting the economic principles of law and economics, for example, the Supreme Court in the mid-seventies changed its mind and today no longer thinks that market consolidation through the merger of competitors inherently reduces competition. Similarly, the court changed its view on vertical arrangements and no longer thinks that a manufacturer's attempt to dictate terms to retailers necessarily creates monopoly dynamics.

Posner's work in antitrust during the seventies helped bring these changes about. Antitrust specialist William Baxter of the Stanford Law School describes Posner's achievement: "What he really did was to explain to the antitrust bar what the economic implications of what they were doing really were. The little book he did in 1976 on antitrust had just been enormously influential in a wide variety of ways. He changed the way the antitrust bar thought of the world, and that showed up quickly enough in the cases. The earlier work of Bork, myself and Phil Areeda tended to be specialists talking to specialists, whereas Posner took the trouble to say it in a way that anyone in the antitrust bar could really understand and all the judges could understand it."[4]

The cornerstone of Posner's work in law and economics is his *Economic Analysis of Law*, first published in 1973. George Priest of the Yale Law School says that "in his first book he put forth this proposition that the common law is efficient, that it had some characteristics which achieved economically efficient ends. This was at the same time an extremely simple and extremely ambitious attempt at explaining the common law system."[5]

"Basically," Priest says, "Posner's law and economics approach is a heightened, intensified form of functionalism. It asks about the effects of the law and what effects will one legal rule have on one another. That approach has been pursued for a long period of time. It wasn't always called law and economics, but it was part of legal realism in a way. What Posner did was to really intensify the focus of effects of legal rules and legal institutions and then to show how important economic analysis was for evaluating those effects. To say that he changed the way people saw the law may well be right, but it was a change that caused the legal scholars to have to address in much more serious form what the effects of the law were."[6]

The principle of wealth maximization—the notion that individuals as consumers of goods, services, and intangibles make rational choices and are what Posner calls "rational maximizers of their satisfactions"—undergirds law and economics and has led critics to argue that the discipline's premise is flawed and that to accept it and to work out its applications is to strike a blow for the Orwellian state.

Not so, says Posner. "A theory that sought faithfully to reproduce the complexity of the empirical world in its assumptions would not be a theory—an explanation—but a description." The value of the economic approach to law, he writes, is that it "elaborates an overarching concept of justice that will both explain judicial decision making and place it on an objective basis."[7]

Other of Posner's critics accept the importance of law and economics but argue for one version over another and question Posner's general contribution to the field. Ackerman says that "Posner's contribution to law and economics is very mixed and is as much the problem as the cure. It's tended to give law and economics a bad name as a form of free market ideology, and I think that's a misconception of law and economics, which is at least as important a tool for progressive liberals as it is for free market conservatives."[8]

Critics have mounted unusually vituperative attacks on Posner, seeming at times to demonize him. His critics, Baxter thinks, hate him "because he's so brilliant and so effective. He is demonized because he's touched so many fields, written so many things that he sort of spit in the eye of these people time and time again. They don't know how to answer him, and it comes out in this kind of personalized venom by people who have never laid eyes on him."[9]

Priest thinks Posner "is something of a lightning rod, that he attracts extraordinary support among a lot of law and economics people, not all, but a lot, and he attracts a lot of criticism too because of the ambitiousness and the power of the arguments."[10]

Brown University philosophy professor Martha Nussbaum, who has been working in law from the angles of philosophy and feminism, thinks that "some people do demonize him because he's a law and economics person." "Some of the critics," she adds, "have been hasty, overly sharp, unwilling to come to grips with the complexity in what he does."[11]

Posner matched the ambitiousness of his thesis with the scope of its exploration and dissemination. Never had an academic so examined a field through scholarly literature. The numbers—nine books and ninety-three articles—for the dozen years beginning in 1969 are staggering. Yet he also found time to teach and to found and edit for nine years the *Journal of Legal Studies*, which consistently published law and economics articles. For the quantity and quality of his scholarly production, according to Becker, Posner had no parallel.

There was nothing in Posner's background that destined him for the embrace of law and economics. Educated first in public and private schools in and around New York City, Posner graduated from Yale University in 1959. He earned Phi Beta Kappa honors there in his junior year and wrote his senior thesis under Cleanth Brooks on Yeats's later poetry. He went to the Harvard Law School, principally because he had heard that its program was the most rigorous. He graduated first in his class and was president of the law review. While at Harvard, the legendary Paul Freund acted as his unofficial advisor.

Posner went to Washington in 1962 as a law clerk to Justice William Brennan. He then worked at the Federal Trade Commission for Philip Elman. Next Posner worked for two years as an assistant to the solicitor general, first Thurgood Marshall and then Erwin Griswold. He wrote forty briefs and argued nine cases before the High Court, winning six of them.

If the one word for Dustin Hoffman in *The Graduate* was plastics, for the young graduate Posner the word was economics. Posner's link to law and economics was forged serendipitously. He had taken a teaching position at the Stanford Law School beginning in the fall of 1968. When he first arrived at Stanford that summer, he noticed Aaron Director's name on one of the faculty offices. Director, the renowned University of Chicago economist, had retired to Los Altos Hills and Stanford had given him an office as a courtesy. As a developing antitrust specialist from his time in the Federal Trade Commission and at the solicitor general's office, Posner recognized the name and introduced himself to Director. They became close friends, and when future Nobel-prize winning economist George Stigler visited the Hoover Institution that winter, Director introduced Posner to Stigler. The rest is history. Baxter remembers that "a few weeks after Stigler and Posner met they were having lunch together day after day after day. Aaron Director was also at that lunch table on many occasions. Posner learned economics that spring from George Stigler, and within just a matter of months he was writing economically analytical material. It was just an amazing thing to watch."[12]

And just what was it about law and economics that caught Posner's fancy? Baxter thinks that it was "simply the rigor of the thinking, the logical structure of the social science of economics." But Stigler was also a brilliant and charming man, Baxter says, which also had something to do with the conversion.[13]

Posner's interest in economics continued when he moved the next year, 1969, to the University of Chicago Law School as the youngest tenured professor in the school's history. He hired a graduate student to tutor him in differential and integral calculus, linear algebra, and econometrics and continued the education in economics begun by Stigler. The assault on the citadel then proceeded in earnest. Nine books and ninety-three articles later, Posner, to the surprise of everyone, found himself on the circuit court bench.

On the Circuit Court Bench

For Posner, who had shown no interest in going on the bench, the opportunity in 1981 to join the bench of the Seventh Circuit of the U.S. Court of Appeals was unexpected. Baxter, who now headed the antitrust division of the Justice Department in the Reagan administration and who was working with the attorney general in filling judicial appointments, called and offered the job to Posner. The offer was a "bolt from the blue," Posner remembers, and at first he was inclined to turn it down, but after two days of deliberation and consultation with his wife, Charlene, he accepted.[14] He was just forty-two years old.

Posner himself, commenting on the change from academe to the judiciary, feels he is where he should be. In going onto the bench, Posner explains, he exchanged the administrative and other chores of academia and an extensive consulting practice for judging. He continues not only with his prolific pace of scholarly production but with teaching as a senior lecturer at the University of Chicago Law School. In an academic year of three quarters, he teaches a course in one quarter and a seminar in another.

The most important question about Posner as a judge was the extent to which he would put his academic ideas on law and economics into practice. After all, in deciding cases, Posner would have to contend with precedent and doctrine. But he took to the Seventh Circuit's diet of cases with enthusiasm, taking particular delight in diversity cases, which gave him the chance to work in common law areas such as torts and contracts. But his zeal appears everywhere, whether the case involves bankruptcy, the tax code, administrative law, or the host of federal statutes that the courts are called on to interpret. He also finds jurisdictional questions compelling and frequently raises them, when the parties have not, as a routine housekeeping matter. He guards the entrance to the federal courts zealously.

Posner's encounter with doctrine was not a collision of matter and antimatter. Rather than change the law with doses of radical law and economics theory, Posner uses his opinions to show, especially in common law areas, how the established underlying configuration of dynamic principles that seek balance and efficiency reflect the concerns of law and economics. "I think my emphasis," Posner explains as a more general matter, "has been on using economics to explain the structure of legal rules and institutions rather than on using it to change behavior."[15] This is his confrontation and exploration of doctrine—doctrine Posnerized, if you will. When he explicitly applies law and economics principles, it is usually as an extension of already established principles in the law, such as Hand's famous formula for negligence.

That Posner has not been more aggressive in applying law and economics has surprised some. Ackerman says that Posner "has changed on the bench. He is not nearly as much of a partisan of law and economics as I would have hoped, actually." Ackerman goes so far as to say that what "Posner has done is abandon or retreat massively both in his work off the court and on the court from the sustained engagement with law and economics."[16] He does this, for example, by not applying law and economics to areas such as the First Amendment.

Ackerman says that "this is a surprise from the writer of the first and second editions of the *Economic Analysis of Law,* which tried to sustain the claim that the common law, as well as much else, is a poor man's law and economics, and I don't think he has pursued this thought on the bench."[17]

Posner himself has written that it would be improper for an academic to "smuggle onto the bench" his scholarly ideas, but for Ackerman, Posner's earlier academic work "stood for the proposition that judges were already doing it. That the logic of the common law has been efficiency, so that the smuggling had been done in the spirit of the common law."[18] Hence the surprise.

And if there was little in Posner's academic writing to suggest that he would apply law and economics less than zealously, there was also little to suggest that Posner would take to the genre of the judicial opinion as he has.

Posner and the Judicial Opinion

First, there has never been a federal judge as productive as Posner. In thirteen years of service, he has written more than thirteen hundred opinions. In his first few months on the bench, in fact, he wrote so many opinions to clear up the court's docket, that he provoked the ire of some colleagues.

Posner's opinions on the Seventh Circuit are like no others that have been written by a federal judge. Posner follows the lead of Jerome Frank in eschewing legal language and writing in the style of an essay. But while Frank worked at deconstructing the judicial opinion, Posner works to strengthen it as a genre of legal literature. Posner distinguishes himself and his opinion in several ways. First, he is one of only three or four federal judges who writes every word of every opinion. And while we know that judges and justices in the past, such as Holmes and Hand, wrote their own opinions, no other judge has written his opinions in Posner's fashion, although one wonders what Holmes, with his promptness and speed, would have done if word-processing technology had been available to him.

At oral argument Posner asks pointed questions designed to isolate the key issues and occasionally makes notes to be used later. The panel votes on the cases and then opinions are assigned by the presiding judge. Sitting on a panel of three, hearing six appeals during a day of oral argument, Posner is assigned to write two opinions for the panel, as are the other two judges sitting that day. His practice, as astonishing as it sounds, is to write complete drafts for both opinions that evening. That he also writes more opinions per year than any federal judge in the country by a sizable margin makes his writing ability even more astonishing. He writes not in longhand but on a Macintosh computer. He has three of these—one for his office, one for his home in Hyde Park, and one for his vacation house. Going through the first draft, he indicates where more research has to be done, although he is able to provide most of the research and citations from cases he has already written and which are readily available. Sometimes a first draft will go to the printer virtually unchanged. When more work is called for, he directs his law clerks to research points of law to provide authority for various propositions. They assemble the research on a library cart for his convenience. The clerks also are encouraged to make comments and suggestions on the draft. He uses two law clerks, although most circuit court judges use three. With the additional research he or his law clerks have done, Posner then revises the opinion on his computer until he has what he wants. He writes every word of his opinions and has read all of the authorities cited in them.

Second, Posner has reshaped the genre of the opinion itself. He revels in facts. He absorbs all of a case's details and then releases onto the page a swiftly moving, compelling narrative of just what happened in the case. He writes with an audience in mind. He writes without footnotes and with an engaging style distinguished by the colloquial, the conversational, and the figurative. He pares away the trappings of ersatz scholarship and discards the conventional structure of the opinion. For him the purpose of the opinion is not justification but exploration.

Priest says that in Posner's opinions there "is the extraordinary power and clarity with which he gets to the bottom of an issue. In the first few paragraphs of an opinion he basically gives the issue in a nutshell, very sharply. A lot of other opinions are written almost as briefs—this side claims this, that side responds this, we decide this. None of that with Posner. He gets to the heart of what the issue is and then talks about the legal precedent going one way or the other and makes a decision. There's a tremendous power."[19]

Nussbaum, who is frequently critical of Posner's work, nevertheless thinks Posner is "a remarkable and wonderful writer. He has the intellectual depth, no matter what topic he's going into, whether it's libel law, or homosexuality, or nude dancing. He does thorough research on the subject." Giving perhaps the highest praise an intellectual can give, she says that "he reads whatever there is to read on a topic, so every time I read one of his opinions I learn something quite new about a whole field."[20]

Judge Alex Kozinski of the Ninth Circuit, himself a talented writer, says, "he has a real gift for expression and for analysis. When you have that, it's a real advantage in trying to explain things in an opinion or in anything else you are writing. Posner sees things very clearly. He is a very fast thinker, and he can translate things into concrete language. The clearer you see things, the easier it is to explain them." Moreover, Kozinski says, "he manages brilliant opinions. He makes all of these recondite, mundane subjects sound interesting, exciting. He really has a gift. There's no doubt about it."[21]

As to Posner's habit of writing his opinions on the evening of oral argument, Kozinski says, "most of us get some pizza on Friday night. It shows a remarkable self-discipline and remarkable stamina. After the week of oral argument I'm ready to go to sleep."[22]

Posner impresses his individual, personal self on the reader in this genre of writing that has so often been distinguished by impersonality. He wants to close the gap between reader and writer and uses a number of techniques to achieve this. He directly addresses the reader on occasion and is always writing with the expectation that he will be read by an interested, inquiring audience. He anticipates the reader's response and uses it to move him or her closer to understanding the case. He creates a feeling of intimacy in doing this. Sometimes he addresses the reader directly. For example, he writes, "CERCLA, as amended by SARA (please forgive our heavy use of acronyms, but it is unavoidable because the full names of the statutes are both cumbersome and uninformative)."[23] Sometimes he acknowledges how the litigants themselves, or their counsel, will react when they read an opinion. Even more effective, he describes the scene as it has unfolded, either in the facts of the case as they developed, at the trial, or at the appellate level. By commenting about the demeanor or performance of counsel at oral argument, Posner provides atmospherics for the judging process itself. Consider these two examples: "[a]t argument Mrs. Colby's lawyer, staring fixedly at the members of this panel, likened the head of household rule to a rule disqualifying bald persons,"[24] and "[t]o this Adamses' counsel replies absurdly that a warning *would* have been costly—it might have scared guests away! The loss of business from telling the truth is not a social loss; it is a social gain."[25] He also tells us how he, the reader, responded to a transcript, writing for example: "[y]et in the closing argument, the defendant's counsel, with a passion that fairly breathes through the transcript, make much of the financial impact that a judgment against the defendants would have on them."[26]

Posner further distinguishes himself as a writer by using a variety of tones in his prose. His inquiring, expository voice dominates the opinions, but at other times he becomes witty, funny, angry, sarcastic, satiric, mischievous, biting, compassionate, and, on occasion, bored. Here he is witty: "[t]here is no doubt that the parties could cancel the Universal Agreement any time they wanted. It may have been universal, but it was not eternal."[27] Here he is angry: "Judge Dumbauld's opinion for this court is concise—one might say summary—and not without wit. I admire witty and concise opinions, remembering Holmes' adage that a judge doesn't have to be heavy in order to be weighty. But I question the appropriateness of treating the consent decree [between the FBI and a public interest group to monitor and control FBI investigations] as if it were a contract between two flour dealers one of whom had 'improvidently' agreed to the provision that the other is seeking to enforce, when in fact it is a federal court order circumscribing the FBI's investigative powers—and not with respect to particular individuals or groups but across the board, and not in some neighborhood or small town but in America's third-largest city, and at a time not of domestic tranquility but of justifiable public anxiety about domestic as well as international terrorism."[28] Here he is sarcastic: "neither the Commission nor the employer has favored us with a brief; we are touched by their faith in our ability to resist the blandishments of an unopposed advocate";[29] and "the world's largest Ford dealer(!) testified that he *always* gets the certificate of origin when. . . ."[30] But he can also write with compassion. For example, "[p]ersons who would go ahead and rob a bank in the face of my hypothetical 20–year sentence are unlikely to be deterred by tightening the punishment screws still further. A civilized society locks up such people until age makes them harmless but it does not keep them in prison until they die."[31] Also, "[w]e shall step outside our judicial role for a moment and express our concern and hope that Mr. DeFrancesco will pay more attention to his health problems, which are debilitating as well as life threatening."[32]

The bar rather than his brethren have often been the object of Posner's attacks. No judge in the country, with the possible exception of Easterbrook, his colleague on the Seventh Circuit, more often comments upon and attacks the substandard performance of lawyers than does Posner. Here are some examples: "[a] brief observation, finally, on the brief submitted to this court by Pearce's counsel, Mr. Burt L. Dancey of Pekin, Illinois.

The brief is execrable. The argument portion is a paltry six pages of extra-large type, with nary a citation. Mr. Dancey was heard to grumble that this court allotted him a mere ten minutes to present his argument. He was lucky that we did not dismiss the appeal for failure to present issues properly. It is not enough for an appellant in his brief to raise issues; they must be pressed in a professionally responsible fashion. . . . This was not done here, and we warn that the penalty for a perfunctory appeal brief can be dismissal of the appeal";[33] "[i]n making this argument the City, in an ill-mannered brief bristling with ad hominem criticisms of its adversary, presents the facts as it would have liked the jury to find them rather than the facts that a rational jury might have found against the appellants";[34] and "[a] final point. We are disturbed that the Department of Justice, in submitting Judge Hart's opinion as an appendix, as it was required to do by Fed. R. App. P. 30(a), submitted a copy on which the department's lawyer had scribbled critical marginalia, such as the word "WRONG" beside several findings of fact of Judge Hart with which she took particular issue. This is indecorous and unprofessional conduct, which we have noticed in other cases and remark publicly today in the hope it will not recur";[35] and "the parties and the amici have favored us with more than two hundred pages of briefs, rich in detail that we can ignore."[36]

Posner's personality appears in his close attention to individual words. True to his theory of free-wheeling candor in judicial opinion writing, he outspokenly comments on the imprecision of legal language. He writes, for example, "[t]he reigning formula of course is 'deliberate indifference' (citation omitted), but the term is not self-defining. Indeed, like other famous oxymorons in law—'all deliberate speed' for example or 'substantive due process'—it evades rather than expresses precise meaning";[37] and "'Willfully' is, however, a classic legal weasel word. Sometimes it means with wrongful intent but often it just means with knowledge of something or other."[38] Not surprisingly, he deprecates euphemism in legal language and writes bluntly at times. For example, "[t]he fact that jurors, several or all, knew that Gutman's codefendant had pleaded guilty was not a ground for a mistrial, as we have held many times (citation omitted). When a codefendant drops out in the course of trial, a juror would have to be pretty stupid not to surmise that he had pleaded guilty";[39] and "[t]he facts of this case are surprisingly lurid for a bankruptcy case."[40] He acknowledges, though, that at times legalese serves a function. He writes, "the linguistically fastidious may shudder at 'nexus,' that hideously overworked legal cliche, but there can be no quarrel with the principle [here]."[41]

He comes to the defense of the language whenever he finds writers abusing it, taking to task those who fail to write clear, grammatical English, regardless of whether they are legislators, lawyers, bureaucrats, or other judges. Some examples are: "[w]e do not condone the draftsmen's sloppy use of the English language—especially the mayhem committed on the word 'transcend'—but redundant and heavy-handed and bureaucratic as it is, the code adequately conveys its concern that an employee not conduct himself in a way likely to bring public obloquy upon HUD";[42] "[t]he indictment charged that the conspiracy lasted 'from in or about May 1985 through at least July 1985.' (What clumsy and ungrammatical prose! The government could have avoided the problems in this case by treating the English language with more respect.)";[43] "[t]he record contains a letter from Fuller's physician suggesting (in the fractured prose that is the hallmark of physicians' epistolary endeavors)";[44] and "[i]t is plain from the above discussion that the main grounds raised in these appeals are frivolous; the other grounds, which we have not bothered to discuss, are even more frivolous. In addition, plaintiffs' briefs, other than those filed by the Public Defender, representing Mr. Kitsos in his appeal from the judgment of criminal contempt, are replete with misrepresentations; with syntactical, grammatical, and lexical errors; and with much sheer gobbledygook."[45]

Posner, however, is no pedant. He writes colloquially and goes so far as to use slang often in his opinions. For example, "[t]he statute forces the owner to either 'fess up or kiss half his money goodbye."[46] People are "in cahoots with each other,"[47] the government can get a "bigger bang for the buck" by prosecuting blatant offenders,[48] criminals "will sing for their freedom,"[49] and the "proof of the pudding is indeed in the eating."[50] He uses the phrases "hogtied,"[51] "winkled,"[52] and "well tanked."[53] In two more examples Posner writes, "[b]ut the arbitrators did not go around it. They did not say, Article XIX means something different from what it says. They said, Article XIX is inapplicable—obsolete—kaput. And this looks like modification rather than interpretation";[54] and "[t]hat is the practical content of all that high falutin' talk of utmost good faith and loyalty, full disclosure, the punctilio of an honor most sensitive, etc., (citations omitted)."[55]

Posner adds to the mix of his prose style an aptitude for figurative language. At various times he uses epigrams, aphorisms, analogies, metaphors and similies. He also draws upon his extensive reading for apt literary and historical allusions. He does not use figurative language to show off but to be emphatic. The effect is to personalize the opinion. Consider some of these examples. For epigrams: "[t]he spirit of Scrooge does not inform the establishment clause";[56] "'heads I win, tails you lose,' is not the spirit that animates the principle that latent ambiguity is a ground for recision of a contract";[57] and "honor among thieves is more an aspiration than a presumption."[58] For aphorisms: "[t]hree appeals in a case about a goatee are enough";[59] "the publication of books is not at the sufferance of juries";[60] "the government is not permitted to play cat and mouse with the prisoner, delaying indefinitely the expiation of his debt to society and his reintegration into the free community. Punishment on the installment plan is forbidden";[61] "[o]n the other hand, *not bricht Eisen* ["necessity breaks iron"]."[62] For analogies: "[i]n short there is no indication either that Mrs. Mayo has been injured by the order barring her from visiting Illinois prisons (and so might obtain damages) or that she would derive a benefit from recision of the order (and so might be aided by the injunction she seeks). She is like a person who is in a room locked from the outside but does not know the room is locked and does not attempt to leave during the time it is locked. More precisely, she is like a person standing outside a locked room, neither knowing the room is locked nor desiring to enter it. Such person incurs no harm from the fact that the door is locked";[63] "[t]he default judgments were worthless, Wallenmeyer being an assetless bankrupt and S.M.F. what the Germans call an *ausgeblasenes Ei* (an eggshell from which the contents have been sucked out through a hole)."[64] For metaphors: "[b]y rejecting that characterization here, my brethren have sawn off the only limb on which they might have sat comfortably";[65] "[e]quity is not a roving commission to redistribute wealth from large companies to small ones. The Lanham Act was not written by Robin Hood";[66] "[t]he Fourteenth Amendment is a vast umbrella, and to preserve a claim under it for consideration by an appellate court you must tell the court just what spot of ground under the umbrella you're standing on."[67] On allusions: "to take the period of limitations from one statute and the accural date from another, however, is like grafting a giraffe's head onto an alligator's body";[68] "[l]ater Barkauskas visited Galson and urged him to act soon, as Joanne was about to visit a lawyer about getting a divorce. Barkaukas requested Galson to shoot Joanne below the neck so that she could have an open-casket funeral. Thus does life imitate art; for Othello had told the sleeping Desdemona, 'Be thus when thou art dead, and I will kill thee, / And love thee after'";[69] "[t]he Commissioner's purpose would be set at naught if the insurance company could avoid the duty to extend benefits by the extremely simple expedient of not writing an extension of benefits clause into the policy. In fact, the regulation would be rendered completely nugatory. Maybe it was meant to be nugatory—a promise to the eye only, like the grapes of Tantalus";[70] "[i]t is true that Senator Wagner, the author of the bill, was present and corrected Senator Walsh on some other matters; but since Homer nods, maybe Senator Wagner did too, on this occasion";[71] "[b]ut it is apparent that the insiders on the board, in particular the chairman, decided to block the tender offer, before its ramifications for shareholder welfare were considered; judgment first, trial later, as the Queen of Hearts said in *Alice in Wonderland*";[72] and "[t]his is a rather sorry excuse for an anti-trust case. . . . To imply that a person is not a dealer in Vermont Castings' free-standing woodburning stoves is not to place the commercial equivalent of the mark of Cain on him."[73]

His style is active, extremely brisk, and fluid. Undergirding all of this is Posner's reliance on narrative and his gift at exposition. He sets out the facts of a case, reducing them to their essentials, and carries the reader along with the developing story as if he were writing fiction or good journalism. Motives are exposed and occasionally commented upon. For example, "[a]s is typical in labor disputes (the genre to which this case belongs), the employer, Union Oil, is on the side of delay. The general reason employers resort so frequently to delaying tactics is to make the laws for the protection—actual or apparent—of workers appear impotent."[74] He is not shy about making his own reading of the narrative known to the reader. The facts do not exist in isolation and end up being anything but the "cold written record" that appellate judges decry when they describe what they have to work with as they attempt to reconstruct events at trial.

His exposition of facts and analyses suggests effortless composition. It seems that he has simply absorbed all of the information, that it has all fallen into place in his mind, and that he is just releasing onto the page these fully formed, seamlessly woven descriptions and thoughts. Most remarkably, the style never eases up. He maintains the same effect regardless of an opinion's length. A twenty- or thirty-page opinion does not seem to be made up of sections, as would be the case with the work of anyone else. And this is true not just because he does not employ subheadings. He begins with a brief observation or two about the nature of the case and the basic problems it presents, often remarking that the case contains interesting or fascinating questions, and then he is off. Reading a Posner opinion, especially a lengthy one, is a whirlwind experience. To read several at one sitting can become almost dizzying. Nothing is perfunctory. Everything is challenged, examined, analyzed, and resolved.

Critical commentary of Posner's judicial work to date has focused on comparing and contrasting the views he articulated as an academic and as a leader of the conservative and controversial law and economics movement with the views he has set out on the bench. Commentators such as Ian Shapiro[75] have looked carefully at Posner's handling of economic cases, especially antitrust and labor cases, to show that he does not consistently apply the principles he had advocated as an academic. This, however, misses the point. There is no requirement that an academic bring to the bench the same philosophy or agenda that made up his academic writings. In Posner's case, he addressed the issue early on in his judicial career, writing that

> [I]t would be quite wrong to imagine that a professor would become a judge in order to smuggle into judicial reports the ideas he had developed as a professor, or that having become a judge, for whatever reason he had done so, he would then set about to see how much of his academic writing he could as it were enact into positive law. He will want to be thought a good judge, and he will not if he uses his position to peddle his academic ideas. . . . [I]t will be hard for the judge, whatever his background, to superimpose the very different role of the law professor. And it would be quite silly and futile anyway, unless he happens to be a Supreme Court justice, because less attention is paid to opinions of lesser judges than is paid to books and major articles.[76]

Posner has resisted the urge to use his own academic work as the catalyst for change. Only on two occasions has he cited his scholarly publications in his opinions. It is important to note, first, that he does cite with great frequency and regularity the work of others in the law and economics movement as authority in those cases in which he is trying to advance an economic slant. University of Chicago economists Stigler and Coase, with fellow Chicago economist Becker not far behind, are frequently cited in Posner's economic opinions. Moreover, Posner often refers to articles that appeared in either his own journal, the *Journal of Legal Studies*, or in the other University of Chicago law and economics organ, the *Journal of Law and Economics*. To the extent that Posner is smuggling economic ideas onto the bench, this is how he is doing it. Second, Posner cites to his own cases, if he has written on the subject before, modestly not giving his own name in parentheses, and so developing a complete, self-contained jurisprudence. His jurisprudence is such a part of him that he can write two entire opinions in one sitting on the same day as oral argument.

Reading the whole of Posner's opinions reveals a wide range of sources beyond law and economics. He cites, for example, certain judges by name when he uses their opinions. Most cited are Holmes, Hand, Friendly, and Cardozo. Their influence on him runs deep. Posner has written a book on Cardozo and edited a Holmes anthology. He also wrote movingly about Friendly when he died. Moreover, Posner, between the time he was contacted about and ultimately confirmed in his position on the Seventh

Circuit, read many of Holmes's opinions and traces the liveliness of his own opinions to this Justice.

Posner's knowledge of past opinions enriches his judicial work. But, in addition, his interest in bringing the insights of economics to bear on law is changing the nature of the judicial opinion and the nature of legal discourse by using the languages of economics and statistics. This is especially true for issues such as causality and damages. In negligence cases he uses the Hand Formula as often as he can to ascertain the costs and duty of care. When called on to apply state law in diversity cases that do not expressly acknowledge the Hand Formula, he will use it nonetheless. In *McCarty v. Pheasant Run, Inc.*,[77] he writes that:

> We are not authorized to change the common law of Illinois, however, and Illinois courts do not cite the Hand Formula but instead define negligence as failure to use reasonable care, a term left undefined (citations omitted). But as this is a distinction without a substantive difference, we have not hesitated to use the Hand Formula in cases governed by Illinois law (citations omitted). The formula translates into economic terms the conventional legal test for negligence. This can be seen by considering the factors that the Illinois courts take into account in negligence cases: the same factors, and in the same relation, as in the Hand Formula (citations omitted). Unreasonable conduct is merely the failure to take precautions that would generate greater benefits in avoiding accidents than the precautions would cost.

But he has gone further and fashioned a mathematical formula along the lines of the Hand Formula to determine whether a preliminary injunction should issue.[78] In addition, he applies the Hand Formula to the question of whether a civil commitment runs afoul of constitutional protections, making an analogy between the commitment for forty-eight hours on a psychiatrist's initial observations to the Fourth Amendment and a *Terry* stop.[79] On the use of the Hand Formula generally, he explains that "an algebraic formulation of legal rules . . . has value in expressing rules compactly, in clarifying complex relationships, in identifying parallels between diverse legal doctrines, and in directing attention to relevant variables that might otherwise be overlooked. It is not, however, a panacea for the travails of judicial decision-making. In practice, the application of standards that can be expressed in algebraic terms still requires the exercise of judgment, implying elements of inescapable subjectivity and intuition in the decisional calculus."[80]

Posner shuns traditional definitions and turns to the language of economics for his. Thus, in tort, we find that "[w]hat is due care depends on the cost of an increment of care in relation to its expected benefits."[81] For the meaning of contract law, Posner again turns to economics: "[a] principal purpose of contracts and contract law is to allocate the risk of the unexpected in accordance with the parties' respective preference for or aversion to risk and their ability or inability to prevent the risk from materializing—not to place it always on the promisee."[82] He uses this language as well for criminal law.

> Thus in my view "entrapment" is merely the name we give to a particularly unproductive use of law enforcement resources, which our system properly condemns. If this is right, the implementing concept of "predisposition to crime" calls less for psychological conjecture than for a common sense assessment of whether it is likely that the defendant would have committed the crime anyway—without the blandishments the police used on him—but at a time and place where it would have been more difficult for them to apprehend him and the state to convict him, or whether the police used threats or promises so powerful that a law-abiding individual was induced to commit a crime. If the latter is the case, the police tactics do not merely affect the timing and location of a crime; they cause crime.[83]

The principles of cost-benefit analysis and efficiency pervade Posner's opinions. In this example, he explains why a patent holder's damages are unjustified. He writes:

> Everyone knew there was a market for a quick-release wrench; everyone knew the elements of such a wrench—the pin and ball device for holding the socket in place and the push button for releasing the old socket and locking in the new. It was just a question of coming up with a workable embodiment of these ideas, a task for which no special training, expensive equipment, or prolonged testing and refining were necessary. Patent protection would overcompensate the inventor in these circumstances and by doing so would both draw excessive resources into the making of minor improvements and impose unnecessary costs of monopoly on the community.[84]

In some of his extrajudicial writings Posner has argued that all law students should emerge from their respective institutions with a working knowledge of statistics and an understanding of probability theory. In his opinions he makes great use of these tools. In a criminal case, for example, he writes:

> Purely for the sake of illustration, assume that in *Beck* the probability that the jury would convict the defendant of capital murder if there was no lesser-included-offense instruction was 90 percent and the probability of ac-

quittal 10 percent, but that if the lesser-included-offense instruction (felony murder) had been given the probability of conviction of capital murder would have been 50 percent, of felony murder 45 percent, and of acquittal 5 percent. On these assumptions Beck might well have been harmed by the failure to instruct on the lesser included offense. Assume that in the present case, with no lesser-included-offense instruction given, the probability of conviction was 60 percent and of acquittal 40 percent, but that if the instruction had been given the probability of conviction of rape would have been 40 percent, of conviction of attempted rape 50 percent, and of acquittal 10 percent. Weighing the greatly reduced probability of acquittal if the instruction was given against the enhanced probability of a shorter sentence if he was convicted, Nichols might think himself better off without the instruction. Of course these figures are conjectural but they illustrate why it is less clear here than in *Beck* that the defendant was hurt by the omission of the instruction.[85]

The economic analysis of law and its driving force of wealth maximization cannot be applied roughshod to the workings of society, his critics contend, because it rejects, for example, the notion of human individuality. This is the thrust of Robin West's criticism of Posner's economic approach, which she finds illustrated in the fiction of Franz Kafka, whose characters, she argues, are motivated by minimalist self-interest.[86] But in his opinions, with his distinctly personal, casual voice, and with his abundant literary and historical allusions, Posner has shown that he is anything but a technician, a detached observer mechanically applying what he considers to be the right values. More important than his language, Posner's approach that he is anything but an ideologue. In his opinions he everywhere makes clear that it is the process, not the result, that matters most. Posner's understanding of an opinion's purpose is not that it rationalizes a result. In one case he explicitly states this. Criticizing a district court judge who had written an opinion only after one of the litigants filed an appeal from his oral decision, Posner wrote, "[b]esides throwing off the appellate timetable, the practice of writing opinions only in cases that the judge knows have been appealed converts the opinion-writing process from exploration to rationalization."[87]

Posner's opinions abound with questions as he talks to the reader. In working through problems there is always tentative questioning. His opinions are filled with "maybe," "perhaps," "but what if," "now it might seem," "suppose," "but forget that and assume." Here he is working his way through a civil rights problem:

Not all state-authorized coercion is government action. This cannot be the end of the case. That Socrates was prosecuted by private denouncer does

133

not place the prosecution of crime in Illinois today outside the core of governmental functions. Every function performed by government has an analogue that was performed privately when government was rudimentary, or before there *was* government—for social order is older than government. The tradition that establishes a core of exclusive governmental functions does not reach back so far. But history is relevant. The question we are trying to answer is whether a private person is doing the state's business and should be treated as an employee or other formal agent of the state. So we ask, is there a tradition of treating civil commitment of the mentally disturbed as a governmental function and, if so, how well established is it?[88]

He asks why certain doctrines exist, what function they serve, whether they still serve that function, and what might be gained by discarding the doctrine for something else. He explains and reveals the reasoning undergirding whatever doctrine he is looking at and only at the end cites cases to support his position. With each case he reasons through the doctrine and then applys facts, always questioning the usefulness of the doctrine. This is not to say that he is quick to discard precedent when he disagrees with it. Firm principles dictate the extent to which a lower court can ignore Supreme Court precedent, and Posner adheres strictly to them.

When it comes to decisions of his or other circuit courts, however, he aggressively examines the reasoning supporting the decisions and rejects it if inadequate. Everything should be questioned. He writes, "although Socrates said that the unexamined life is not worth living, not a few judicial doctrines have become well established by assumption rather than analysis."[89] He attacks those who pass off conclusions as reasoning. For example, he writes, "[t]he common law did not enforce agreements such as section 2-209(2) authorizes. The 'reasoning' was that the parties were always free to agree orally to cancel their contract and the clause forbidding modifications not in writing would disappear with the rest of the contract when it was cancelled. 'The most iron clad written contract can always be cut into by the acetylene torch of parol modification supported by adequate proof.' (citation omitted). This is not reasoning; it is a conclusion disguised as a metaphor";[90] "[m]y brethren find such a duty implicit in the fiduciary relationship between a closely held corporation and its shareholders. By this approach, what should be the beginning of the analysis becomes its end."[91]

Much of what he writes are dicta, which is to say that the commentary can be excised from the opinion without changing its essential holding. He comments sometimes offhandedly, but at other times he digresses or simply steps back and asks whether, as an original matter, it makes sense to follow certain doctrines. Here he considers a principle of appellate review:

> When the company refused to arbitrate the union brought this section 301 suit, arguing that the company's refusal violated the collective bargaining agreement. The district judge ruled that the dispute was not within the scope of the arbitration clause, and he therefore dismissed the suit. Appellate review of the judge's ruling is plenary, since the only issue is the meaning of a written contract, and such an issue is still treated as a question of law when no evidence other than the contract itself is before the court. Many cases hold with specific reference to arbitration clauses. . . . As neither party questions the principle in this case, we shall repress our own doubts about its good sense. Appellate judges can read a document as well as trial judges, but now that appellate review of findings of fact based solely on documentary evidence has been held to be governed by the clearly erroneous standard, . . . it is not obvious why the old practice of plenary ("de novo") appellate review of contract interpretation should persist. Plenary review of questions of law is necessary to assure that the law is reasonably uniform and predictable. This goal has less appellate application to issues of contractual interpretation, although not zero application, for often either the same contract or identical language in different contracts gives rise to a number of lawsuits, and it is desirable that they be decided the same way. That is a common situation with insurance contracts—and with arbitration clauses as well, as we shall see. But the question of the continued appropriateness of the practice of plenary review of contractual interpretation is for another day.[92]

Frequently an opinion becomes the occasion for an essay within the opinion. We find discursive discussions on a host of procedural and substantive questions, including laches and the abuse of discretion standard;[93] the directed verdict;[94] the constitutionality of magistrates trying cases and entering judgment with the consent of the parties;[95] the *Doyle* doctrine;[96] the relationship between antitrust and patent law;[97] and on standing in antitrust cases.[98] He can work through elaborate analyses of problems that he himself has created, only to say at the end that the court need not consider these matters. In *Olson v. Paine, Webber, Jackson & Curtis, Inc.*,[99] for example, Posner performs a tour de force in his arguments for discarding the *Enelow-Ettleson* doctrine. He prefaces the long analysis with the rule regarding a lower court's ability to effectively overrule Supreme Court precedent. He next lists events subsequent to the establishment of the doctrine indicating that the High Court would almost certainly overrule itself on this point if the matter came to them again. But then, after the long analysis that demonstrates without doubt that the doctrine has no current utility, if it ever did, he invokes Hand's famous observation about the caution that lower courts should exercise in overruling the Supreme Court. Posner then concludes by saying that the job of discarding the doctrine must be done by someone else, which in fact happened when the Supreme Court recently rejected its long held doctrine.[100]

As an academic, Posner did not engage in doctrinal analysis of the sort we find in his opinions. At that time he was interested in nontraditional legal scholarship, which for him was the application of economic principles to various areas of the law. Nor, for that matter, is the exploration of doctrine in Posner's opinions like the doctrinal analysis we find in law reviews, which Posner has described this way: "[i]t involves the careful reading and comparison of appellate opinions with a view to identifying ambiguities, exposing inconsistencies among cases and lines of cases, developing distinctions, reconciling holdings, and otherwise exercising the characteristic skills of legal analysis."[101] Rather, his exploration of doctrine is on a more fundamental level. His interest is not as much in matching the case against the doctrine as it is in testing the validity of the doctrine with respect to its application in the particular case in front of him. He searches for the animating principles of the doctrine and then tests them against rules of common sense. Readers are the beneficiaries of this approach because they observe the doctrines taken apart, tested, and then reassembled. More important, they see the entire landscape of the law at one time. Doctrines do not exist in isolation. Rather, they exist in relationship with each other. Posner's explorations of doctrine are really explorations in the ways various doctrines fit together.

Quoting one case, *Rardin v. T&D Mach. Handling, Inc.*,[102] in its entirety illustrates Posner's methodology.

Jack Rardin, the plaintiff, bought for use in his printing business a used printing press from Whitacre-Sunbelt, Inc. for $47,000. The price included an allowance of $1,200 to cover the cost of dismantling the press for shipment and loading it on a truck at Whitacre's premises in Georgia for transportation to Rardin in Illinois. The contract of sale provided that the press was to be "Sold As Is, Where Is," that payment was to be made before removal of the press from Whitacre's premises, and that Whitacre was to be responsible only for such damage to the press as might be "incurred by reason of the fault or negligence of [Whitacre's] employees, agents, contractors or representatives." To dismantle and load the press, Whitacre hired T&D Machine Handling, Inc., which performed these tasks carelessly; as a result the press was damaged. Not only did Rardin incur costs to repair the press; he lost profits in his printing business during the time it took to put the press into operating order. He brought this suit against Whitacre, T&D, and others; settled with Whitacre; dismissed all the other defendants except T&D, and now appeals from the dismissal of his case against T&D for failure to state a claim. (The facts we recited are all taken from the complaint.) The only issue is whether Rardin stated a claim against T&D under Illinois law, which the parties agree controls this diversity suit.

The contract indemnified Rardin against physical damage to the press caused by the negligence of Whitacre's contractor, T&D, and the settlement with Whitacre extinguished Rardin's claim for the cost of repairing the damage. The damages that Rardin seeks from T&D are the profits that he lost as a result of the delay in putting the press into operation in his business, a delay caused by T&D's negligence in damaging the press. Rardin could not have sought these damages from Whitacre under the warranty, because consequential damages (of which a loss of profits that is due to delay is a classic example) are not recoverable in a breach of contract suit, with exceptions not applicable here. Rardin had no contract with T&D, and his claim against T&D is a tort claim; consequential damages are the norm in tort law.

We agree with the district judge that Illinois law does not provide a tort remedy in a case such as this. We may put a simpler version of the case, as follows: A takes his watch to a retail store, B, for repair. B sends it out to a watchmaker, C. Through negligence, C damages the watch, and when it is returned to A via B it does not tell time accurately. As a result, A misses an important meeting with his creditors. They petition him into bankruptcy. He loses everything. Can he obtain damages from C, the watchmaker, for the consequences of C's negligence? There is no issue of causation in our hypothetical case; there is none in Rardin's. We may assume that but for C's negligence A would have made the meeting and averted the bankruptcy, just as but for T&D's negligence the press would have arrived in working condition. The issue is not causation; it is duty.

The basic reason why no court (we believe) would impose liability on C in a suit by A is that C would not estimate the consequences of his carelessness, ignorant as he was of the circumstances of A, who is B's customer. In principle, it is true, merely to conclude that C was negligent is to affirm that the costs of care to him were less than the costs of his carelessness to all who might be hurt by it; that, essentially, is what negligence means, in Illinois as elsewhere. See *McCarty v. Pheasant Run, Inc.*, 826 F.2d 1554, 1556–57 (7th Cir.1987). So in a perfect world of rational actors and complete information, and with damages set equal to the plaintiff's injury, there would be no negligence: the costs of negligence would be greater to the defendant than the costs of care and therefore it would never pay to be negligent. And if there were no negligence, the scope of liability for negligence would have no practical significance. But all this is a matter of abstract principle, and it is not realistic to assume that *every* responsible citizen can and will avoid *ever* being negligent. In fact, all that taking care does it make it less likely that one will commit a careless act. In deciding how much effort to expend on being careful—and therefore how far to reduce the probability of a careless accident—the potential injurer must have at least a rough idea of the extent of liability. C in our example could not form such an idea. He does not know the circumstances of the myriad owners of watches sent him to repair. He cannot know what costs he will impose if through momentary inattention he negligently damages one of the watches in his charge.

Two further points argue against liability. The first is that A could by his contract with B have protected himself against the consequences of C's negligence. He could have insisted that B guarantee him against all untoward consequences, however remote or difficult to foresee, of a failure to redeliver the watch in working order. The fact that B would in all likelihood refuse to give such a guaranty for a consideration acceptable to A is evidence that liability for all the consequences of every negligent act is in fact not optimal. Second, A could have protected himself not through guarantees but simply by reducing his dependence on his watch. Knowing how important the meeting was he could have left himself a margin of error or consulted another timepiece. Why impose liability for a harm that the victim could easily have prevented himself?

The present case is essentially the same as our hypothetical example. T&D is in the business of dismantling and loading printing presses. It is not privy to the circumstances of the owners of those presses. It did not deal directly with the owner, that is, with Rardin. It knew nothing about his business and could not without an inquiry that Rardin would have considered intrusive (indeed bizarre) have determined the financial consequences to Rardin if the press arrived in damaged condition.

The spirit of *Hadley v. Baxendale*, 9 Ex. 341, 156 Eng. Rep. 145 (1854), still the leading case on the nonrecoverability of consequential damages in breach of contract suits, broods over this case although not cited by either party or by the district judge and although the present case is a tort case rather than a contract case. The plaintiffs in *Hadley v. Baxendale* owned a mill, and the defendants were in business as a common carrier. The defendants agreed to carry the plaintiffs' broken mill shaft to its original manufacturer, who was to make a new shaft using the broken one as a model. The defendants failed to deliver the broken shaft within the time required by the contract. Meanwhile, the plaintiffs, having no spare shaft, had been forced to shut down the mill. The plaintiffs sued the defendants for the profits lost during the additional period the mill remained closed as a result of the defendants' delay in delivering the shaft to the manufacturer. The plaintiffs lost the case. The defendants were not privy to the mill's finances and hence could not form an accurate estimate of how costly delay would be and therefore how much care to take to prevent it. The plaintiffs, however, as the court noted, could have protected themselves from the consequences of a delay by keeping a spare shaft on hand. See 9 Ex. at 355, 156 Eng. Rep. at 151. Indeed, simple prudence dictated such a precaution, both because a replacement shaft could not be obtained immediately in any event (it had to be manufactured), and because conditions beyond the defendants' control could easily cause delay in the delivery of the broken shaft to the manufacturer should the shaft ever break. See also *EVRA Corp. v. Swiss Bank Corp.*, 673 F.2d 951, 957 (7th Cir.1982); *Afram Export Corp. v. Metallurgiki Halyps, S.A.*, 772 F.2d 1358, 1368–69 (7th Cir.1985). Rardin, too, could have taken measures to protect himself against the financial consequences of unexpected delay. He could have arranged in advance to contract out some of his printing work, he could have bought business insurance, or he could have negotiated for a liquidated damages clause in his contract with Whitacre that would have compensated him for delay in putting the press into working condition after it arrived.

As we noted in *EVRA Corp. v. Swiss Bank Corp.*, supra, 673 F.2d at 956, Illinois follows *Hadley v. Baxendale*. So if this were a contract case, Rardin would lose—and this regardless of whether the breach of contract were involuntary or, as he alleges, due to the promisor's negligence. See 673 F.2d at 957; *Siegel v. Western Union Tel. Co.*, 312 Ill. App. 86, 37 N.e.2d 868 (1941). It is a tort case, but so was *EVRA*, where, applying Illinois law, we concluded that the plaintiff could not recover consequential damages. The plaintiff had instructed its bank to deposit a payment in the bank account of a firm with which the plaintiff had a contract. The bank telexed its correspondent bank in Geneva—which happened to be Swiss Bank Corporation—to make the transaction. As a result of negligence by Swiss Bank, the transaction was not completed, whereupon the plaintiff lost its contract because the other party to it declared a default. The plaintiff sued Swiss Bank for the lost contract profits, and lost. We held that the principle of *Hadley v. Baxendale* is not limited to cases in which there is privity of contract between the plaintiff and the defendant. Swiss Bank could not have estimated the consequences of its negligence and the plaintiff, like the plaintiffs in *Hadley*, could have averted disaster by simple precautions. See 673 F.2d at 955–59. This case differs from both *Hadley* and *EVRA* in that there is no suggestion that Rardin was imprudent in failing to take precautions against damage or delay. But as in those cases the defendant was not put in a position to assess the consequences of its negligence. In this respect the present case and *EVRA* are actually stronger for defendants even though these are tort rather than contract cases since neither case involves a defendant who is dealing face-to-face with the plaintiff. While it is generally true that consequential damages are recoverable in tort although not in contract law, *EVRA* shows that the classification of a case as a tort case or a contract case is not decisive on this question.

We are reinforced in our conclusion that T&D is not liable to Rardin by a series of cases—beginning with *Moorman Mfg. Co. v. National Tank Co.*, 91 Ill.2d 69, 61 Ill.Dec. 746, 435 N.E.2d 443 (1982)(decided only a few weeks before *EVRA*, and not cited to or by us in that case), continuing in cases like *Redarowicz v. Ohlendorf*, 92 Ill.2d 171, 65 Ill.Dec. 411, 441 N.E.2d 324 (1982), and discussed by this court in *Chicago Heights Venture v. Dynamit Nobel of America, Inc.*, 782 F.2d 723, 726–29 (7th Cir.1986), and *Dundee Cement Co. v. Chemical Laboratories, Inc.*, 712 F.2d 1166 (7th Cir.1983)—in which the Supreme Court of Illinois has held that damages for "purely economic loss" cannot be recovered in tort cases. (See also *Kishwaukee Community Health Services Center v. Hospital Building & Equipment Co.*, 638 F. Supp. 1492, 1495–1504). The doctrine is not unique to Illinois. Originating in Chief Justice Traynor's opinion in *Seely v. White Motor Co.*, 63 Cal.2d 9, 45 Cal. Rptr. 17, 403 P.2d 145 (1965), it has become the majority rule (see the thorough discussion of the case law in *Spring Motors Distributors, Inc. v. Ford Motor Co.*, 98 N.J. 555, 489 A.2d 660 [1985]), and was adopted as the rule for admiralty as well in *East River S.S. Corp. v. Transamerica Delaval, Inc.*, 476 U.S. 858, 106 S.Ct. 2295, 90 L.Ed.2d 865 (1986). We need not consider the outer boundaries of the doctrine; it is enough that it bars liability in a suit for lost profits resulting from negligence in carrying out a commercial undertaking.

The doctrine (called in Illinois the *Moorman* doctrine) rests on the insight, which is consistent with the analysis in *EVRA*, that contractual-type limitations on liability may make sense in many tort cases that are not contract cases only because there is no privity of contract between the parties. The contractual linkage between Rardin and T&D was indirect but unmistakable, and Rardin could have as we have said protected himself through his contractual arrangements with Whitacre, while there was little that T&D could do to shield itself from liability to Whitacre's customer except be more careful—and we have explained why a finding of negligence alone should not expose a defendant to unlimited liability.

The *Moorman* doctrine goes further than is necessary to resolve this case. Once a case is held to fall within it, the plaintiff has no tort remedy. In our hypothetical case about the watch the plaintiff could not sue the repairer even for property damage. *Anderson Electric, Inc. v. Ledbetter Erection Corp.*, 115 Ill.2d 146, 104 Ill.Dec. 689, 504 N.E.2d 246 (1986). *Moorman* itself was a case in which there was a contract between the parties, so there was no reason to allow a tort remedy. The present case, like *Anderson*, is one where, although there is no contract, the policies that animate the principle which denies recovery of consequential damages in contract cases apply fully and forbid a tort end-run around that principle. The "economic loss" doctrine of *Moorman* and its counterpart cases in other jurisdictions is not the only tort doctrine that limits for-want-of-a-nail-kingdom-was-lost liability. It is closely related to the doctrine, thoroughly discussed in *Barber Lines A/S v. M/V Donau Mary*, 764 F.2d 50 (1st Cir. 1985), that bars recovery for economic loss even if the loss does not arise from a commercial relationship between the parties—even if for example a negligent accident in the Holland Tunnel backs up traffic for hours, imposing cumulatively enormous and readily monetizable costs of delay. See *Petition of Kinsman Transit Co.*, 388 F.2d 821, 825 n. 8 (2d Cir. 1968). Admittedly these doctrines are in tension with other doctrines of tort law that appear to expose the tortfeasor to unlimited liability. One is the principle that allows recovery of full tort damages in a personal injury suit for injury resulting from a defective or unreasonably dangerous product—a form of legal action that arises in a contractual setting and indeed originated in suits for breach of warranty. Another is the principle, also of personal injury law, that the injurer takes his victim as he finds him and is therefore liable for the full extent of the injury even if unforeseeable—even if the person he runs down is Henry Ford and sustains huge earnings loss, or because of a preexisting injury sustains a much greater loss than the average victim would have done. See e.g., *Stoleson v. United States*, 708 F.2d 1217, 1221 (7th Cir. 1983). Both are doctrines of personal-injury law, however, and there are at least three differences between the personal injury case and the economic-loss case, whether in a stranger or in a contractual setting. The first difference is that the potential variance in liability is larger when the victim of a tort is a business, because businesses vary in their financial magnitude more than individuals do; more precisely, physical capital is more variable than human capital. The second is that many business losses are offset elsewhere in the system: Rardin's competitors undoubtedly picked up much or all of the business he lost as a result of the delay of putting the printing press into operation, so that his loss overstates the social loss caused by T&D's negligence. See *Grip-Pak, Inc. v. Illinois Tool Works, Inc.*, 694 F.2d 466, 473–74 (7th Cir. 1982). Third, tort law is a field largely shaped by special considerations involved in personal injury cases, as contract law is not. Tort doctrines are, therefore, prima facie more suitable for the governance of such cases than contract doctrines are.

True, the "thin skull" principle illustrated by *Stoleson* is sometimes invoked to allow recovery of lost profits in cases where there is physical damage to property. See, e.g. *Consolidated Aluminum Corp. v. C.F. Bean Corp.*, 772 F.2d 1217, 1222–24 (5th Cir. 1985). The thinking here seems to be that the requirement of physical damage at least limits the number of plaintiffs. Rardin could appeal to that principle here—since title had passed to him before T&D began dismantling and loading the press—were it not that the *Moorman* line rejects it, as we explained in *Chicago Heights Venture* (see 782 F.2d at 726–29), when the injury is the consequence of a sudden, calamitous accident as distinct from a mere failure to perform up to expectations. *Consolidated Aluminum* illustrates this exception, which is related to the principle that allows consumers injured by a defective product to sue the supplier in tort whether or not the consumer has a contract with him. There are other exceptions. The largest perhaps is the familiar principle that allows a suit for fraud against a person with whom the plaintiff has a contract, while the closest to the present case is the principle that allows a suit against an attorney or accountant for professional malpractice or negligent misrepresentation that causes business losses to the plaintiff. See *Rozny v. Marnul*, 43 Ill.2d 54, 250 N.E.2d 656 (1969); *Pelham v. Griesheimer*, 92 Ill.2d 13, 64 Ill.Dec. 544, 440 N.E.2d 96 (1982); *Greycas, Inc. v. Proud*, 826 F.2d 1560, 1563 (7th Cir. 1987). These cases are distinguishable, however, as ones in which the role of the defendant is, precisely, to guarantee the performance of the other party to the plaintiff's contract, usually a seller. The guaranty would be worth little without a remedy, necessarily in tort (or in an expansive interpretation of the doctrine of third-party beneficiaries) against the guarantor.

Although cases barring the recovery, whether under tort or contract law, of consequential damages in contractual settings ordinarily involve smaller potential losses than pure stranger cases do (such as the Lincoln Tunnel hypothetical discussed in *Kinsman*), this is not always so. In our watch hypothetical, in *EVRA*, and for all we know in *Hadley* and in the present case, the financial consequences of a seemingly trivial slip might be enormous. And it is in contractual settings that the potential victim ordinarily is best able to work out alternative protective arrangements and need not rely on tort law. Our conclusion that there is no tort liability in this case does not, therefore, leave buyers in the plaintiff's position remediless. Rardin could have sought guarantees from Whitacre (at a price, of course), but what he could not do was require the tort system to compensate him for business losses occasioned by negligent damage to his property.

A final example will nail the point down. The defendant in *H.R. Moch Co. v. Rensselaer Water Co.*, 247 N.Y. 160, 159 N.E. 896 (1928), had agreed to supply the City of Rensselaer with water of specified pressure for the city's mains. There was a fire, the company was notified but failed to keep up the pressure, and as a result the fire department could not extinguish the fire, which destroyed the plaintiff's building. In a famous opinion denying liability, Chief Judge Cardozo stated that even if the failure of pressure was due to negligence on the defendant's part, the plaintiff could not obtain damages. The city was acting as the agent of its residents in negotiating with the water company, and the water company was entitled to assume that, if it was to be the fire insurer for the city's property, the city would compensate it accordingly. Similarly, in dealing with T&D, Whitacre was acting in effect as Rardin's agent, and T&D was entitled to assume that, if it were to be an insurer of Rardin's business loses, Whitacre on behalf of Rardin would compensate it accordingly. Rardin in short could protect itself against T&D's negligence by negotiating appropriate terms with Whitacre.

The protracted analysis that we have thought necessary to address the parties' contentions underscores the desirability—perhaps urgency—of harmonizing the entire complex and confusing pattern of liability and nonliability for tortious conduct in contractual settings. But that is a task for the Supreme Court of Illinois rather than for us in this diversity case governed by Illinois law. It is enough for us that Illinois law does not permit a tort suit for profits lost as the result of the failure to complete a commercial undertaking.

Rardin is in some ways not the best example of a Posner opinion. He is not as colloquial and there is little figurative language here. And as for tone, there is not as much of the whirlwind flavor and glee that infects so many of Posner's other opinions, although his opening hypothetical has some of this. Here he is doing more applying than exploring, working through doctrines to show how they function. The key is that Posner is setting out an argument for the application of the tort doctrine on consequential damages. The *EVRA* case that Posner relies on is one of his cases, as is *Afram Export Corp. v. Metallurgiki Halyps, S.A.* He covered this territory before, but rather than just cite his cases and be done with it, he demonstrates, with some delight, how all of the pieces fit together. He takes the strands of various tort and contract doctrines to show the reasonableness of extending the doctrine of consequential damages from one area to another. Relying, as he does, on his analysis of *Hadley* and on the complementary extension to the existing *Moorman* doctrine, Posner creates the impression of a straightforward exposition. I am not suggesting he is being dishonest, or that he is smuggling his academic ideas onto the bench. Rather, he constructs his analysis along such unobjectionable lines that the result can hardly be quarreled with. But more important, for the reader at least, Posner presents the entire case, from its facts to its analysis, in a way that teaches and informs. In an age in which the Socratic method still finds significant pockets of support in legal education, Posner in his opinions accomplishes more by relying on narrative skill and sheer exposition.

One Posner opinion, even given in its entirety, does not convey his complete methodology. A random sampling of fifty of his opinions enlarges our understanding of Posner's judicial work. I began with the first volume of the third series of the *Federal Reporter* and collected the next fifty cases, which coincidentally concluded in 15 F.3d of the series. Each Posner opinion averaged 4.14 pages. Each page of *Federal Reporter* text contains approximately 750 words. Therefore a typical Posner opinion is approximately three thousand one hundred words long.

Posner averaged slightly more than twenty-one citations per case. He cited at least one of his own opinions—though not naming himself as the author—in all but three of the fifty cases. Each of these three cases was exceedingly short. They contained only a few citations and easily disposed of a single issue. Posner cited law review articles in eleven of his fifty opinions and treatises in seventeen. Two of the law review articles were by Friendly. Treatises included works by Moore and by Wright and Miller on civil procedure, Prosser on torts, Farnsworth on contracts, Tiffany on real property, the Restatements on torts and contracts, as well as treatises and specialized works on bankruptcy, taxation, and a variety of other topics. Posner cited to opinions of Holmes in four cases, to opinions by Hand in three cases, and to opinions by Friendly in five cases.

Posner explored legal doctrines in several of these fifty cases. He examined the law of the case doctrine,[103] tolling doctrines,[104] the mend the hold doctrine,[105] the doctrine of equitable reformation of contracts,[106] the doctrine of inquiry notice in statute of limitations cases,[107] and the innocent construction doctrine in libel cases.[108] This last case is an especially good example of Posner using traditional doctrinal analysis, that is, following and reconciling cases on a particular point of law.

What is missing from this random sampling are good examples of Posner dismantling a legal doctrine and testing its underpinnings against the insights of law and economic analysis. But for this we need only go back a few volumes in the *Federal Reporter* to *Rodi Yachts, Inc. v. National Marine, Inc.*,[109] an admiralty case involving damage caused by a barge that had slipped from its moorings. At the heart of the case were the doctrines in tort law relating to the respective obligations of the parties to avoid the injury causing the damage. Put differently, the case involved doctrines relating to the standard of care in tort cases. Posner quotes from Holmes's *The Common Law* as part of his exposition and turns for his primary authority to Hand's decision in *T.J. Hooper*,[110] which Posner describes as the canonical expression of the principle that compliance with custom is no defense to a tort claim. In the same paragraph, Posner links Hand with one of his favorites in law and economics, Ronald Coase, citing Coase's seminal article, "The Problem of Social Cost."[111] Against this background,

Posner then explores the particular facts of the case, identifying the responsibilities of the respective parties to aid the district judge to whom the case needs to be remanded for further fact finding.

Influence on the Bench

Posner's judicial contribution is already apparent. In the area of legal doctrine it is usually as an expositor, with his vocabulary of economics, but sometimes it is as an innovator. Perhaps most important has been Posner's view on the "charter of negative liberties" that is the Bill of Rights when it comes to the dimensions of civil rights law. In a series of cases he crafted the principle that the state has an affirmative obligation to protect a citizen only when it assumes control or responsibility of that citizen. When the High Court affirmed his decision in the famous *Deshaney* case a few years ago, Chief Justice Rehnquist followed Posner's lead step by step.[112]

When it comes to his influence on other judges, "one of the most telling things," Kozinski says, "is how often he is cited by name, either when you add his name in parenthesis, or say, 'Judge Posner says.' You see a lot more of that with him than with any other judge. A Posner opinion carries more weight. You can cite Posner dissents. I think it's hard to quantify, but it is obvious he has substantial influence."[113] A computer search, in fact, reveals that Posner, of those working today, is by far the circuit judge most cited by name. Of all circuit court judges, only Friendly and Learned Hand have been cited by name more often.

Ackerman calls Posner "a giant, a genuine intellectual, a great legal academic and great federal judge. He is and ought to be an extremely influential judge, both for his intelligence, his learning, and the fact that he does his own work."[114]

Off the Bench

Posner is a working intellectual the likes of which has never been seen before on the federal bench. The numbers bear repeating. Aside from the twelve hundred opinions he has written, since becoming a judge Posner has written ninety-five articles and thirteen books. A brief look at a few of the books reveals the breadth of his interests. *The Federal Courts*[115] challenges the system to be more efficient and responsive to changing times. *Law and Literature*[116] argues that legal academics are distorting literary texts in an attempt to have them support their own ideological arguments. *The Problems of Jurisprudence*[117] canvasses the whole of legal philosophy in order to argue for a pragmatic jurisprudence and against the idea of law as an autonomous discipline. *Cardozo*[118] analyzes the phenomenon of reputation quantitatively and qualitatively, with Benjamin Cardozo as the example. *The Essential Holmes*[119] collects the best of Holmes's writing with an appreciative introduction revealing Posner's ability to read for nuance. *Sex and Reason*[120] is a comprehensive survey and analysis of law and regulation relating to sexual practices. It argues that the law and economics approach best reveals society's ability and inability to fashion law that conforms to the realities of sexual interactions.

"I don't know," Becker says, "that one can mention anyone else who can be doing such high level academic work and be writing some hundred odd decisions each year, many of them influential."[121]

Nussbaum identifies the combination of breadth and depth as Posner's gift and his unique contribution as an intellectual. She says, "he has both theoretical depth and range which is absolutely extraordinary. He doesn't just speak philosophically about the law in the way that, say, Dworkin does, but unlike Dworkin, he also goes out and finds out all the facts about everything. That makes some of his contributions, let's say in areas having to do with sex, quite a lot sharper than Dworkin's. I think he's really a unique figure. There's no one else like him in intellectual life. The way he can bring this to bear on immediate social issues is also enormously valuable."[122]

Ironically, the variety and quantity of Posner's extrajudicial writing make an assessment of his work difficult. Priest thinks that "it's hard for any single scholar or especially commentator to follow all of it. You can follow those things precisely in your field but it's very tough to see all of it. So that I think his reputation will continue to expand as he goes on."[123]

Posner says that his productivity is a function of his efficiency and his Prussian soul. Those who have worked with him, such as academics Stephen Barnett of the University of California at Berkeley Law School and John Langbein of the Yale Law School, begin their descriptions of Posner with, "he's a genius, you know." Justice Scalia, customarily requesting that he not be quoted verbatim, also thinks Posner is a genius and adds that he cannot do what Posner does. Posner, he says, has a global vision.

G. Edward White, University of Virginia Law School legal historian and biographer of Holmes, restricts use of the "genius" label to Holmes, Hand, and Friendly but thinks Posner has "incredible powers of assimilation and a very well developed world view."[124] He considers Posner a visionary who saw the future in the 1970s. Geoffrey Stone, Dean of the University of Chicago Law School, is not alone in thinking that Posner "is the most important and original legal thinker since Oliver Wendell Holmes."[125]

Becker also thinks Posner is a visionary and adds that he was a risk taker as well. "At that time it wasn't obvious that the field was going to be as successful as it turned out to be. He gambled on it. He had a vision. He believed."[126]

Posner disclaims genius status and says that if anyone in the law is a genius, it is his Seventh Circuit colleague Frank Easterbrook. Easterbrook has a photographic memory, Posner reports, while he only scans documents well.

The cost of Posner's productivity is his unfamiliarity with popular culture. He watches little television and listens to books-on-tape for commuting to work, though when he did watch television he recalls watching *Kojak*. Not a sports fan, he learned of Michael Jordan's existence only last year. When Greta Garbo died, he recalls, he rented a few of her films, but for the most part doesn't watch movies either.

He has a wide circle of correspondents and tends to return letters within a week. Nussbaum, defining an important aspect of academic collegiality, says that Posner "is, among all the academics I know anywhere, the most generous with his time and with giving comments on manuscripts. Any time I write anything, whether it's about the emotions or literature or whatever, comments from him are always enormously valuable, and he's more reliable than just about anyone else." "The amazing thing," she continues, "is that I can send him something I'm writing on, say, Aristotle, and within three days he sends back enormously helpful comments."[127]

He has eclectic reading taste and is as likely to move through all of Joyce as he is to read spy novels by John Le Carré or books of Russian history. He rereads much of Shakespeare each year and reads *The American Scholar, Commentary, The Times Literary Supplement*, the *New York Review of Books, The Economist, Raritan, The Public Interest*, and the *New Republic* regularly.

The Tyranny of Labels

To discuss Posner is to discuss his chances of advancing to the Supreme Court. Like Robert Bork and Antonin Scalia, Posner was appointed to the circuit court to advance the conservative agenda of the Reagan White House. He was short-listed for nominations in the 1980s, but his stock seemed to fall after the Bork fiasco. With his extraordinary paper trail dotted with provocative positions, Posner would be vulnerable to soundbite attacks. Griswold says, "I shudder at the things Posner has written which could be thrown against him if he ever came before the Senate judiciary committee. The balance to a fair-minded person would make a lot of sense. But when you take individual sentences and read them out of context, he's written a lot of stuff which would be very shocking to the right wingers."[128] He has, in fact, surprised and disappointed many conservatives. Members of the arch-conservative Federalist Society were so disenchanted with a speech Posner gave a few years ago that they heckled him. This and a rejection of their extremist, strict constructionist views have led Posner to distance himself from the Society.

Posner may have been mislabeled as a conservative from the beginning. Baxter, head of the search committee that put Posner on the bench, says that "Posner is basically a libertarian, a nineteenth-century liberal. This implies that the government leaves people alone. It implies that the government leaves them alone in their economic lives unless there's an actual problem. Posner has been totally faithful to that philosophical position. So [his work on the bench] certainly didn't surprise me. It couldn't have surprised Attorney General William French Smith because I described him to Bill in precisely those terms and he understood the difference between a social conservative and a libertarian."[129]

The most conservative member of the Seventh Circuit when he was appointed, Posner now considers himself the fourth most conservative. This is the result, he says, of his mellowing and the influence of his law clerks.

For Griswold, Posner is now "certainly more liberal than he was when he was in his late twenties in my office when I was solicitor general." Some people, he adds, "would think that he does now write in an extremely liberal fashion." Nevertheless, Griswold is certain that Posner "would be attacked by the liberals and by the fundamentalists who are strong on the Republican side."[130]

Ironically, winning a Nobel prize in economics might not help him reach the High Court. Griswold thinks that the Nobel prize "would be hard to get over, I'm afraid. That would be the death knell to any further legal advancement. That would be regarded as highly theoretical and way out."[131]

The current right-tilting Supreme Court has rejected Posner's positions on several occasions. In a recent First Amendment involving nude dancing, the High Court reversed a Seventh Circuit decision in which Posner had written an eloquent concurring opinion that acts as a primer in the arts.[132]

The Supreme Court also affirmed a Seventh Circuit decision holding that for sentencing purposes in a drug case involving LSD, the amount of the drug to be considered is the combined weight of the drug and the medium on which it is placed for sale. Posner had argued that such an approach led to absurd and inequitable results.[133] In a similar case a few years before, Posner had written the majority opinion holding that the combined weight approach was right. When he came to the issue the second time, he forthrightly explained in his dissent why the conclusion no longer made sense to him.

Triumvirate of Heroes

HOLMES

As one who saw the young lawyer maturing, Griswold thinks that Posner considered Holmes, Hand, and Friendly to be role models. Posner displays in his office photographs of Hand and Holmes. He knew Friendly personally at the end of his life and wrote eloquently about him in the *Harvard Law Review*.[134] He believes that each was the greatest appellate judge of his generation.

As a trio, Holmes, Hand, and Friendly were each distinguished by prodigious intellectual abilities, graceful and effective writing styles, and the ability to master complex factual and legal matters quickly and efficiently. Each in his own way was the most efficient judicial engine of his generation. Posner, following his role models, has these traits in spades.

The parallels between Holmes and Posner are especially striking. Posner, who considers Holmes the greatest judge of the century, read him intensively in the six months between his appointment to the circuit bench and his confirmation. Writing opinions without footnotes, in a style reminiscent of Holmes, and on the day they are assigned to him, are all tips of the hat to Holmes. But Posner eschews Holmes's penchant for self-indulgent obscurantism, aiming instead for full-blown exploration, readability, and scholarship. If Holmes, the great reader, wrote about his reading in personal correspondence, Posner, an even greater reader, writes about it publicly.

Priest thinks that Posner is the most important and influential legal figure of the last twenty-five years and that his contributions in many respects are greater than those of Holmes. "Posner," he says, "likes Holmes's style and manner. He likes his intellectual toughness, but I think Posner's ideas are much more sophisticated than those of Holmes. Holmes's *Common Law* is really about how legal doctrines begin from ancient historical sources, and though the reasons for them change, the doctrine is transmuted in some way that it serves. That's a pretty mild proposition in comparison to what Posner has shown us about the law."[135]

Though a hero of his, Posner does not blindly follow Holmes. Posner has occasionally pointed out instances in which Holmes—the "great man" as he calls him—got it wrong. He got it wrong, for example, in formulating the "stop, look, and listen" principle in railroad crossing negligence law, which allocates the burden of preventing crossing accidents to the traveller who fails to make the necessary sensory observations.[136]

Posner has a compassion Holmes lacked. Holmes, remember, had a sufficiently ugly side to him that Grant Gilmore could not bring himself to complete the third and final volume of the biography started by Mark DeWolf Howe. Holmes believed that a society defines itself in part by its willingness to kill its members. In a deportation case recently decided by Posner, Holmes probably would have permitted the deportation even though the deportee would likely have been executed by his native Iran because of an American drug conviction. Posner, on the other hand, reminded the Immigration and Naturalization Service, when he remanded the case for further factual determinations, of the dimensions of the "hardship" provisions in the applicable law. "Death," he wrote in the opinion's concluding sentence, "is a hardship."[137]

HAND

Hand, the giant of the Second Circuit, appears more often in Posner's opinions than any other judge and in the practical, day-to-day chores of judging has had the greatest affect on Posner. Posner has taken Hand's formula for determining negligence and used its mathematical underpinning in a variety of other situations, such as in fashioning his own formula to determine if a preliminary injunction should issue. Once understood, Hand's economic approach to accident law, according to Posner, reveals that "the implicit structure of much legal reasoning is economic."[138]

Posner is certainly not Learned Hand, according to Baxter. His view is that "Hand did some important work in antitrust, but Dick would disagree with almost all of it. Hand was by and large very anti-economic in his antitrust orientation. He regarded the antitrust laws as a mistake. He though that government regulation was a superior solution. In his most famous opinion he made catastrophic analytical errors." "The notion," Baxter continues, "that Posner is patterning himself after them I don't think is true. I think he's just his own person, and he is a person of incredible genius."[139]

One reason Posner looks to Holmes and Hand is that they share with him an interest in the economic perspective, in doctrinal analysis, and in the common law. In his introduction to *The Essential Holmes*, for example, he writes that "he was a deep student of the common law and skillful legal analyst, and—much like Learned Hand, the greatest lower-court judge in the history of the federal judiciary—he had a considerable intuitive feel for the economic and other policy implications of legal doctrine."[140]

Posner may have outstripped, at least according to Priest, Holmes's contributions to understanding the common law, based as the common law is, on economic efficiency. Certainly Posner has gone beyond both Hand and Holmes as an opinion writer because of his interest in exposition and exploration. He remains their student, however, in matters of style. Hand and Holmes were great essayists, so much so that they probably made their most important contributions to law in this form. Taking a step back from the form and function of the judicial opinion as they understood them, Holmes and Hand better expressed their views of law to the general audience of the essay, giving those essays a warmth and texture that their opinions lacked. But while Posner's extrajudicial essays do not have these engaging characteristics, his opinions have perhaps the final say in the measure of his writing, whether judicial or extrajudicial.

◆   ◆

Considering Posner in the context of Holmes and Hand suggests the significance of his achievements, but his contributions to the judicial opinion is really understood against the background of the Supreme Court and the development of the common law in America, which has produced what Karl Llewellyn called the Grand Style of judging.

Posner's judicial writings are important in part because they show the limitations of Supreme Court opinions. As I argued in my discussion of the greatest or most important Supreme Court opinions, the Court at its most influential uses opinions as a means of communication between it and the people. These opinions are legal literature in the limited sense of announcing conclusions or in describing how discrete results were reached. Posner's opinions are legal literature of a different sort. They aim for exposition and exploration of the process of law, of how law works, with its strengths and weaknesses, in contemporary society. And because Posner expresses himself as the expositor and explorer, the opinions move beyond legal literature and find a place in literature generally. He is the writer, a person sifting through life, which, in his case, is defined primarily as a legal life.

Posner's opinions also, by extension, show the limitations of most lower federal court opinions today. Distinguishing opinions with introductions and figurative language to enliven them is admirable, but it is not enough.

Judges must go further and engage the reader throughout the opinion. They need to break free of the typical structure, in which the judge responds to the points raised by the litigants, and treat the issues as occasions for discussion. There are, to be sure, a handful of judges aside from Posner engaged in opinion writing of this sort. A short list includes Alex Kozinski of the Ninth Circuit, Edward Becker of the Third, Guido Calabresi of the Second, Michael Boudin of the First, Richard Arnold of the Eighth, and Frank Easterbrook of the Seventh. But in a federal judiciary with nearly a thousand judges, this small group is not enough to hide the limitations of lower federal court opinions generally.

A greater significance, though, of Posner's opinions is their connections to Hand and Holmes as common law judges and to the common law tradition in America. As was noted above in chapter 3, this tradition spawned the Grand Style of judging and here we find that the major strands of the judicial opinion story come together. We tend to forget in this regard that Holmes was a great common law judge on the highest court of Massachusetts for twenty years before going onto the High Court bench in 1902. Hand was, as well, a great common law judge. At the beginning of his common law study Llewellyn listed a handful of great common law judges from the seventeenth, eighteenth, nineteenth, and twentieth centuries. Writing in 1960, Llewellyn placed Hand as the second and last common law judge of the twentieth century.

Llewellyn's Grand Style of judging described the way state court judges were fashioning the common law in the first half of the nineteenth century. He found no parallels on either the Continent or in England for the American practice of considering the constituent policy and doctrinal questions that were part of the resolution of each common law question that the courts addressed.

Llewellyn did not address the economic aspect of the common law, but it is clear today, to some scholars at least, that the common law has always had an economic component. For instance, the case of *Anon.* in 1480,[141] discussed in chapter 2, can be taken as the starting point of a line of cases showing both the Grand Style in action and the economic impetus propelling the decisions. Remember that when the English court decided *Anon.*, the year book opinion was only eight lines long, contained no pertinent facts, and displayed no reasoning leading to the conclusion that a landowner whose animals stray onto his neighbor's land is liable for damage. As truncated as the opinion was, we saw that the English courts throughout the centuries blindly accepted the decision of *Anon.* and used it as support for related legal principles. Furthermore, English courts considered *Anon.* dispositive each time it undertook the animal trespass issue. As late as 1947 with *Searle v. Wallbank*,[142] the English reaffirmed the validity of *Anon.*, even though conditions within England had so changed that that the principle of *Anon.* was anachronistic. The common law and the English interpretation of it were so inadequate, in fact, that the English needed to pass legislation in 1971 to get around the historic stranglehold that *Anon.* held over the country.

In the nineteenth century the question for the American state courts when first dealing with the animal trespass issue was whether they should simply accept the English common law, as Blackstone said they should if the common law was "applicable" to the colonies,[143] or whether they should reevaluate the merits of the issue and reach their own conclusion. Those courts that followed the common law considered that it was applicable to them because they had the same legal system as the English.[144] Those courts that rejected a sheeplike deference to the British looked at the key idea of "applicability" in a different way.[145] They tested the geographical, demographic, and land use aspects of their land and population and tested whether the animal trespass rule made the most sense. Frequently it did not and the common law rule was rejected. In a series of decisions from states from all parts of the country, the courts engaged in empirical analyses and examined the issue of economic efficiency. While not employing any of today's law and economics jargon, the judges in these decisions were motivated by the same principles as the law and economics advocates of today.

Posner's pedigree, ultimately, is in the common law tradition, as described by Llewellyn and his Grand Style and as exemplified by common law cases, such as those testing the animal trespass doctrine in America, that flesh out economic principles. Following Holmes and Hand, with their economic sensibilities, Posner takes the essential nature of the American system to its fullest development. With Posner there is not only reasoning, there is also exploration and exposition.

What, then, if Posner were to go to the Supreme Court? Those who recognize his unique contributions and place in the legal and judicial worlds would bemoan a promotion to the High Court because there he would not be handling common law issues in the way that he does on the circuit court with its diversity jurisdiction. But while federal statutes and their interpretation would dominate his work, Posner has said that he would not change his approach to opinion writing if he were to go to the High Court.[146] He would need to accommodate the views of others more than now, he says, because of the Court's greater size. But aside from that modification, not much would change. The result would be that Supreme Court opinions would assume a new function and place in legal literature. The new voice would startle readers at first, given what Supreme Court opinions have been and are, but soon exposition and exploration would carry the day and Supreme Court opinions would never be the same.

Finally, what do we make of Posner and his connection to Henry Friendly? It was from Judge Friendly, the third of Posner's heroes, that Posner learned the surprising truth that Holmes was wrong when he said that you can live greatly in the law. Posner shared with Friendly a love for railroad law and got to know him in his last years. He thought Friendly a very matter-of-fact person. He had great common sense, something Posner feels is often lacking in intellectuals.

Posner considers Friendly to be Hand's successor as the greatest appellate judge of his generation. But as great as his achievements were, Posner considers them limited because they were rooted solely in his judging. With judging, Posner feels, you cannot know enough about one thing. The knowledge is too much on the surface because so much is required.

To live greatly as an intellectual contributor, Posner has determined that he must go beyond law. His remarkable productivity makes sense when understood this way. He is not the first judge to write extensively off the bench. Justice William O. Douglas, who comes closest to Posner for sheer intellectual ability, was another such extrajudicial voice. But Douglas's books were self-indulgent while Posner's concern themselves with the larger world of the social sciences, which, Posner argues, judges should know more about. As does his work on the bench, Posner's work off the bench ultimately attempts to explain the objective workings of our world. His opinions and books are but the micro and macro approaches to the same problem.

It has been clear from the beginning of Posner's tenure on the bench that he saw matters differently from others. His opinions have had the distinguishing characteristics of style and approach that I have outlined in this chapter, but in addition the opinions have been distinctively different in that Posner has never used footnotes. In part the reason for this is that Posner, being against smuggling academic ideas onto the bench, is against smuggling ideas into footnotes that should be stated in the text. The reader senses that for Posner footnotes represent a sort of insidious, truth-obscuring force. In one of his dissents, he finds the majority not directly confronting what he considers an important issue. With subtle criticism he writes, "[m]y brethren, to their credit, are troubled by this point, for they remark in a footnote (naturally) that . . ."[147] On a broader level, Posner's disdain for footnotes significantly furthers his attempt to bridge the gap between the reader and the writer. Footnotes do not get in the way with him. All of this is important because as an academic Posner used footnotes with the best. Even the academic work he has continued to do since joining the bench is strewn with footnotes. Some commentators, in fact, have criticized his attempt to canvass all existing scholarship in his footnotes. That he does not write with footnotes on the bench indicates that he sees his role as judge quite differently from his role as an academic.

Footnotes are the convention in academic writing, but they have not always been so in judicial opinions. For the most part they are the product of the age of the law clerk. The clearest indication we get that Posner sees his judicial self differently from his academic self is that as a judge he has steadfastly resisted the all but pervasive movement in the judiciary today, which is from being a writer to being a supervisor of law clerks. Posner writes all of his own opinions. His job is to reason to a conclusion and then to write about that process. The act of writing is, almost by definition, the act of exploration. Posner of course had written all of his own work as an academic, but now, freed of the restraints of the academy and of perhaps feeling obligated to defend an ideological position, Posner finds himself daily confronting real cases presenting real issues of law needing resolution. There is nothing academic about what he does on the bench, and perhaps this is the principal reason he has been able to thrive in his new territory, with a voice and mind distinctly his own.

◆   ◆

It is, ironically, Posner's individual voice that has led critics and commentators away from his work on the bench. Ours is an age of academic critical theory in law—whether it is the critical legal studies school, or the reader-response school, or the schools of deconstructionism or feminism—which is not hospitable to appreciations of judging because the act of judging is the anathematic exercise of power. But it must be recognized as power. The more individual the judging voice, the more emphatic the idea that an individual is deciding a case. True, judges such as Posner are speaking for panels of three or for a court en banc, but the result is the same: one voice is articulating how law is being fashioned. The more a judge uses euphemistic language, or the more a judge disguises his voice with the bland, homogeneous tone of law clerks, the less pointed is the act of judging. When we look at judicial opinions without the edges of current critical theory, however, we can recognize judicial opinions generally and Posner's specifically as legal literature that can soar to the level of literature generally.

Notes

Preface

1. Quoted in KAPLAN, THE TENTH JUSTICE 200 (1986).
2. Rodell, *Goodbye to Law Reviews*, 22 VA. L. REV. 38 (1936).
3. CARDOZO, *Law and Literature, in* LAW AND LITERATURE 6 (1931).
4. See reviews in *The Nation*, 25 Apr. 1994, 569; *Times Literary Supplement*, 3 June 1994, 22.
5. WYZANSKI, JR., *Brandeis: The Independent Man, in* WHEREAS—A JUDGE'S PREMISES 50 (1965).
6. Quoted in KLUGER, SIMPLE JUSTICE 706 (1971).
7. LLEWELLYN, THE COMMON LAW TRADITION 333–34 (1960).

Introduction

1. For examples of these approaches, see WHITE, JUSTICE AS TRANSLATION (1990); Symposium, *Legal Storytelling*, 87 MICH. L. REV. 2073 (1989); Delgado and Stefancic, *Scorn*, 35 WM. & MARY L. REV. 1061 (1994); Tushnet, *Style and the Supreme Court's Educational Role in Government*, 11 CONST. COMM. 215 (1994); Falk, *Against the Tyranny of the Text*, 78 CORNELL L. REV. 163 (1993); Symposium, *Humor in the Law*, 17 NOVA L. REV. 899 (1993).
2. See, for example, BOSMAJIAN, METAPHOR AND JUDICIAL REASON IN JUDICIAL OPINIONS (1992); Boudin, *Antitrust Doctrine and the Sway of Metaphor*, 75 GEO. L.J. 395 (1986); Winter, *The Metaphor of Standing and the Problem of Self-Governance*, 40 STAN. L. REV. 1371 (1988); Henly, *"Penumbra": The Roots of a Legal Metaphor*, 15 HASTINGS CONST. L.Q. 81 (1987); BALL, LYING DOWN TOGETHER: LAW, METAPHOR AND THEOLOGY (1985).
3. Berky v. Third Ave. Ry. Co., 155 N.E. 58, 61 (1926) (Cardozo, J.).
4. McCollum v. Board of Education, 333 U.S. 203, 247, 68 S. Ct. 461, 482, 92 L. Ed. 649 (1948) (Reed, J., dissenting).
5. Bell, *Style in Judicial Writing*, 15 J. PUB. L. 214 (1966).

6. See POSNER, LAW AND LITERATURE: A MISUNDERSTOOD RELATION 281–89 (1988); CARDOZO: A STUDY IN REPUTATION (1990).

7. Epstein, "Where the Action Is: Congresss, Not the Supreme Court," *Wall Street Journal*, 20 Apr. 1994, A15.

Chapter 1: Reporting and Publishing Judicial Decisions

1. See Joyce, *The Rise of the Supreme Court Reporter*, 83 MICH. L. REV. 1291 (1985).

2. The first volumes, *Dallas's Reports*, were followed by those bearing the names of his successors until 1875 when the title became *U.S. Reports*. The reporters, their volumes, and the correspondingly renumbered *U.S. Reports* are as follows:

Reporter	Eponymous Volumes	*U.S. Reports* Volumes
Dallas	1–4	1–4
Cranch	1–9	5–13
Wheaton	1–12	14–25
Peters	1–16	26–41
Howard	1–24	42–65
Black	1–2	66–67
Wallace	1–23	68–90

3. 26 U.S. (1 Pet.) iii–iv (1828).

4. 4 Stat. 213, 19th Cong., 2d Sess. (1827).

5. Proposals for publishing by subscription, The Cases in the Supreme Court of the United States, From its organization to the close of January term, 1827 (1828), Record, at 9–11, Wheaton v. Peters, 33 U.S. (8 Pet.) 591 (1834).

6. Wheaton v. Peters, 33 U.S. (8 Pet.) 668.

7. Easterbrook, *Insignificant Justices*, 50 U. CHI. L. REV. 481, 487n.18 (1983).

8. *Article III. Reports of Cases Argued and Adjudged in the Supreme Court of the United States, February Term, 1818, by Henry Wheaton, vol. 3*, 8 NORTH AMERICAN REVIEW (hereafter N. AM. REV.) 63–71 (1818); *Article VI. Reports of Cases Argued and Adjudged in the Supreme Court of the United States, February Term, 1819, by Henry Wheaton, vol. 4.*, 10 N. AM. REV. (n.s.) 83–115 (1820); *Article VI. Law Reports*, 18 N. AM. REV. (n.s.) 371–82 (1824); *Article V. Condensed Reports of Cases in the United States Supreme Court, from Its Organization to the Commencement of Peter's Reports, at January Term, 1827, by Richard Peters, vol. 1, from April Term, 1791, to February, 1826*, 7 AMERICAN QUARTERLY REVIEW (hereafter AM. Q. REV.) 111–36 (1830); *Article VII. Reports of Cases Argued and Adjudged in the Supreme Court of the United States, January Term, 1837, by Richard Peters*, 46 N. AM. REV. (n.s.) 126–56 (1838); *Article IX. Reports of Cases Argued and Determined in the Circuit Court of the United States, for the Second Circuit, Comprising the Districts of New York, Connecticut, and Vermont, by Elijah Paine. vol.*

1, 1827, 27 N. Am. Rev. (n.s.) 167–91 (1828); *Article VII. Reports of Cases Argued and Determined in the Supreme Judicial Court of Massachusetts, September Term 1822 to October Term 1823*, 11 N. Am. Rev. (n.s.) 180–91 (1825); *Article X. Reports of Cases Adjudged in the Court of Chancery of New York, by William Johnson, vols. 1, 2, and 3 (1816, 1818, 1819)*, 11 N. Am. Rev. (n.s.) 140–66 (1820); *Article IX. Reports of Cases Adjudged in the Supreme Court of Pennsylvania, by Thomas Sergeant and William Rawle, vol. 12*, 2 Am. Q. Rev. 185–214 (1827); *Article VIII. Reports of Cases Argued and Determined in the Supreme Judicial Court of Massachusetts, vol. 14, Containing the Cases for the Year 1817, by Dudley Atkins Tyng, 1818*, 7 N. Am. Rev. (n.s.) 184–97 (1818); see also *Article V. Reports of Cases Argued and Determined in the English Courts of Common Law. Edited by Thomas Sergeant and John Lowrer, 1822–1825*, 24 N.Am. Rev. (n.s.) 377–88 (1825).

9. Review of *Wheaton's Reports*, vol. 3, in 8 N. Am. Rev. (n.s.) 67 (1818).

10. Quoted in *Cases in the United States Courts*, 27 N. Am. Rev. (n.s.) 183 (1828).

11. *Id.* at 69.

12. *Quoted id.* at 183.

13. *Id.* at 182.

14. *Article XXI. Reports of Cases Argued and Determined in the Supreme Court of the United States, February Term, 1823, by Henry Wheaton, 1823*, 43 N. Am. Rev. (n.s.) 371, 378 (1824).

15. For the best general account of the plea rolls and the yearbooks that followed them, see Baker, *Records, Reports and the Origins of Case-Law in England, in* Judicial Records, Law Reports, and the Growth of Case Law 15–46 (Baker ed., 1989).

16. [1861–73] All E.R. 1 (1868).

17. Y.B. 20 Edw. 4, fo. 10, pl. 10.

18. As translated in Rylands v. Fletcher, [1861–73] All E.R. 1, 8 (1868).

19. [1861–73] All E.R. 1, 7 (1868).

20. 13 The Works of Francis Bacon 65 (Ellis and Spedding eds. 1827).

21. 34 Mass. Rep. (17 Pick.) 9–10 (1835).

22. Von Nessen, *Law Reporting*, 48 Mod. L. Rev. 412, 417 (1985).

23. Quoted in Moran, The Heralds of the Law 44 (1948).

24. Details of the Curtis-Taney correspondence come from A Memoir of Benjamin Robbins Curtis 212–42 (1879).

25. *The Dred Scott Case*, 85 N. Am. Rev. 392–93 (1857).

26. 42 Stat. 816, 67th Cong., 2d Sess., chap. 267 (1922).

27. 62 Cong. Rec. 7756 (1922).

28. *Id.*

29. Banks Law Pub. Co. v. Lawyers Cooperative Pub. Co., 169 F. 386, 389 (2d Cir. 1909).

30. See Woxland *"Forever Associated with the Practice of Law": The Early Years of the West Publishing Company*, 5 L. Ref. Ser. Q. 115, 120, 122 (1985).

31. Quoted in Preface, 1 THE FEDERAL CASES iii (1884).

32. An example of an indexed volume is *Robb's Patent Cases*, A Collection of patent cases decided in the Supreme and circuit courts from 1789 to 1859, with notes, by James B. Robb, counselor at law, 2 vols. (Boston: Little, Brown, 1854).

33. Preface, 1 F. 3 (1880).

34. *New York Times*, 17 June 1880.

35. See, for example, Internal Operating Procedure Rule 5.5 (Publication of Opinions) of the Third Circuit: "Rule 5.5.3 Forwarding by Clerk. The Clerk promptly forwards for publication to any publisher designated by the court all opinions designated for publication for the information of the bench and bar. These publishers include the West Publishing Company in its Federal Reporter, certain other legal publishers, the Equity Publishing Corporation in its Virgin Island Reports, (Virgin Islands cases), and companies providing computer assisted legal research."

36. Garfield v. Palmieri, 297 F.2d 526, 527–28 (2d Cir. 1962).

37. 36 Stat. 1155, 61st Cong., 3d Sess. (1911).

38. SOLOMON, HISTORY OF THE SEVENTH CIRCUIT, 1891–1941 (1976).

39. 1 FEDERAL COURTS STUDY COMMITTEE: WORKING PAPERS AND SUBCOMMITTEE REPORTS, JULY 1, 1990 81 (1990).

40. Filings per year per circuit and district court judge (from POSNER, THE FEDERAL COURTS, Appendix B, 358–60 [1985]):

	Circuit Judge	District Judge
1910	51	325
1920	46	676
1930	64	929
1940	63	415
1950	42	387
1960	57	341
1970	127	370
1980	193	432
1988	240	494

41. 1 FEDERAL COURTS STUDY COMMITTEE: WORKING PAPERS AND SUBCOMMITTEE REPORTS, JULY 1, 1990 29, 31 (1990).

42. REPORT OF THE FEDERAL COURTS STUDY COMMITTEE 171–83 (1990).

43. See Vestal, *Federal District Court Opinions*, 20 Sw. L.J. 63, 75–76 (1966).

44. West Publishing Co. v. Mead Data Cent., Inc., 616 F. Supp. 1571 (D.Minn. 1985).

45. "U.S. Drops Legal Number Idea," *Minneapolis Star Tribune*, 14 Feb. 1995.

46. See United States v. Detroit Lumber Co., 200 U.S. 321, 337, 26 S. Ct. 282, 50 L. Ed. 499 (1905), in which the Court held that the Reporter's syllabus had no precedential authority.

47. Hester v. Intern. Union of Operating Engineers, 742 F. Supp. 1522, 1525 (N.D.Ala. 1990) (Acker, J.).

48. After this book went to press, West Publishing was bought, subject to regulatory approval, by Thomson Corp. of Canada, which already owns Lawyers Cooperative Publishing Company, publishers of the *Lawyers' Edition of the Supreme Court Reports*. See "Thompson to Purchase West Publishing for $3.45 Billion," *Wall Street Journal*," 27 Feb. 1996, A3.

Chapter 2: Who Writes Judicial Opinions

1. Tidewater Oil Co. v. United States, 409 U.S. 151, 174 (1972) (Douglas, J., dissenting).

2. Carrizosa, "O'Connor Says Justices Still Working Hard," *Los Angeles Daily Journal*, 17 Aug. 1994, p. 1, col. 1.

3. *Justice Rehnquist Holds Court*, 37 HARV. L. SCH. BULL. 28 (1986).

4. Quoted in SCHWARTZ, SUPER CHIEF: EARL WARREN AND HIS SUPREME COURT 68 (1983).

5. JEFFRIES, JUSTICE LEWIS F. POWELL, JR.: A BIOGRAPHY 295 (1994).

6. WILKINSON, JR., SERVING JUSTICE 91–93 (1974).

7. Toobin, "The Burden of Clarence Thomas," *New Yorker*, 27 Sept. 1993, at 46–47.

8. Barrett, "If There Is Blood, We Know Who Wrote It," *Wall Street Journal*, 4 Oct. 1993, A1.

9. See Joyce, *The Rise of the Supreme Court Reporter*, 83 MICH. L. REV. 1291, 1304n.77 (1985).

10. See, generally, WHITE, THE MARSHALL COURT AND CULTURAL CHANGE (1988).

11. Trustees of Dartmouth College v. Woodward, 17 U.S. (4 Wheat.) 518 (1819).

12. Currie, *The Most Insignificant Justice*, 50 U. CHI. L. REV. 466 (1983). In a rejoinder, Currie's colleague Frank Easterbrook argued that the insignificance of Thomas Todd (1807–26) surpassed that of Duvall. Easterbrook, *Insignificant Justices*, 50 U. CHI. L. REV. 481 (1983).

13. Currie, *The Most Insignificant Justice*, 50 U. CHI. L. REV. 472 (1983).

14. Quoted in FRANK, JUSTICE DANIEL DISSENTING: A BIOGRAPHY OF PETER V. DANIEL, 1784–1869 at 174 (1964).

15. Quoted in BRODHEAD, DAVID J. BREWER: THE LIFE OF A SUPREME COURT JUSTICE, 1837–1910 at 78 (1994).

16. *Id.* at 79.

17. *Id.*

18. Interview with Justice Douglas by Professor Walter Murphy, Seeley G. Mudd Manuscript Library, Princeton University, at 213, 239 (9 June 1962).

19. Interview with Justice Douglas by Professor Walter Murphy, Seeley G. Mudd Manuscript Library, Princeton University, at 246–47 (18 Dec. 1962).

20. Quoted in Brodhead, David J. Brewer 79–80 (1994).

21. *Id.* at 80.

22. Quoted in Pringle, The Life and Times of William Howard Taft 311 (1939).

23. Quoted in Bowen, Yankee from Olympus 429 (1945).

24. Williams, *The 1924 Term: Recollections of Chief Justice Taft's Law Clerk,* 1989 Yearbook of Supreme Court History 40, 44.

25. Mason, Harlan Fiske Stone 327 (1956).

26. 2 Holmes-Laski Letters 1296 (Howe ed., 1953).

27. Holmes-Einstein Letters 21 (Peabody ed., 1964).

28. *Id.* at 97.

29. *Id.* at 35.

30. 1 Holmes-Laski Letters 755 (Howe ed., 1953).

31. McCraw, *Louis D. Brandeis Reappraised,* 54 Am. Schol. 525 (1985).

32. Rodell, Nine Men 218–19 (1955).

33. Williams, *The 1924 Term: Recollections of Chief Justice Taft's Law Clerk,* 1989 Yearbook of Supreme Court History 40, 44.

34. Mason, Harlan Fiske Stone 275 (1956).

35. Pusey, *Charles Evans Hughes, in* Mr. Justice 161–62 (Dunham and Kurland eds. 1964).

36. Quoted in Newman, Hugo Black: A Biography 325 (1994).

37. *Id.* at 273–74.

38. *Id.* at 275.

39. Black, My Father 135 (1975).

40. Quoted in Newman, Hugo Black: A Biography 325–26 (1994).

41. Stevens, *Mr. Justice Rutledge, in* Mr. Justice (Dunham and Kurland eds., 1964).

42. Urofsky, *Getting the Job Done, in* "He Shall Not Pass This Way Again": The Legacy of Justice William O. Douglas 46 (Wasby ed., 1990).

43. Schwartz, Super Chief: Earl Warren and His Supreme Court 61 (1983).

44. Urofsky, *Getting the Job Done, in* "He Shall Not Pass This Way Again" 34 (Wasby ed., 1990).

45. *Id.* at 34, quoting interview with C. David Ginsburg.

46. Interview with Justice Douglas by Professor Walter Murphy, Seeley G. Mudd Manuscript Library, Princeton University, at 54 (27 Dec. 1961).

47. Urofsky, The Douglas Letters: Selections from the Private Papers of Justice William O. Douglas 70 (1987).

48. 24 Stat. 254, 49th Cong., 1st Sess. (1886).

49. Hughes, The Autobiographical Notes of Charles Evans Hughes 153 (1973).

50. Biddle, A Casual Past 271 (1961).

51. See Newland, *Personal Assistants to Supreme Court Justices,* 40 Or. L. Rev. 312 (1961).

52. *Id.*

53. Fine, Frank Murphy: The Washington Years 162 (1984).

54. Schwartz, Super Chief: Earl Warren and His Supreme Court 68 (1983).

55. *Id.*

56. Atkinson, *Opinion Writing on the Supreme Court, 1949–1956: The Views of Justice Sherman Minton,* 49 Temp. L.Q. 105, 113 (1975).

57. Yarborough, John Marshall Harlan: Great Dissenter of the Warren Court 143 (1992).

58. Rehnquist, "Who Writes Decisions of the Supreme Court," *U.S. News & World Report,* 13 Dec. 1957, p. 75.

59. "Sway of Clerks on Court Cited," *New York Times,* 10 Dec. 1957, p. 23, col. 4.

60. Rogers, "Clerks' Work Is 'Not Decisive of Ultimate Result,'" *U.S. News & World Report,* 21 Feb. 1958, pp. 142–43.

61. Bickel, "The Court: An Indictment Analyzed," *New York Times,* 27 Apr. 1958, sec. 6, p. 16.

62. Duke, *Justice Douglas and the Criminal Law, in* "He Shall Not Pass This Way Again" 142 (Wasby ed., 1990).

63. Posner, *Democracy and Distrust Revisited,* 77 Va. L. Rev. 641, 651 (1991).

64. 46 Stat. 774, 71st Cong., 2d Sess. (1930).

65. 49 Stat. 1140, 74th Cong., 2d Sess. (1936).

66. Gunther, Learned Hand 288 (1994).

67. Posner, The Federal Courts: Crisis and Reform 102–19 (1985).

68. Interview with Judge Posner, Chicago (6 Feb. 1991).

69. Interview with Justice Scalia, Washington, D.C. (6 Sept. 1990).

70. Coffin, On Appeal: Lawyering and Judging at the Appellate Court 193–209 (1994).

71. Swygert, *Swygert's Story,* 11 Chi. Law. 16–17 (1988).

72. Wald, *The Problem with the Courts,* 42 Md. L. Rev. 766, 777–78 (1983).

73. Wald, *Selecting Law Clerks,* 89 Mich. L. Rev. 152, 153 (1990).

74. Acceptance Ins. Co. v. Schafner, 651 F. Supp. 776, 778 (N.D.Ala. 1986).

75. 2 Federal Courts Study Committee: Working Papers and Subcommittee Reports, July 1, 1990 71 (1990).

76. *Id.*

77. *Id.* at 72–73.

78. *Id.* at 73.

79. *Id.*

80. *Id.*

81. Letter, 13 Jan. 1939, to Charles Burlingham, Robert Jackson Papers, box 10, Manuscript Division, Library of Congress, Washington, D.C.

82. Judicial Staff Directory, 1995; The American Bench, 1993–1994.

83. Quoted in Schick, Learned Hand's Court 107 (1970).

84. GUNTHER, LEARNED HAND 141 (1994).

85. *Id.* at 620.

86. DILLIARD, ED., THE SPIRIT OF LIBERTY: PAPERS AND ADDRESSES OF LEARNED HAND 36 (3d ed., 1960).

87. GUNTHER, LEARNED HAND 24 (1994).

88. The Reminiscences of Judge Learned Hand, Oral History Research Office, Columbia University (1958).

89. *Id.* at 80–82.

90. *Id.* at 102.

91. *Id.* at 100.

92. SHAKESPEARE, JULIUS CAESAR, I, ii, 192–210.

93. The Reminiscences of Judge Learned Hand, 103–6.

94. Telephone interview, 30 Dec. 1993, with Erwin Griswold.

95. Freund, *Henry Friendly*, 99 HARV. L. REV. 1715 (1986).

96. Quoted in *id.*

97. Ackerman, *Henry J. Friendly*, 99 HARV. L. REV. 1709 (1986).

98. *Id.* at 1719.

99. In his review of GUNTHER, LEARNED HAND, Posner relates that while Hand wrote some three thousand opinions, only 1359 of them were signed majority opinions. The others were very brief per curiam opinions and ephemeral concurrences. Posner, *The Learned Hand Biography and the Question of Judicial Greatness*, 104 YALE L.J. 511, 522n.38 (1994).

Chapter 3: Style and Substance in Supreme Court Opinions

1. Boskey and Gressman, *The Supreme Court Bids Farewell to Mandatory Appeals*, 121 F.R.D. 81.

2. City of Cincinnati v. Discovery Network, Inc., 507 U.S. 410, 113 S. Ct. 1505, 123 L. Ed. 2d 99 (1993).

3. U.S. v. Hill, 506 U.S. 546, 113 S. Ct. 941, 122 L. Ed. 2d 330 (1993).

4. Building & Trades Council v. Associated Builders, 507 U.S. 218, 113 S. Ct. 1190, 122 L. Ed. 2d 565 (1993).

5. Sale v. Haitian Centers Council, Inc., __ U.S. __, 113 S. Ct. 2549, 125 L. Ed. 2d 128 (1993).

6. Godinez v. Moran, __ U.S. __, 113 S. Ct. 2680, 125 L. Ed. 2d 321 (1993).

7. Buckley v. Fitzsimmons, __ U.S. __, 113 S. Ct. 2606, 125 L. Ed. 2d 209 (1993).

8. U.S. v. Dixon, __ U.S. __, 113 S. Ct. 2849, 125 L. Ed. 2d 556 (1993).

9. Parke v. Raley, 506 U.S. 20, 113 S. Ct. 517, 121 L. Ed. 2d 391 (1992).

10. Richmond v. Lewis, 506 U.S. 40, 113 S. Ct. 528, 121 L. Ed. 2d 411; Johnson v. Texas, 113 S. Ct. 2658, 125 L. Ed. 2d 290 (1993).

11. Sodal v. Cook County, 506 U.S. 56, 113 S. Ct. 538, 121 L. Ed. 2d 450 (1992).

12. C.I.R. v. Soliman, 506 U.S. 168, 113 S. Ct. 701, 121 L. Ed. 2d 634 (1993).

13. Nixon v. U.S., 506 U.S. 224, 113 S. Ct. 732, 122 L. Ed. 2d 1 (1993).

14. Herrera v. Collins, 506 U.S. 390, 113 S. Ct. 853, 122 L. Ed. 2d 203 (1993).

15. Itel v. Containers Int'l Corp. v. Huddleston, 507 U.S. 60, 113 S. Ct. 1095, 113, 122 L. Ed. 2d 421 (1993).

16. Edenfield v. Fane, 507 U.S. 761, 113 S. Ct. 1792, 123 L. Ed. 2d 543 (1993).

17. 508 U.S. 384, 113 S. Ct. 2141, 124 L. Ed. 2d 352 (1993).

18. 403 U.S. 602, 91 S. Ct. 2105, 29 L. Ed. 2d 745 (1971).

19. 2 U.S. (2 Dall.) 419 (1792).

20. 5 U.S. (1 Cranch) 137 (1803).

21. Currie, The Constitution in the Supreme Court: The First Hundred Years, 1789–1888 at 125–26 (1985).

22. 36 U.S. (11 Pet.) 420 (1837).

23. Newmyer, Supreme Court Justice Joseph Story 112–13 (1985).

24. *Id.* at 85.

25. Vol. 26. The Telephone Case, 126 U.S. 1 (1887) (Waite, J.). This description is somewhat inaccurate, as preliminary matters go to page 531. Waite's opinion is actually fifty-three pages long. It is followed by an *In Memoriam* appendix occasioned by his death on 23 Mar. 1888.

26. Letter, 29 Oct. 1879, quoted in Fairman, Mr. Justice Miller and the Supreme Court 408–9 (1935).

27. *Id.*

28. Llewellyn, The Common Law Tradition (1960).

29. Viterbo v. Friedlander, 120 U.S. 707, 714, 7 S. Ct. 962, 965, 30 L. Ed. 776 (1887).

30. "To the same general effect are many other cases, some of which, for convenience of reference, are given in the margin." Union Pacific Railway Co. v. McDonald, 152 U.S. 262, 278, 14 S. Ct. 619, 625, 38 L. Ed. 434 (1894).

31. Pratt, *Rhetorical Styles on the Fuller Court*, 24 Am. J. Legal Hist. 190 (1980).

32. *Id.* at 191.

33. Springfield Gas Co. v. Springfield, 257 U.S. 66, 42 S. Ct. 24, 66 L. Ed. 131 (1921).

34. Wilson, Patriotic Gore 743 (1962).

35. 236 U.S. 133, 35 S. Ct. 279, 59 L. Ed. 501 (1915).

36. 236 U.S. at 134, 35 S. Ct. at 279.

37. Buck v. Bell, 274 U.S. 200, 207, 47 S. Ct. 584, 585, 71 L. Ed. 1000 (1927).

38. Panhandle Oil Co. v. Knox, 277 U.S. 218, 223, 48 S. Ct. 451, 453, 72 L. Ed. (1928) (Holmes, J., dissenting).

39. Southern Pacific Co. v. Jensen, 244 U.S. 205, 222, 37 S. Ct. 524, 531, 61 L. Ed. 1086 (1917).

40. Compania de Tabacos v. Collector, 275 U.S. 87, 100, 48 S. Ct. 100, 105, 72 L. Ed. 177 (1904) (Holmes, J. dissenting).

41. Northern Securities Co. v. United States, 193 U.S. 197, 400, 24 S. Ct. 436, 468, 48 L. Ed. 679 (1904).

42. 2 HOLMES-LASKI LETTERS 961 (Howe ed., 1953).

43. 208 U.S. 412, 28 S. Ct. 324, 52 L. Ed. 551 (1908).

44. Quoted in Wyzanski, *Brandeis: The Independent Man, in* WHEREAS—A JUDGE'S PREMISES 52 (1965).

45. Acheson, *Recollections of Service with the Federal Supreme Court,* 18 ALA. LAW. 355 (1957), describing Ruppert v. Caffey, 251 U.S. 264, 40 S. Ct. 141, 64 L. Ed. 260 (1920).

46. See, generally, Simpson, *The Rise and Fall of the Legal Treatise,* 48 U. CHI. L. REV. 632 (1981).

47. Rodell, *Goodbye to Law Reviews,* 22 VA. L. REV. 38 (1936).

48. Olmstead v. United States, 277 U.S. 438, 48 S. Ct. 575, 72 L. Ed. 944 (1928) (Brandeis, J., dissenting).

49. Letter, 17 Aug. 1938, from Robert Jackson to Irving Dilliard, Robert Jackson Papers, Manuscript Division, Library of Congress, Washington, D.C.

50. Diary of Mark De Wolf Howe's year as Justice Holmes's law clerk, in the Howe Papers, Harvard Law School Library, Ms. box 29, folder 1, p. 9.

51. Anon Y Mous, *The Speech of Judges,* 29 VA. L. REV. 625 (1943).

52. Graves v. People of State of New York, 306 U.S. 466, 59 S. Ct. 595, 83 L. Ed. 927 (1939).

53. GLENNON, THE ICONOCLAST AS REFORMER: JEROME FRANK'S IMPACT ON AMERICAN LAW 203n.103 (1985).

54. Milk Wagon Drivers Union v. Meadowmoor Dairies, 312 U.S. 287, 302, 61 S. Ct. 552, 559, 85 L. Ed. 836 (1941) (Black, J., dissenting).

55. UROFSKY, THE DOUGLAS LETTERS: SELECTIONS FROM THE PRIVATE PAPERS OF JUSTICE WILLIAM O. DOUGLAS 120 (1987).

56. Stewart, *Jackson on Federal-State Relationships, in* MR. JUSTICE JACKSON: FOUR LECTURES IN HIS HONOR 63 (1969).

57. 314 U.S. 160, 186, 62 S. Ct. 164, 172, 86 L. Ed. 119 (1941) (Jackson, J., concurring).

58. SCHWARTZ, SUPER CHIEF 96–97 (1983).

59. *Justice Rehnquist Holds Court,* 37 HARV. L. SCH. BULL. 28 (1986).

60. Earl Warren, speaking extemporaneously during retirement ceremonies, 395 U.S. xi (1969).

61. 1 HOLMES-LASKI LETTERS 646–47 (1953).

62. 402 U.S. 490, 109 S. Ct. 3040, 106 L. Ed. 2d 410 (1989).

63. 402 U.S. at 537, 559–60, 109 S. Ct. at 3067, 3079.

64. 448 U.S. 445, 109 S. Ct. 693, 102 L. Ed. 2d 835 (1989).

65. 448 U.S. at 466, 109 S. Ct. at 704–5.

66. 489 U.S. 189, 109 S. Ct. 998, 103 L. Ed. 2d 249 (1989).

67. 489 U.S. 212–13, 109 S. Ct. at 1012–13.

Chapter 4: The Canon

1. LEFLAR, INTERNAL OPERATING PROCEDURES OF APPELLATE COURTS (1961).

2. Currie, The Constitution in the Supreme Court: The First Hundred Years, 1789–1888 (1985); Currie, The Constitution in the Supreme Court: The Second Century, 1888–1986 (1990).

3. 17 U.S. (4 Wheat.) 316 (1819) (Marshall, C.J.).

4. 250 U.S. 624, 40 S. Ct. 20, 63 L. Ed. 1173 (1919) (Holmes, J., dissenting).

5. 309 U.S. 227, 60 S. Ct. 472, 84 L. Ed. 716 (1940) (Black, J.).

6. Youngstown Sheet & Tube Co. v. Sawyer, 343 U.S. 579, 72 S. Ct. 863, 96 L. Ed. 1153 (1952) (Black, J.).

7. 347 U.S. 483, 74 S. Ct. 686, 98 L. Ed. 873 (1954) (Warren, C.J.).

8. 384 U.S. 436, 86 S. Ct. 1602, 16 L. Ed. 2d 694 (1966) (Warren, C.J.)

9. 319 U.S. 624, 63 S. Ct. 1178, 87 L. Ed. 1628 (1943) (Jackson, J.).

10. 372 U.S. 335, 83 S. Ct. 792, 9 L. Ed. 2d 799 (1963) (Black, J.).

11. 388 U.S. 1, 87 S. Ct. 1817, 18 L. Ed. 2d 1010 (1967) (Warren, C.J.).

12. 410 U.S. 113, 93 S. Ct. 705, 35 L. Ed. 2d 147 (1973) (Blackmun, J.).

13. 316 U.S. 535, 62 S. Ct. 1110, 86 L. Ed. 1655 (1942).

14. 310 U.S. 586, 60 S. Ct. 1010, 84 L. Ed. 1375 (1940).

15. West Virginia State Board of Education v. Barnett, 319 U.S. 624, 634, 63 S. Ct. 1178, 1183, 87 L. Ed. 1628 (1943); 319 U.S. at 640–41, 63 S. Ct. at 1186–87.

16. 319 U.S at 642, 63 S. Ct. at 1187.

17. Skinner v. State of Oklahoma, 316 U.S. at 536, 62 S. Ct. at 1111.

18. 309 U.S. at 227, 60 S. Ct. at 473.

19. 384 U.S. at 339, 86 S. Ct. at 1609.

20. 316 U.S. at 541, 62 S. Ct. at 1113.

21. 309 U.S. at 240–41, 60 S. Ct. at 479.

22. 388 U.S. at 2, 87 S. Ct. at 1818–19.

23. 388 U.S. at 12, 87 S. Ct. at 1824.

24. 347 U.S. at 493, 74 S. Ct. at 691.

25. Id.

26. 347 U.S. at 495, 74 S. Ct. at 691.

27. 410 U.S. at 116, 93 S. Ct. at 708.

28. 384 U.S. at 458, 86 S. Ct. at 1619.

29. 384 U.S. at 471–72, 86 S. Ct. at 1626.

30. 372 U.S. at 344, 83 S. Ct. at 796.

31. Id.

32. Id.

33. 343 U.S. at 582, 72 S. Ct. at 864.

34. 343 U.S. at 597, 72 S. Ct. at 867.

35. 343 U.S. at 589, 72 S. Ct. at 867.

36. 17 U.S. (4 Wheat.) at 421.

37. 17 U.S. (4 Wheat.) at 431.

38. 17 U.S. (4 Wheat.) at 436.

39. Two Leaflets and an Experiment, in The Mind and Faith of Justice Holmes 306 (Lerner ed., 1945).

40. 250 U.S. at 630, 40 S. Ct. at 22.

41. See Posner, Law and Literature: A Misunderstood Relation 281–89 (1988).

42. See Posner, Sex and Reason 337 (1992).

43. 381 U.S. 479, 85 S. Ct. 1678, 14 L. Ed. 2d 510 (1965) (Douglas, J.).

44. 418 U.S. 683, 94 S. Ct. 3090, 41 L. Ed. 2d 1039 (1974).

45. 376 U.S. 254, 84 S. Ct. 710, 11 L. Ed. 2d 686 (1964).

46. 377 U.S. 533, 84 S. Ct. 1362, 12 L. Ed. 2d 506 (1964).

47. 319 U.S. at 641, 63 S. Ct. at 1187.

Chapter 5: Style and Substance in Lower Federal Court Opinions

1. American Medical Systems, Inc. v. Medical Engineering Corporation, 794 F. Supp. 1370 (E.D.Wis. 1992).

2. United Sweetener USA, Inc. v. Nutrasweet Co., 760 F. Supp. 400 (D.Del. 1991).

3. Bristol-Myers Squibb Co. v. McNeil-P.P.C., Inc., 786 F. Supp. 182 (E.D.N.Y. 1992).

4. Lotus Development Corp. v. Paperback Software International, 740 F. Supp. 37 (D.Mass. 1990).

5. Newton v. National Broadcasting Company, Inc., 930 F.2d 662 (9th Cir. 1990), cert. denied, 502 U.S. 866 (1991).

6. Karl Rove & Co. v. Thornburgh, 824 F. Supp. 662, 676 (W.D.Tex. 1993), aff'd, 39 F.3d 1273 (1994).

7. Lish v. Harper's Magazine Foundation, 807 F. Supp. 1090 (S.D.N.Y. 1992).

8. Hatter v. United States, 953 F.2d 626 (Fed. Cir. 1992).

9. New York Times Company v. National Aeronautics and Space Administration, 782 F. Supp. 628 (D.D.C. 1991).

10. Nixon v. United States, 782 F. Supp. 634 (D.D.C. 1991), rev'd, 978 F.2d 1269 (1992).

11. Booker v. Lehigh University, 800 F. Supp. 234 (E.D.Pa. 1992), aff'd, 995 F.2d 215 (3d Cir. 1992).

12. Dranoff-Perlstein Associates v. Shlar, 967 F.2d 852 (3d Cir. 1992).

13. U.S. v. Prince, 938 F.2d 1092, 1093 (10th Cir. 1991), cert. denied, 502 U.S. 961 (1991).

14. U.S. v. Dowdy, 960 F.2d 78 (8th Cir. 1992).

15. Citizens v. New England Aquarium, 836 F. Supp. 45 (D.Mass. 1993).

16. McClendon v. OMI Offshore Marine Service, 807 F. Supp. 1266 (E.D.Tex. 1992).

17. 961 F.2d 145 (9th Cir. 1992).

18. 956 F.2d 63 (4th Cir. 1992).

19. 10 F.3d 1327 (7th Cir. 1993).

20. Worm v. American Cyanamid Co., 5 F.3d 744 (4th Cir. 1993).

21. 100 F. 795 (S.D.Ga. 1900).

22. 100 F. 180, 196 (S.D.N.Y. 1900).

23. 200 F. 80 (S.D.N.Y. 1912). Since we are surveying these volumes selectively, this our first encounter with Hand. But his first published opinion was In re McCarthy, 170 F. 859 (S.D.N.Y. 1909).

24. Friendly, *Judge Learned Hand, in* BENCHMARKS 315 (1967).

25. Hand, *Sources of Tolerance, in* THE SPIRIT OF LIBERTY 81 (Dilliard ed., 1952).

26. Friendly, *Judge Learned Hand, in* BENCHMARKS 315 (1967).

27. United States v. Peoni, 100 F.2d 401, 402 (2d Cir. 1938).

28. Harrison v. United States, 7 F.2d 259, 263 (2d Cir. 1925).

29. Spector Motor Service, Inc. v. Walsh, 139 F.2d 809, 823 (2d Cir. 1943).

30. Lehigh Valley Coal Co. v. Yensavage, 218 F. 547, 553 (2d Cir. 1914).

31. Cabell v. Markham, 148 F.2d 737, 739 (2d Cir.), *aff'd*, 326 U.S. 404 (1945).

32. NLRB v. Federbush Co., 121 F.2d 954, 967 (2d Cir. 1941).

33. 250 F. 566 (S.D.N.Y. 1918).

34. Featheredge Rubber Co. v. Miller Rubber Co., 250 F. 255 (N.D.Ohio 1917).

35. Kroger Grocery & Baking Co. v. Retail Clerks' Int'l Assoc., 250 F. 890 (E.D.Mo. 1918) (Trieber, J.).

36. Button v. Cities Fuel & Power Co., 200 F. 280, 300 (4th Cir. 1924).

37. Bank of Commerce & Trusts v. Hatcher, 50 F.2d 719 (4th Cir. 1931).

38. Pueblo De Taos v. Gusdorf, 50 F.2d 721, 722 (10th Cir. 1931).

39. Quittner v. Motion Picture Producers & Distributors of America, 50 F.2d 266 (S.D.N.Y. 1931).

40. U.S. v. Antonelli Fireworks, 155 F.2d 631, 662 (1946).

41. United States v. Rubenstein, 151 F.2d 915, 923 (2d Cir. 1945) (Frank, J., dissenting).

42. Triangle Publications, Inc. v. Rohrlich, 167 F.2d 969, 982 (2d Cir. 1949) (Frank, J., dissenting).

43. Letter, 12 Nov. 1942, quoted in GLENNON, THE ICONOCLAST AS REFORMER: JEROME FRANK'S IMPACT ON AMERICAN LAW 105 (1985).

44. 300 F.2d 345 (2d Cir. 1962); 372 U.S. 391, 83 S. Ct. 822, 9 L. Ed. 2d 837 (1963).

45. See Posner, *Judges' Writing Styles*, 62 U. CHI. L. REV. 1421 (1995).

46. Jenkins v. United Gas Corporation, 400 F.2d 28, 29 (5th Cir. 1968).

47. General Electric Co., Battery Prod., Cap. Dept. v. N.L.R.B., 400 F.2d 713, 715 (5th Cir. 1968).

48. Watson v. Gulf Stevedore Corporation, 400 F.2d 649, 651 (5th Cir. 1968) (Rubin, J.), *cert. denied*, 394 U.S. 976 (1969).

49. Pond v. Braniff Airways, Incorporated, 500 F.2d 161, 165 n.9 (5th Cir. 1974).

50. U.S. v. Phillips, 600 F.2d 535, 540–41 (5th Cir. 1979).

51. Pressroom Unions v. Continental Assurance Co., 700 F.2d 889, 890 (2d Cir. 1983), *cert. denied*, 464 U.S. 845 (1983).

52. Blackman v. Hustler Magazine, Inc., 800 F.2d 1160, 1161 (D.C. Cir. 1986) (Kozinski, J.).

53. U.S. v. Syufy Enterprises, 903 F.2d 659 (9th Cir. 1990) (Kozinski, J.).

54. For a detailed examination of Judge Selya's use of figurative language as a district judge, see Domnarski, *Hearing the Judicial Voices*, 61 Conn. B.J. 155 (1987).

55. Jackson v. Harvard University, 900 F.2d 464, 465 (1st Cir. 1990), *cert. denied*, 498 U.S. 848 (1990).

56. *Id.* at 467.

57. *Id.* at 469.

58. Guglietti v. Secretary of Health & Human Services, 900 F.2d 397, 398 (1st Cir. 1990), *cert. denied*, 498 U.S. 891 (1990).

59. *Id.* at 399.

60. Anderson v. Beatrice Foods Co., 900 F.2d 388, 391 (1st Cir. 1990).

61. *Id.* at 396.

62. *Id.* at 388, 395.

63. Rivera-Gomez v. de Castro, 900 F.2d 1, 3 (1st Cir. 1990).

64. *Id.* at 1, 4.

65. Schiro v. Clark, 963 F.2d 962, 965 (7th Cir. 1992) (Cummings, J.), *aff'd*, 114 S. Ct. 783 (1994).

66. Estate of Sinthasomphone v. City of Milwaukee, 785 F. Supp. 1343, 1345 (E.D.Wis. 1992).

67. U.S. v. Sloan, 939 F.2d 499 (7th Cir. 1991) (Kanne, J.), *cert. denied*, 112 S. Ct. 940 (1992).

68. S.E.C. v. International Loan Network, Inc., 968 F.2d 1304, 1305 (D.C. Cir. 1992) (Henderson, J.).

69. Ritter v. Ross, 992 F.2d 750, 751 (7th Cir. 1993) (Wood, J.) (citation omitted), *cert. denied*, 114 S. Ct. 694 (1994).

70. U.S. v. Green, 964 F.2d 365, 367 (5th Cir. 1992) (Garza, J.), *cert. denied*, 113 S. Ct. 984 (1993).

71. E.E.O.C. v. Boeing Service International, 968 F.2d 549, 551 (5th Cir. 1992) (Goldberg, J.).

72. Lewis v. Lake Region Conference of Seventh Day Adventists, 779 F. Supp. 72, 73 (E.D.Mich. 1991), *aff'd*, 978 F. 2d 940 (1992).

73. Lamont v. Woods, 948 F.2d 825, 827 (2d Cir. 1991) (Oakes, C.J.) (footnotes and citation omitted).

74. Capital Imaging v. Mohawk Valley Medical Assoc., 996 F.2d 537, 538, 539 (2d Cir. 1993) (Cardamone, J.), *cert. denied*, 114 S. Ct. 388 (1993).

75. City of New York v. U.S. Dept. of Commerce, 739 F. Supp. 761, 762–63 (E.D.N.Y. 1990) (McLaughlin, J.).

76. Reuther v. Southern Cross Club, Inc., 785 F. Supp. 1339, 1340 (S.D.Ind. 1992) (Barker, J.).

77. Effects Associates, Inc. v. Cohen, 908 F.2d 555 (9th Cir. 1990) (Kozinski, J.), *cert. denied*, 498 U.S. 1103 (1991).

78. U.S. v. Dumont, 936 F.2d 292, 294 (7th Cir. 1991) (Easterbrook, J.), *cert. denied*, 502 U.S. 950 (1991).

79. U.S. v. Boyll, 774 F. Supp. 1333, 1334 (D.N.M. 1991) (Burciaga, J.).

80. U.S. v. Harper, 928 F.2d 894, 895 (9th Cir. 1991) (Kozinski, J.).

81. U.S. v. Maxwell, 734 F. Supp. 280, 281 (S.D.Tex. 1990) (Hughes, J.).

82. Bowlin v. Deschutes County, 712 F. Supp. 803, 804 (D.Or. 1988) (Burns, J.) (footnotes omitted), *aff'd*, 918 F.2d 181 (1990).

83. Greater Rockford Energy & Technology v. Shell Oil Co., 777 F. Supp. 690, 691 (C.D.Ill. 1991) (Mills, J.).

84. JSG Trading Corp. v. Tray-Wrap, Inc., 917 F.2d 75, 76 (2d Cir. 1990) (Cardamone, J.) (citations omitted).

85. Frigaliment Importing Co. v. B.N.S. International Sales Corp., 190 F. Supp. 116 (S.D.N.Y. 1960).

86. Mississippi Poultry Association, Inc. v. Madigan, 992 F.2d 1359, 1360–61 (5th Cir. 1993) (Wiener, J.), *aff'd*, 9 F.3d 1113 (1993).

87. Stella v. Town of Tewksbury, Mass., 4 F.3d 53, 54 (1st Cir. 1993) (Selya, J.).

88. O'Shea v. City of San Francisco, 966 F.2d 503, 504 (9th Cir. 1992) (Beezer, J.).

89. In re Burzynski, 989 F.2d 733, 736 (5th Cir. 1993) (by the court).

90. Trust Co. Bank v. U.S. Gypsum Co., 950 F.2d 1144, 1146 (5th Cir. 1992) (Johnson, J.).

91. Sabine River Authority v. U.S. Dept. of Interior, 951 F.2d 669, 671 (5th Cir. 1992) (Goldberg, J.), *cert. denied*, 113 S. Ct. 75 (1992); U.S. v. Angueira, 744 F. Supp. 36 (D.Puerto Rico 1990) (Perez-Gimenez, C.J.), *aff'd*, 951 F.2d 12 (1991).

92. Sea-Land Services, Inc. v. Pepper Source, 941 F.2d 519 (7th Cir. 1991) (Bauer, C.J.).

93. Lindsey v. Federal Deposit Ins. Corp., 960 F.2d 567, 568 (5th Cir. 1992) (Jolly, J.).

94. All Service Exportacao v. Banco Bamerindus, 921 F.2d 32, 33 (2d Cir. 1990) (Kaufman, J.).

95. Sea-Land Services, Inc. v. Pepper Source, 941 F.2d 519 (7th Cir. 1991) (Bauer, C.J.).

96. Texas Pig Stands, Inc. v. Hard Rock Cafe International, Inc., 951 F.2d 684 (5th Cir. 1992) (Brown, J.).

97. Solano v. Southeast Bank, 796 F. Supp. 506 (S.D.Fla. 1992) (Paine, J.).

98. 976 F.2d 1249, 1250 (9th Cir. 1992) (Kozinski, J.).

99. Prince v. Zazove, 959 F.2d 1395, 1396 (7th Cir. 1992) (Sharp, J.).

100. United States v. Dunkel, 927 F.2d 955, 956 (7th Cir. 1991) (Easterbrook, J.).

101. N.L.R.B. v. Special Mine Services, Inc., 11 F.3d 88, 90 (7th Cir. 1993) (Easterbrook, J.).

102. U.S. v. Bradley, 892 F.2d 634, 635 (7th Cir. 1990) (Easterbrook, J.), *cert. denied*, 495 U.S. 909 (1990).

103. Hurst v. Union Pacific Railroad Company, 958 F.2d 1002, 1003 (10th Cir. 1992) (Moore, J.).

104. Mercantile-Safe Deposit v. Trans World Airlines, 771 F. Supp. 90, 91 (S.D.N.Y. 1991) (Goettel, J.).

105. U.S. v. Cardascia, 951 F.2d 474, 477 (2d Cir. 1991) (Cardamone, J.).

106. Seevers v. Arkenberg, 726 F. Supp. 1159, 1161 (S.D.Ind. 1989) (Barker, J.).

107. Putnam Resources v. Pateman, 958 F.2d 448, 451 (1st Cir. 1992) (Selya, J.).

108. Magnuson v. City of Hickory Hills, 933 F.2d 562, 563 (7th Cir. 1991) (Bauer, C.J.).

109. U.S. v. Strickland, 935 F.2d 822, 824 (7th Cir. 1991) (Bauer, C.J.), *cert. denied*, 502 U.S. 917 (1991).

110. U.S. v. Siddiqi, 959 F.2d 1167, 1168 (2d Cir. 1992) (Pratt, J.).

111. Thibeault v. Square D Co., 960 F.2d 239, 242 (1st Cir. 1992) (Selya, J.).

112. Autocephalous Church v. Goldberg & Feldman Arts, 917 F.2d 278, 279 (7th Cir. 1990) (Bauer, C.J.).

113. McMillan v. State Mutual Life Assurance Co. of America, 922 F.2d 1073, 1077 (3rd Cir. 1990) (Rosenn, J.); United Thermal Industries, Inc. v. Asbestos Training & Employment, Inc., 920 F.2d 1345, 1347 (7th Cir. 1990) (Cudahy, J.).; Blank v. Bethlehem Steel Corp., 758 F. Supp. 697, 703n.6 (M.D.Fla. 1990) (Melton, J.).

114. United Sweetener USA, Inc. v. Nutrasweet Co., 760 F. Supp. 400, 402 (D.Del. 1991) (Roth, J.) (quoting from E. Stewart, Privileged Lives 315–16 (1988) (detective fiction).

115. For a complete description of the ways judges have used Shakespeare in the more than one thousand times they have quoted his poetry, see Domnarski, *Shakespeare in the Law*, 67 Conn. B.J. 317 (1993).

116. Baylson v. Disciplinary Board of Supreme Court of Pennsylvania, 975 F.2d 102, 111 (3rd Cir. 1992), *cert. denied*, 113 S. Ct. 1578 (1993).

117. Haines v. Liggett Group, Inc., 975 F.2d 81, 89 (3d Cir. 1992) (Aldisert, J.).

118. Albright v. Oliver, 975 F.2d 343 (7th Cir. 1992), *aff'd*, 114 S. Ct. 807 (1994).

Chapter 6: Closing the Circle

1. Quoted in *Wall Street Journal*, 4 Aug. 1986, A1.

2. Telephone interview, 28 Dec. 1993. This and the following interviews were with the author.

3. *Id.*

4. Telephone interview, 4 Jan. 1994.

5. *Id.*

6. *Id.*

7. Posner, Economic Analysis of Law 17 (4th ed., 1992).

8. Telephone interview, 6 Jan. 1994.

9. Telephone interview, 4 Jan. 1994.

10. *Id.*

11. Telephone interview, 13 Jan. 1994.

12. Telephone interview, 4 Jan. 1994.

13. *Id.*

14. Interview with Richard Posner, 6 Feb. 1991.

15. Quoted in Roth, *Law & Economics*, 83 U. Chi. Mag. 31 (1991).

16. Telephone interview, 6 Jan. 1994.

17. *Id.*

18. *Id.*

19. Telephone interview, 4 Jan. 1994.

20. Telephone interview, 13 Jan. 1994.

21. Telephone interview, 3 Jan. 1994.

22. *Id.*

23. U. S. v. Fisher, 864 F.2d 434, 437 (7th Cir. 1988).

24. Colby v. J. C. Penny, 811 F.2d 1119, 1122 (7th Cir. 1987).

25. Wassell v. Adams, 865 F.2d 849, 853 (7th Cir. 1989).

26. Joseph v. Brierton, 739 F.2d 1244, 1246 (7th Cir. 1984).

27. Matterhorn, Inc. v. NCR Corp., 763 F.2d 866, 871 (7th Cir. 1985).

28. Alliance to End Repression v. City of Chicago, 733 F.2d 1187, 1193 (7th Cir. 1984) (Posner, J., dissenting).

29. Miller v. Federal Mine Safety & Health Rev. Com'n, 687 F.2d 194, 196 (7th Cir. 1982).

30. Foy v. First Nat. Bank of Elkhart, 868 F.2d 251, 255 (7th Cir. 1989).

31. U.S. v. Jackson, 835 F.2d 1195, 1200 (1987) (Posner, J., concurring), *cert. denied*, 485 U.S. 969 (1988).

32. DeFrancesco v. Bowen, 867 F.2d 1040, 1044 (7th Cir. 1989).

33. Pearce v. Sullivan, 871 F.2d 61, 64 (7th Cir. 1989).

34. Pieczynski v. Duffy, 875 F.2d 1331, 1332 (7th Cir. 1989).

35. Allen v. Seidman, 881 F.2d 375, 381 (7th Cir.1989).

36. Continental Illinois Corp. v. C.I.R., 998 F.2d 513, 515 (7th Cir. 1993), *cert. denied*, 114 S. Ct. 685 (1994).

37. Duckworth v. Franzen, 780 F.2d 645, 652 (7th Cir. 1985), *cert. denied*, 479 U.S. 816 (1986).

38. American Nurses' Ass'n v. State of Ill., 783 F.2d 716, 726 (7th Cir. 1986).

39. United States v. Gutman, 725 F.2d 417, 421 (7th Cir. 1984), *cert. denied*, 469 U.S. 880 (1984)..

40. In re Wagner, 808 F.2d 542, 544 (7th Cir. 1987).

41. Shondel v. McDermott, 775 F.2d 859, 869 (7th Cir. 1985).

42. Wild v. United States Dept. of Housing & Urban Dev., 692 F.2d 1129, 1131 (7th Cir. 1982).

43. U.S. v. Mancari, 875 F.2d 103, 106 (7th Cir. 1989), *cert. denied*, 499 U.S. 924 (1991).

44. Fuller v. CBT Corp., 905 F.2d 1055, 1057 (7th Cir. 1990).

45. Fox Valley AMC/Jeep, Inc. v. AM Credit Corp., 836 F.2d 366, 368 (7th Cir. 1988).

46. C.I.R. v. Hendrickson, 873 F.2d 1018, 1021 (7th Cir. 1989).

47. Ill. Ex. Rel. Hartigan v. Panhandle E. Pipe Line, 839 F.2d 1206, 1211 (7th Cir. 1988) (Posner, J., concurring and dissenting) (vacated on grant of rehearing en banc), *cert. denied*, 488 U.S. 986 (1988).

48. White v. Elrod, 816 F.2d 1172, 1176 (7th Cir. 1987), *cert. denied*, 484 U.S. 924 (1987).

49. U.S. v. Cerro, 775 F.2d 908, 915 (7th Cir. 1985).

50. Mars Steel v. Continental National Bank & Trust, 834 F.2d 677, 684 (7th Cir. 1987).

51. Williams v. Commissioner of Internal Revenue, 1 F.3d 502, 507 (7th Cir. 1993).

52. Stromberger v. 3M Company, 990 F.2d 974, 978 (7th Cir. 1993).

53. Niehus v. Liberio, 973 F.2d 526, 527 (7th Cir. 1992).

54. Bro. of Locomotive v. Atchison, Topeka & Santa Fe, 768 F.2d 914, 922 (7th Cir. 1985).

55. Olympia Hotels Corp. v. Johnson Wax Dev. Corp., 908 F.2d 1363, 1373 (7th Cir. 1990).

56. American Civil Lib. Union v. City of St. Charles, 794 F.2d 265, 272 (7th Cir. 1986), *cert. denied*, 479 U.S. 961 (1986).

57. Colfax Envelope Corporation v. Local No. 458–3M, Chicago Graphic Communications International Union, AFL-CIO, 20 F.3d 750 (7th Cir. 1994).

58. U.S. v. Lechuga, 994 F.2d 346 (7th Cir. 1993) (en banc), *cert. denied*, 114 S. Ct. 482 (1993).

59. Muscare v. Quinn, 680 F.2d 42, 45 (7th Cir. 1982) (recalling Holmes).

60. Haynes v. Alfred A. Knopf, Inc., 8 F.3d 1222, 1234 (7th Cir. 1993).

61. Dunne v. Keohane, 14 F.3d 335, 336 (7th Cir. 1994), *cert. denied*, 114 S. Ct. 2182 (1994).

62. G. Heileman Brewing Co., Inc. v. Joseph Oat Corp., 871 F.2d 648, 657 (7th Cir. 1989) (en banc) (Posner, J., dissenting).

63. Mayo v. Lane, 867 F.2d 374, 376 (7th Cir. 1989).

64. Ash v. Wallenmeyer, 879 F.2d 272, 273 (7th Cir. 1989).

65. Sally Beauty Co. v. Nexxus Products Co., Inc., 801 F.2d 1001, 1009 (7th Cir. 1986) (Posner, J., dissenting).

66. Louis Vuitton S.A. v. Lee, 875 F.2d 584, 589 (7th Cir. 1989).

67. Yatvin v. Madison Metropolitan School Dist., 840 F.2d 412, 420 (7th Cir. 1988).

68. Singletary v. Continental Illinois National Bank, 9 F.3d 1236, 1242 (7th Cir. 1993).

69. Barkauskas v. Lane, 878 F.2d 1031, 1032 (7th Cir. 1989).

70. Walker v. Maccabees Mut. Life Ins. Co., 753 F.2d 599, 602 (7th Cir. 1985).

71. Haffner v. United States, 757 F.2d 920, 922 (7th Cir. 1985) (Posner, J., dissenting).

72. Dynamics Corp. of America v. CTS Corp., 794 F.2d 250, 257 (7th Cir. 1986), *rev'd in part*, 481 U.S. 69 (1987).

73. Isaksen v. Vermont Castings, Inc., 825 F.2d 1158, 1161, 1166 (7th Cir. 1987), *cert. denied*, 486 U.S. 1005 (1988).

74. McLaughlin v. Union Oil Co. of California, 869 F.2d 1039, 1041 (7th Cir. 1989).

75. Shapiro, *Richard Posner's Praxis*, 48 Ohio St. L. J. 999 (1987). Other examples of this approach include: Cunningham, *Testing Posner's Strong Theory of Wealth Maximization*, 81 Geo. L.J. 141 (1992); Brown, *Posner, Prisoners, and Pragmatism*, 66 Tul. L. Rev. 1117 (1992); Hammer, *Free Speech and the "Acid Bath": An Evaluation and Critique of Judge Richard Posner's Economic Interpretation of the First Amendment*, 87 Mich. L. Rev. 499 (1988); Culp, *Judex Economicus*, 50 Law & Contemp. Probs. 95 (1987); and Cohen, *Posnerian Jurisprudence and Economic of Law: The View from the Bench*, 133 U. Pa. L. Rev. 1117 (1985).

76. Posner, *Wealth Maximization and Judicial Decision-Making*, 4 Int'l Rev. L. & Econ. 131 (1984).

77. 826 F.2d 1554 (7th Cir. 1987).

78. Roland Machinery Co. v. Dresser Industries, Inc., 749 F.2d 380 (7th Cir. 1984).

79. Villanova v. Abrams, 972 F.2d 792, 796 (7th Cir. 1992).

80. *Id.*

81. Western Transp. Co. v. E. I. Du Pont De Nemours, 682 F.2d 1233, 1236 (7th Cir. 1982).

82. Spartech Corp. v. Opper, 890 F.2d 949, 955 (7th Cir. 1989).

83. United States v. Kaminski, 703 F.2d 1004, 1010 (7th Cir. 1983) (Posner, J., concurring).

84. Roberts v. Sears, Roebuck & Co., 697 F.2d 796, 798 (7th Cir. 1983) (vacated on grant of petition for rehearing en banc).

85. Nichols v. Gagnon, 710 F.2d 1267, 1269 (7th Cir. 1983), *cert. denied*, 466 U.S. 940 (1984).

86. West, *Authority, Autonomy, and Choice*, 99 Harv. L. Rev. 384 (1985).

87. In re Jones, 768 F.2d 923, 932 (7th Cir. 1985) (Posner, J., concurring).

88. Spencer v. Lee, 864 F.2d 1376, 1380 (7th Cir. 1989) (en banc), *cert. denied*, 494 U.S. 1016 (1990).

89. Colby v. J. C. Penny, 811 F.2d 1119, 1127 (7th Cir. 1987).

90. Wisconsin Knife Works v. National Metal Crafters, 781 F.2d 1280, 1286 (7th Cir. 1986).

91. Jordan v. Duff and Phelps, Inc., 815 F.2d 429, 445 (7th Cir. 1987) (Posner, J., dissenting).

92. Intern. Ass'n of Machinists, Lodge No. 1000 v. GE, 865 F.2d 902, 905 (7th Cir. 1989).

93. Piper Aircraft Corp. v. Wag-Aero, Inc., 741 F.2d 925 (7th Cir. 1984) (Posner, J., concurring).

94. U.S. v. Kerley, 838 F.2d 932, 937 (7th Cir. 1988).

95. Geras v. Lafayette Display Fixtures, Inc., 742 F.2d 1037 (7th Cir. 1984) (Posner, J., dissenting).

96. Phelps v. Duckworth, 772 F.2d 1410 (7th Cir. 1985) (en banc) (Posner, J., concurring), *cert. denied*, 474 U.S. 1011 (1985).

97. Brunswick Corp. v. Riegel Textile, 752 F.2d 261 (7th Cir. 1985), *cert. denied*, 472 U.S. 1018 (1985).

98. Jack Walters & Sons Corp. v. Morton Building, 737 F.2d 698 (7th Cir. 1984), *cert. denied*, 469 U.S. 1018 (1984).

99. 806 F.2d 731 (7th Cir. 1986).

100. Gulfstream Aerospace Corp. v. Mayacamas Corp., 485 U.S. 271, 108 S. Ct. 1133, 99 L. Ed. 2d 296 (1988).

101. Posner, *The Present Situation in Legal Scholarship*, 90 YALE L.J. 1113 (1981).

102. 890 F.2d 24 (7th Cir. 1989).

103. Brazinski v. Amoco Petroleum Additives Company, 6 F.3d 1176 (7th Cir. 1993).

104. Singletary v. Continental Illinois National Bank, 9 F.3d 1236 (7th Cir. 1993).

105. Patz v. St. Paul Fire & Marine Insurance Co., 15 F.3d 699 (7th Cir. 1994).

106. Hartman v. Prudential Insurance Company of America, 9 F.3d 1207 (7th Cir. 1993).

107. Tregenza v. Great American Communications Co., 12 F.3d 717 (7th Cir. 1993), *cert. denied*, 114 S. Ct. 1837 (1994).

108. Haynes v. Alfred A. Knopf, Inc., 8 F.3d 1222 (7th Cir. 1993).

109. 984 F.2d 880 (7th Cir. 1993).

110. 60 F.2d 737 (2d Cir. 1932).

111. 3 J. LAW & ECON. 1 (1960).

112. 109 S. Ct. 998 (1989).

113. Telephone interview, 3 Jan. 1994.

114. Telephone interview, 6 Jan. 1994.

115. POSNER, THE FEDERAL COURTS: CRISIS AND REFORM (1985).

116. POSNER, LAW AND LITERATURE: A MISUNDERSTOOD RELATION (1988).

117. POSNER, THE PROBLEMS OF JURISPRUDENCE (1990).

118. POSNER, CARDOZO: A STUDY IN REPUTATION (1990).

119. POSNER, ED., THE ESSENTIAL HOLMES: SELECTIONS FROM THE LETTERS,

Speeches, Judicial Opinions, and Other Writings of Oliver Wendell Holmes, Jr. (1992).

120. Posner, Sex and Reason (1992).

121. Telephone interview, 28 Dec. 1993.

122. Telephone Interview, 3 Jan. 1994.

123. Telephone interview, 4 Jan. 1994.

124. Telephone interview, 28 Dec. 1994.

125. Abramowitz, "Sex by the Numbers," *Washington Post*, Aug. 2, 1992, D2.

126. Telephone interview, 28 Dec. 1994.

127. Telephone interview, 13 Jan. 1994.

128. Telephone interview, 30 Dec. 1993.

129. Telephone interview, 4 Jan. 1994.

130. Telephone interview, 30 Dec. 1993.

131. *Id.*

132. Miller v. Civil City of South Bend, 904 F.2d 1081, 1089 (7th Cir.) (Posner, J., concurring), *rev'd* under the name of Barnes v. Glen Theatre, Inc., 501 U.S. 560 (1991).

133. U.S. v. Marshall, 908 F.2d 1312, 1331 (7th Cir.) (en banc) (Posner, J., dissenting), *aff'd*, under the name Chapman v. U.S., 500 U.S. 453 (1991).

134. Posner, *Henry Friendly*, 99 Harv. L. Rev. 1724 (1986).

135. Telephone interview, 4 Jan. 1994.

136. Trevino v. Union Pacific R.R., 916 F.2d 1230 (7th Cir. 1990) (Posner, J.) (commenting on Holmes's principle in Baltimore & Ohio R.R. v. Goodman, 275 U.S. 66 (1927), overruled in Pokora v. Wabash Ry., 292 U.S. 98 (1934).

137. Bastanipour v. I.N.S., 980 F.2d 1129, 1134 (7th Cir. 1992).

138. Posner, Economic Analysis of Law (4th ed., 1992).

139. Telephone interview, 4 Jan. 1994.

140. Posner, The Essential Holmes xxii (1992).

141. Y.B. 20 Edw. 4, fo. 10, pl. 10.

142. All E.R. 12 (1947).

143. Commentaries (18th ed.), bk. 1 at 111.

144. For example, Seely v. Peters, 5 Gilm. 130, 153.

145. For example, Delaney v. Erickson, 10 Neb. 492, 6 N.W. 600 (Neb. 1880); Sanford v. Boring, 12 Cal. 535 (1859); L.R. & F.S. Railway Co. v. Finley, 37 Ark. 562 (1881); and S.F. & W. Railway Co. v. J.H. Geiger, 21 Fla. 669 (1886).

146. Interview, 6 Feb. 1991.

147. Lauer v. Bowen, 818 F.2d 636, 642 (7th Cir. 1987) (Posner, J., dissenting).

Index

WILLIAM DOMNARSKI practices law in Minneapolis and writes on law and the legal profession. He has graduate degrees from the University of Chicago and the University of Connecticut, where he was an adjunct lecturer in English, and a law degree from the University of Connecticut School of Law, where he was also an adjunct lecturer. He is completing a book on the Supreme Court of 1941–54 and Justices Black, Douglas, Jackson, and Frankfurter.